MAKER

DESIGN A GAME!

COMICS

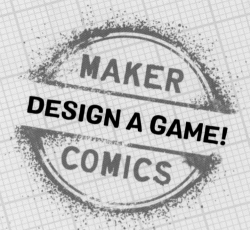

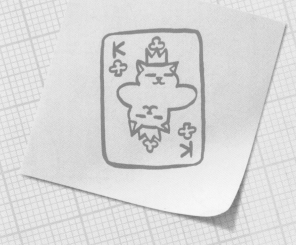

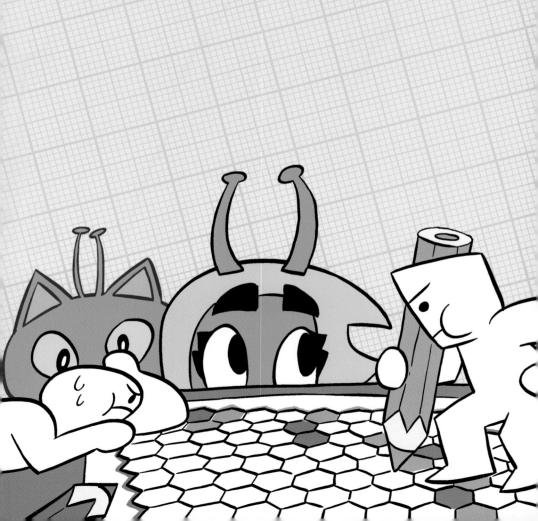

MAKER COMICS

DESIGN A GAME!

Written by Bree Wolf and Jesse Fuchs

Art by Bree Wolf

LV1
LV1
HP: 75
SPD:10
STR:12
DEF: 8

:01

First Second
New York

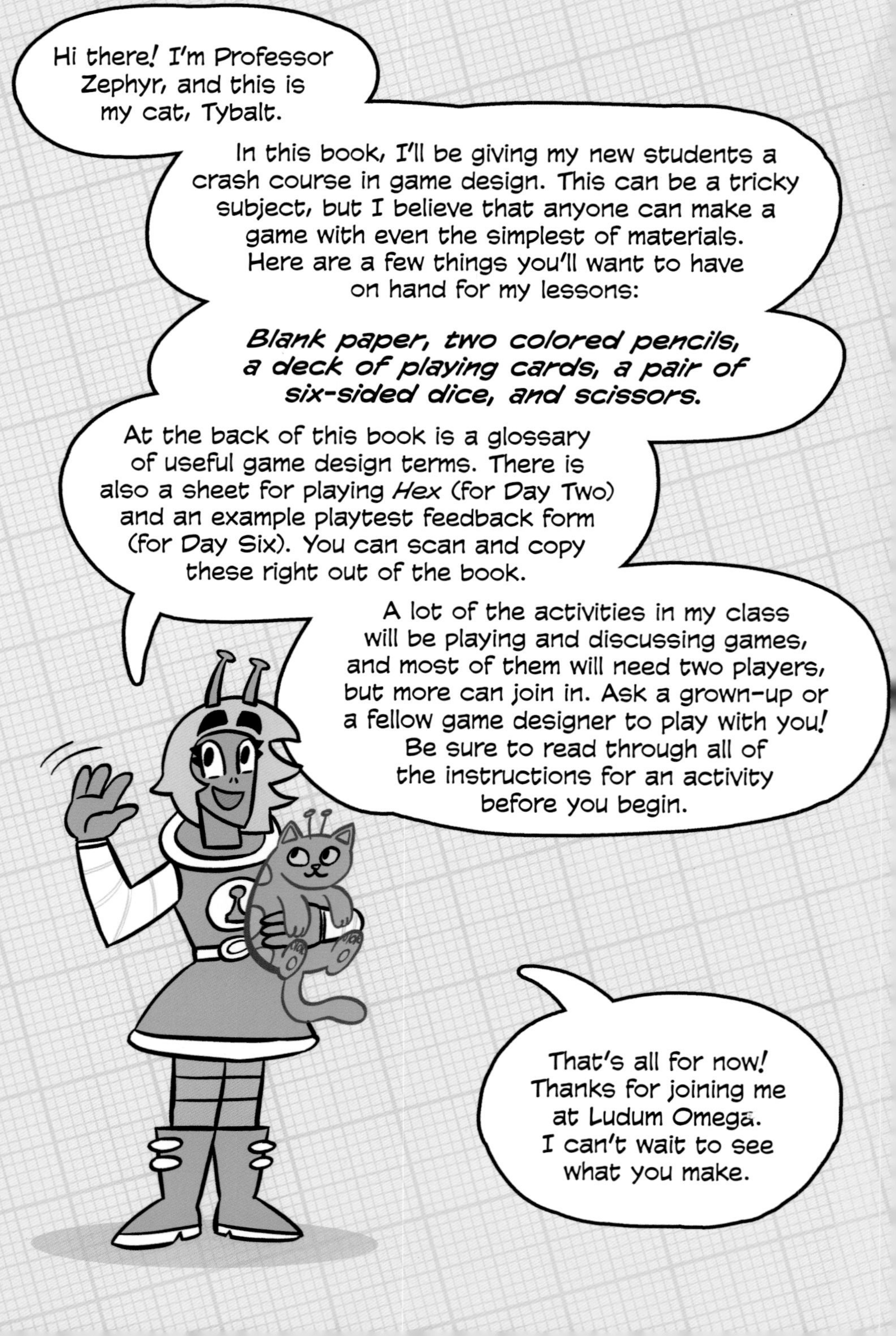
Hi there! I'm Professor Zephyr, and this is my cat, Tybalt.
In this book, I'll be giving my new students a crash course in game design. This can be a tricky subject, but I believe that anyone can make a game with even the simplest of materials. Here are a few things you'll want to have on hand for my lessons:
Blank paper, two colored pencils, a deck of playing cards, a pair of six-sided dice, and scissors.
At the back of this book is a glossary of useful game design terms. There is also a sheet for playing *Hex* (for Day Two) and an example playtest feedback form (for Day Six). You can scan and copy these right out of the book.
A lot of the activities in my class will be playing and discussing games, and most of them will need two players, but more can join in. Ask a grown-up or a fellow game designer to play with you! Be sure to read through all of the instructions for an activity before you begin.
That's all for now! Thanks for joining me at Ludum Omega. I can't wait to see what you make.

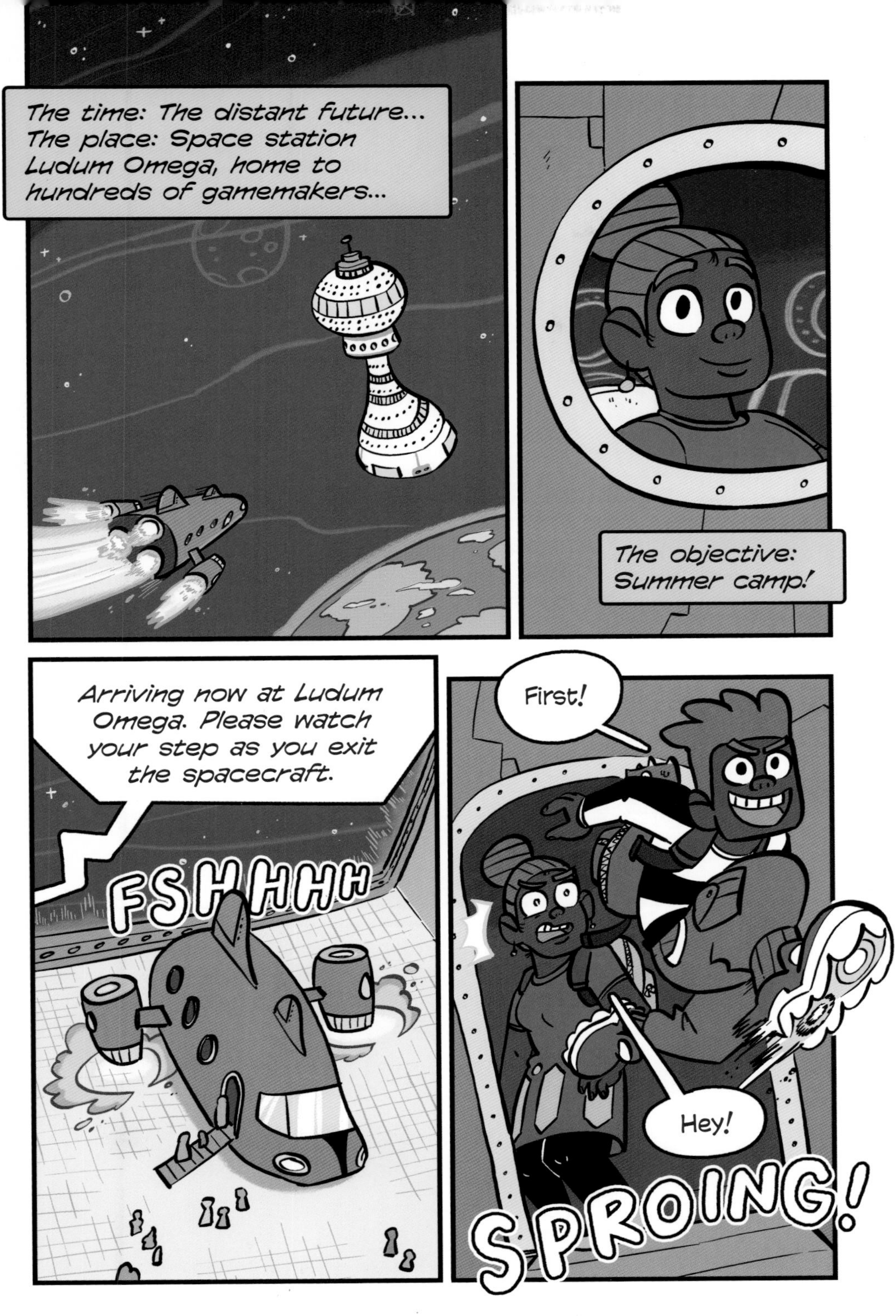
The time: The distant future...
The place: Space station Ludum Omega, home to hundreds of gamemakers...
The objective: Summer camp!
Arriving now at Ludum Omega. Please watch your step as you exit the spacecraft.
FSHHHHH
First!
Hey!
SPROING!

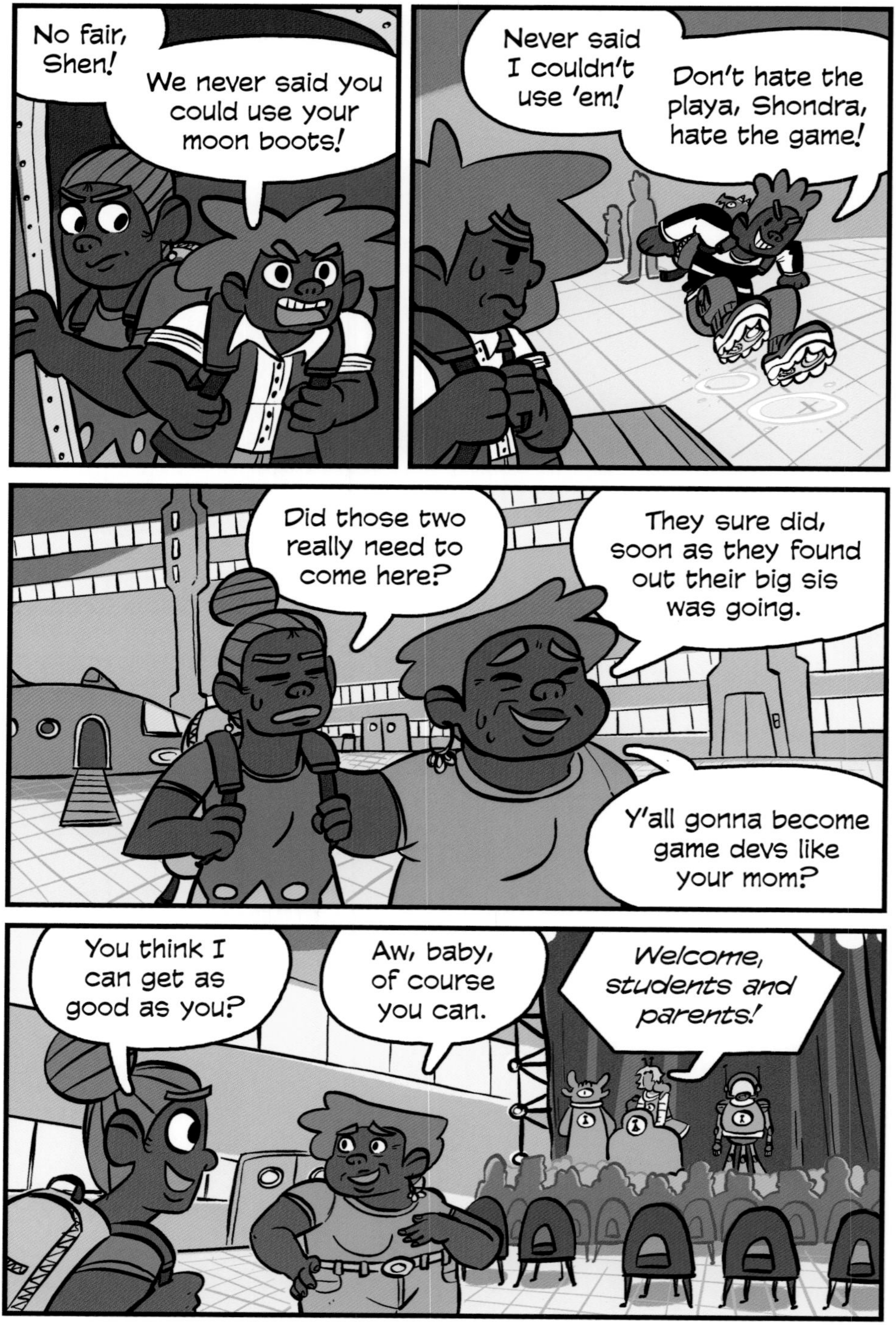
No fair, Shen!
We never said you could use your moon boots!
Never said I couldn't use 'em!
Don't hate the playa, Shondra, hate the game!
Did those two really need to come here?
They sure did, soon as they found out their big sis was going.
Y'all gonna become game devs like your mom?
You think I can get as good as you?
Aw, baby, of course you can.
Welcome, students and parents!

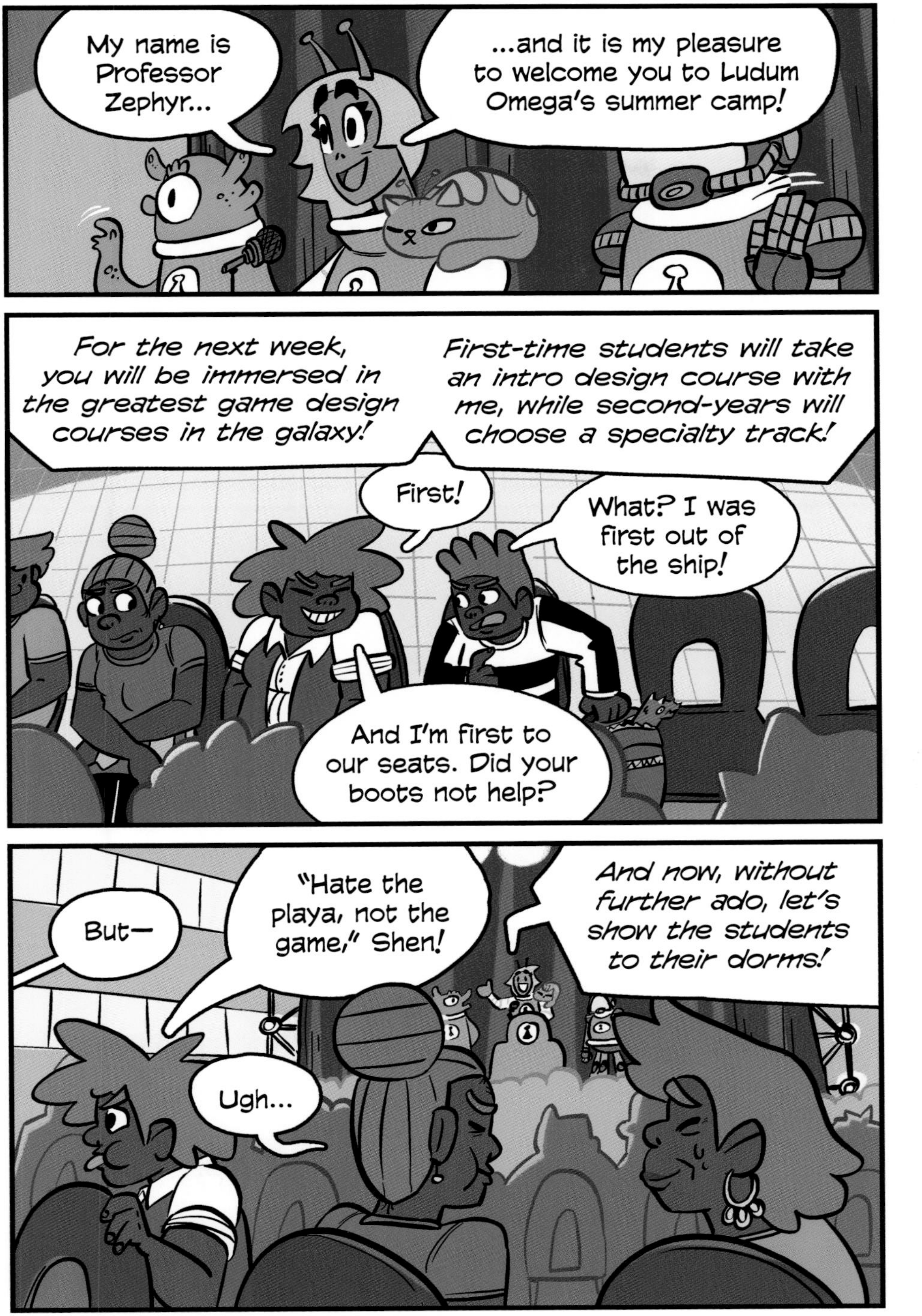
My name is Professor Zephyr...
...and it is my pleasure to welcome you to Ludum Omega's summer camp!
For the next week, you will be immersed in the greatest game design courses in the galaxy!
First-time students will take an intro design course with me, while second-years will choose a specialty track!
First!
What? I was first out of the ship!
And I'm first to our seats. Did your boots not help?
But—
"Hate the playa, not the game," Shen!
Ugh...
And now, without further ado, let's show the students to their dorms!

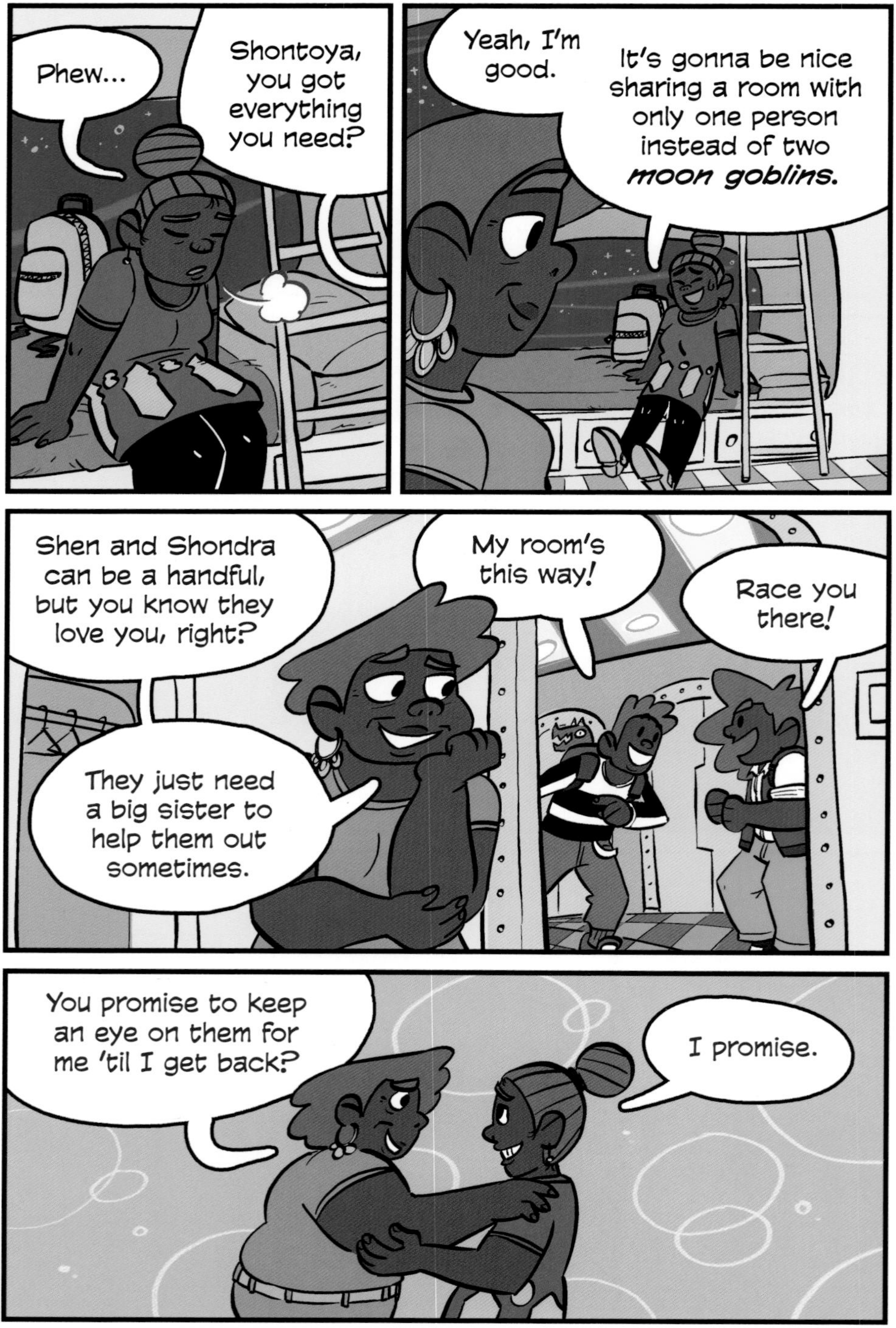
Phew...
Shontoya, you got everything you need?
Yeah, I'm good.
It's gonna be nice sharing a room with only one person instead of two *moon goblins.*
Shen and Shondra can be a handful, but you know they love you, right?
They just need a big sister to help them out sometimes.
My room's this way!
Race you there!
You promise to keep an eye on them for me 'til I get back?
I promise.

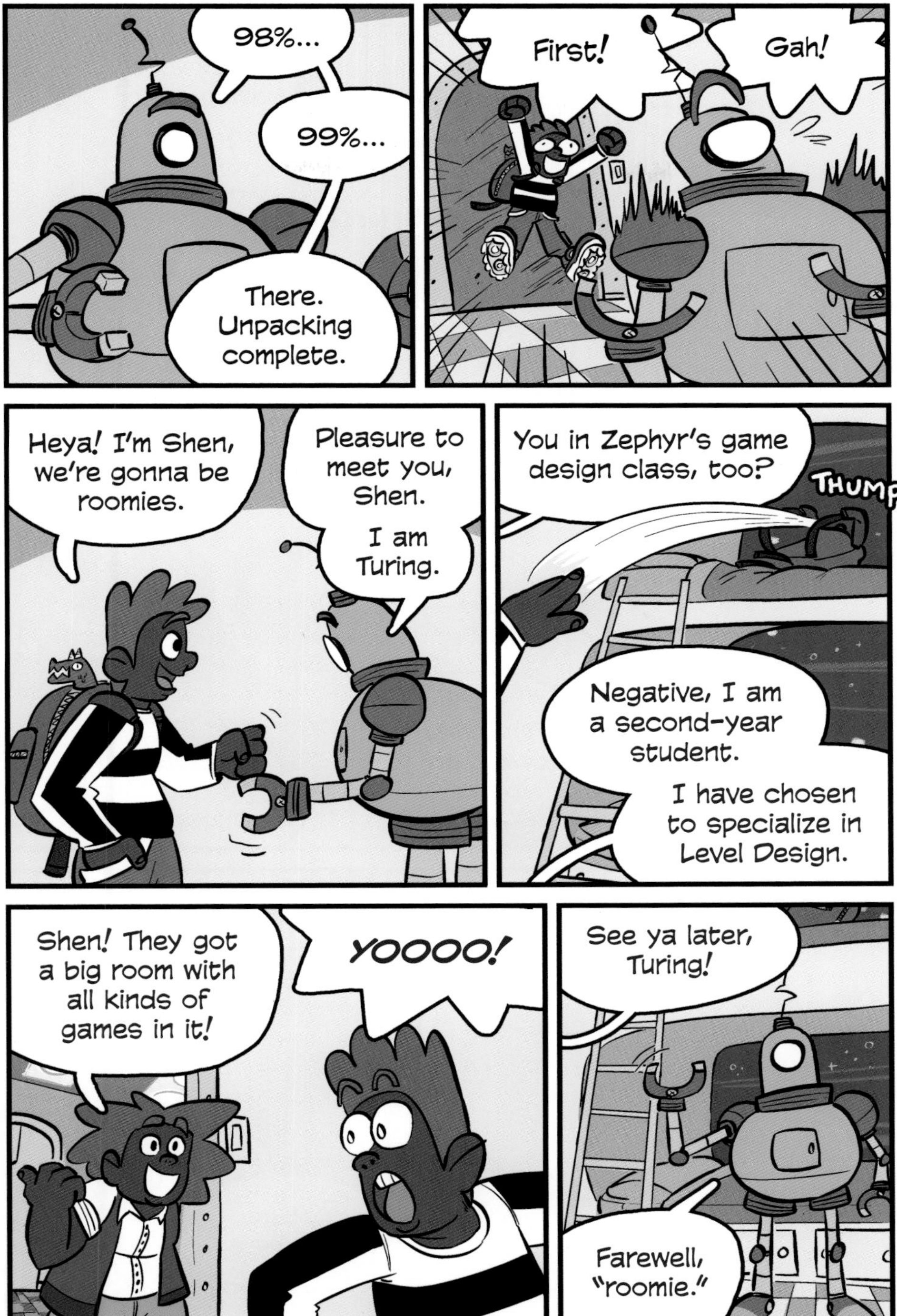
98%...
99%...
There. Unpacking complete.
First!
Gah!
Heya! I'm Shen, we're gonna be roomies.
Pleasure to meet you, Shen.
I am Turing.
You in Zephyr's game design class, too?
THUMP
Negative, I am a second-year student.
I have chosen to specialize in Level Design.
Shen! They got a big room with all kinds of games in it!
YOOOO!
See ya later, Turing!
Farewell, "roomie."

Is this room 404?

Yeah!

I-I mean... yeah.

You must be my roommate.

I'm Vale, second year. Character Animation. You?

Uh... Shontoya. First year.

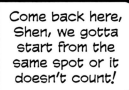

Come back here, Shen, we gotta start from the same spot or it doesn't count!

You got longer legs so I get a head start, that's fairer!

Dang, they seem *pumped* to be here.

D-do they? I don't know those weirdos.

Heya, Shontoya! See you in class tomorrow!

Sigh...

...See you there.

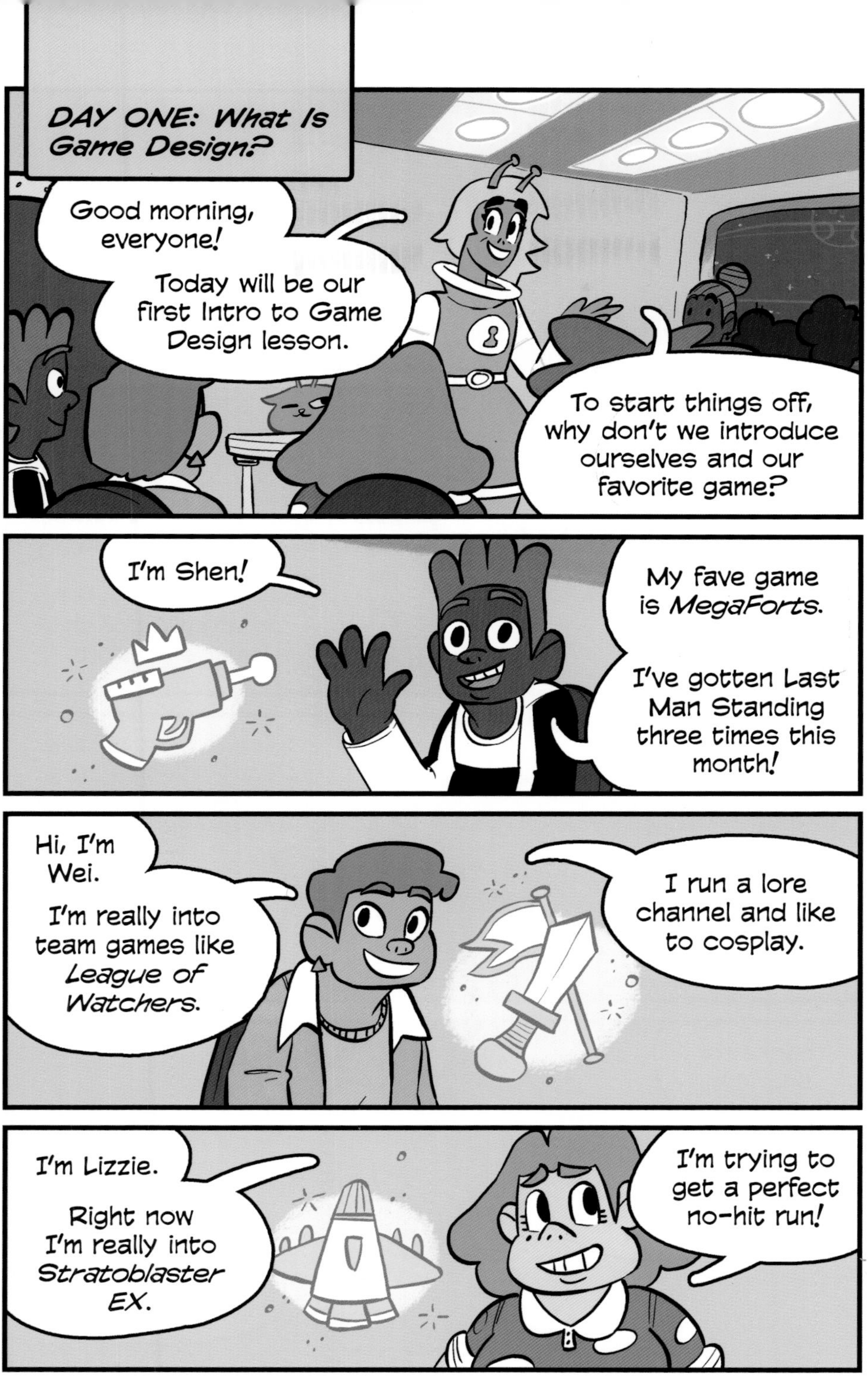
DAY ONE: What Is Game Design?
Good morning, everyone!
Today will be our first Intro to Game Design lesson.
To start things off, why don't we introduce ourselves and our favorite game?
I'm Shen!
My fave game is *MegaForts*.
I've gotten Last Man Standing three times this month!
Hi, I'm Wei.
I'm really into team games like *League of Watchers*.
I run a lore channel and like to cosplay.
I'm Lizzie.
Right now I'm really into *Stratoblaster EX*.
I'm trying to get a perfect no-hit run!

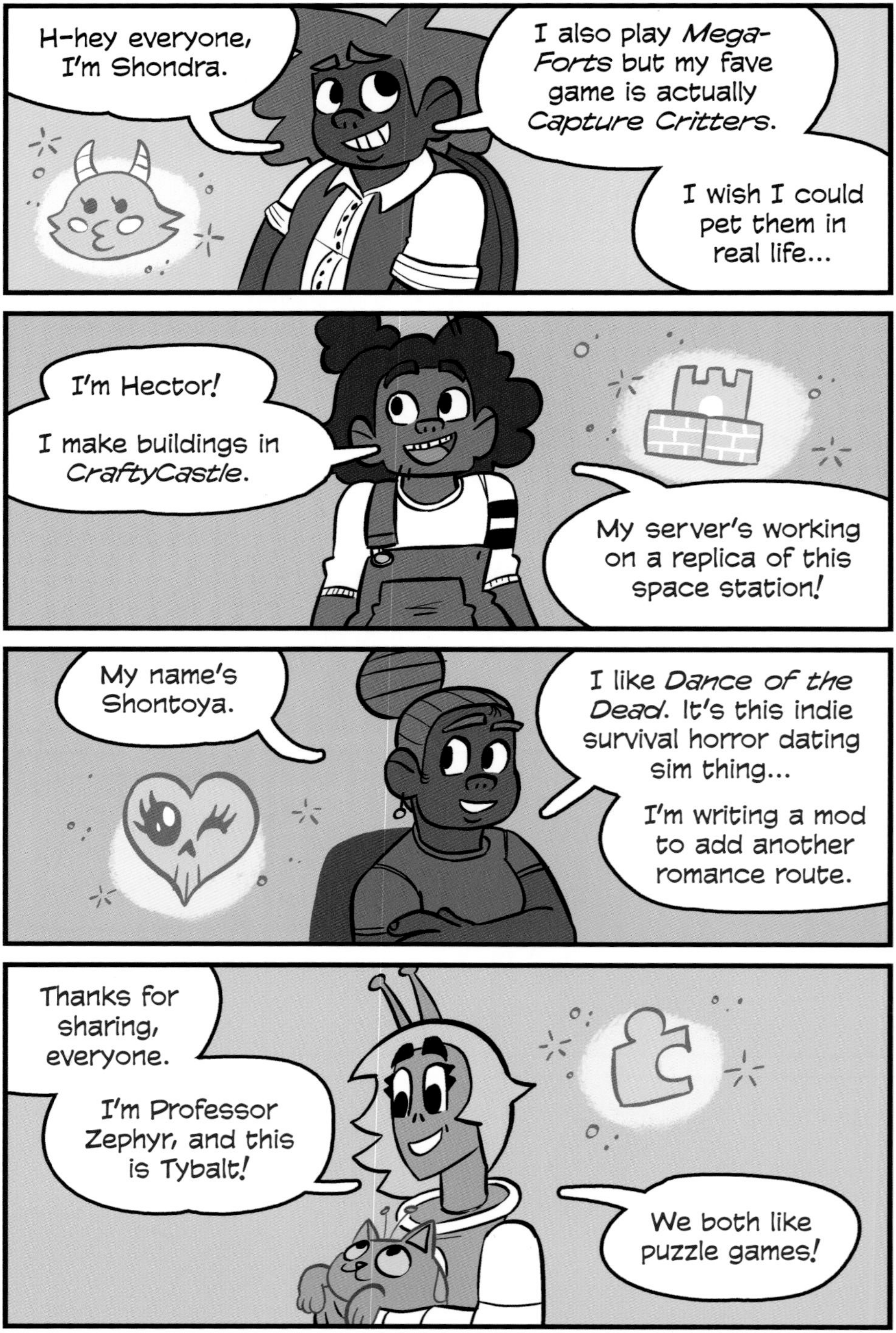
H-hey everyone, I'm Shondra.
I also play *Mega-Forts* but my fave game is actually *Capture Critters*.
I wish I could pet them in real life...
I'm Hector!
I make buildings in *CraftyCastle*.
My server's working on a replica of this space station!
My name's Shontoya.
I like *Dance of the Dead*. It's this indie survival horror dating sim thing...
I'm writing a mod to add another romance route.
Thanks for sharing, everyone.
I'm Professor Zephyr, and this is Tybalt!
We both like puzzle games!

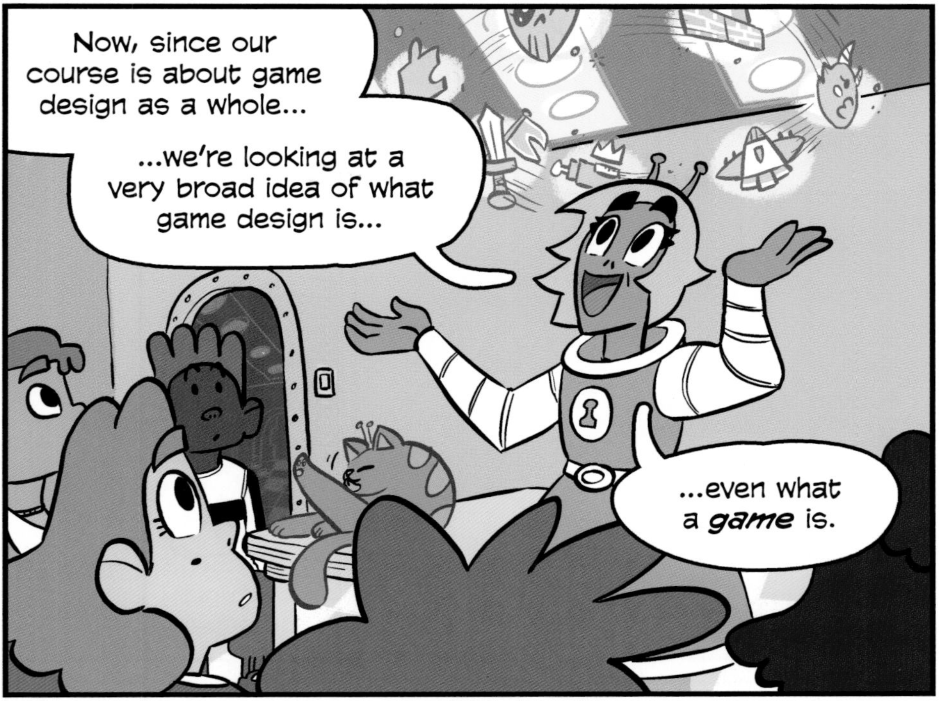
Now, since our course is about game design as a whole...
...we're looking at a very broad idea of what game design is...
...even what a *game* is.

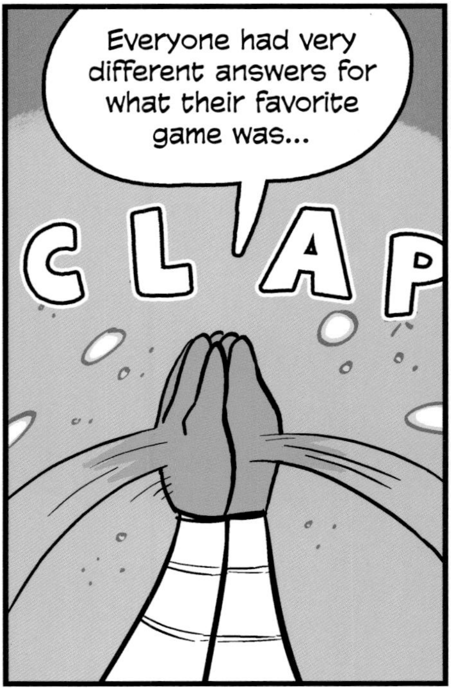
Everyone had very different answers for what their favorite game was...
CLAP

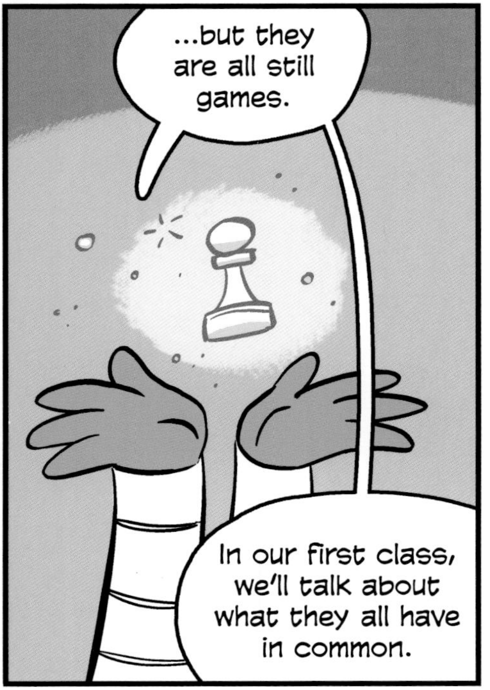
...but they are all still games.
In our first class, we'll talk about what they all have in common.

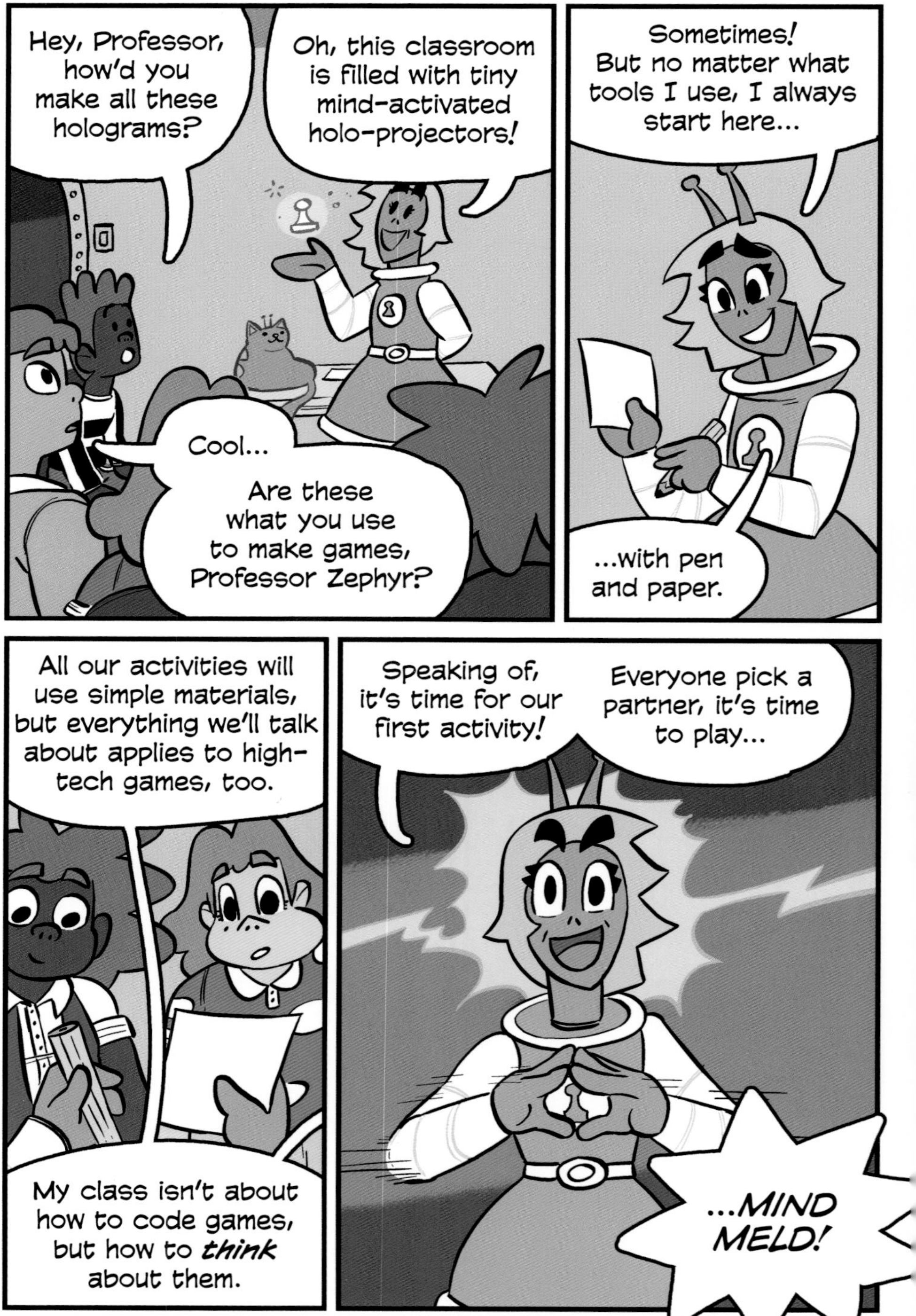
Hey, Professor, how'd you make all these holograms?
Oh, this classroom is filled with tiny mind-activated holo-projectors!
Cool...
Are these what you use to make games, Professor Zephyr?
Sometimes! But no matter what tools I use, I always start here...
...with pen and paper.
All our activities will use simple materials, but everything we'll talk about applies to high-tech games, too.
My class isn't about how to code games, but how to *think* about them.
Speaking of, it's time for our first activity!
Everyone pick a partner, it's time to play...
...MIND MELD!

Let's Play *Mind Meld!*

Players:	Materials:	Time to play:
2+	None	5 minutes

1. Two players stand face-to-face. They count to three, with player A saying "one," player B saying "two," and both players saying "three."

2. After the players say "three," they both simultaneously say any noun they can think of.

3. If both players say the same noun, they both win! If not, they begin a new round and count down again. Play continues until both players say the same noun.

4. Players cannot say the same word twice (or a word that's too similar). Players cannot discuss what words they should say before counting down.

BONUS! Try this game with different people. Take note of how many rounds each game takes and what patterns emerge from each game!

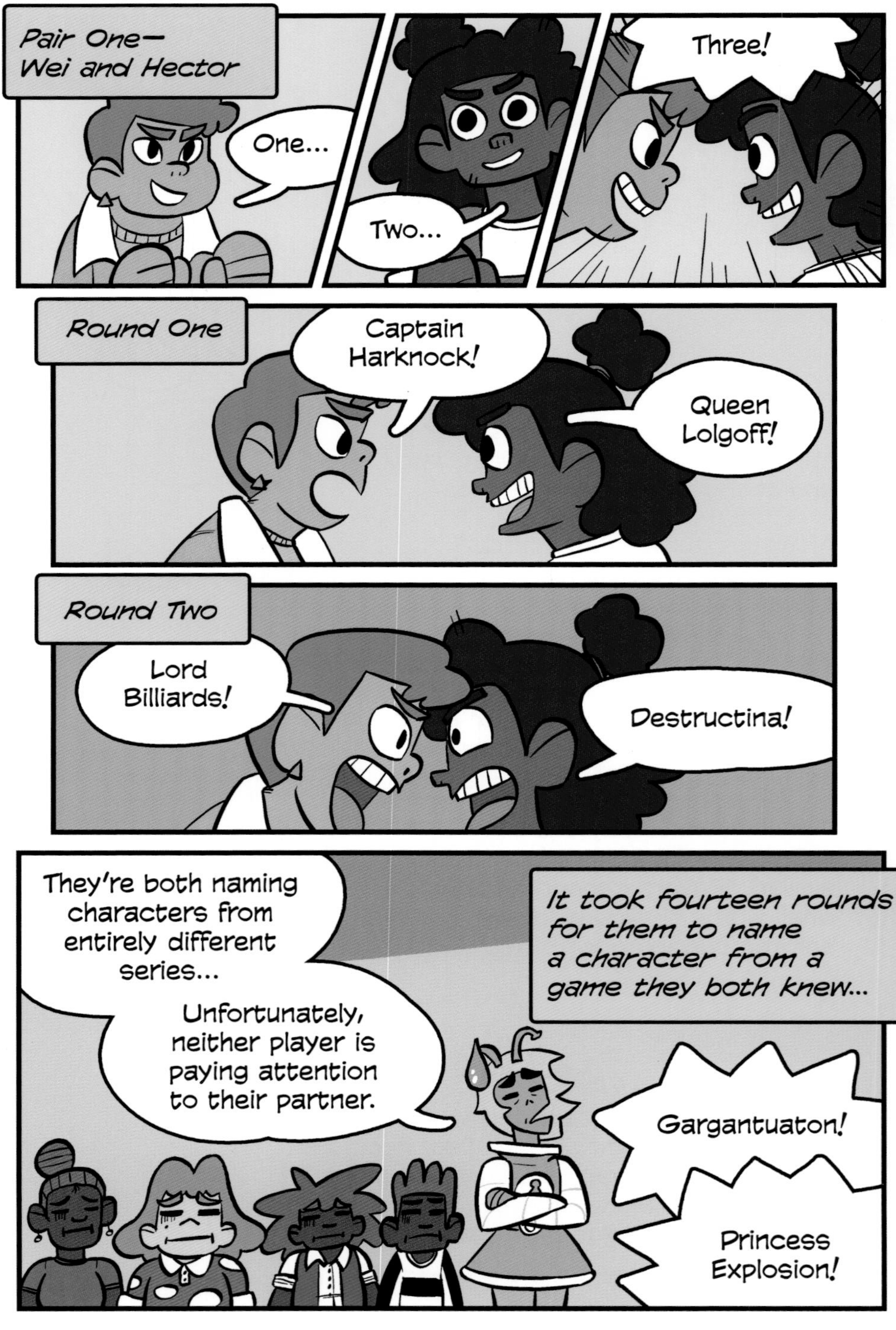
Pair One—
Wei and Hector
One...
Two...
Three!
Round One
Captain Harknock!
Queen Lolgoff!
Round Two
Lord Billiards!
Destructina!
They're both naming characters from entirely different series...
Unfortunately, neither player is paying attention to their partner.
It took fourteen rounds for them to name a character from a game they both knew...
Gargantuaton!
Princess Explosion!

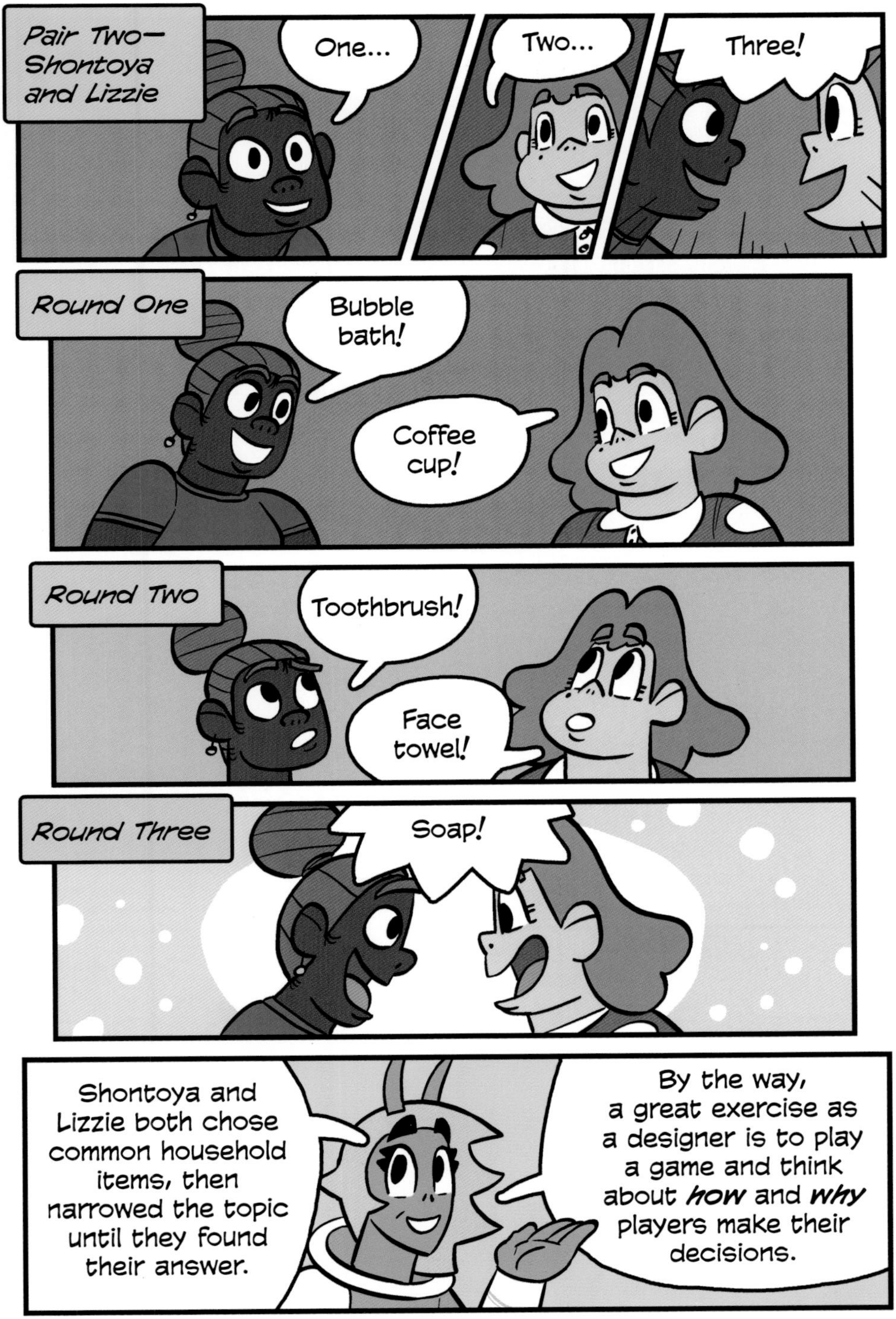
Pair Two— Shontoya and Lizzie
One...
Two...
Three!
Round One
Bubble bath!
Coffee cup!
Round Two
Toothbrush!
Face towel!
Round Three
Soap!
Shontoya and Lizzie both chose common household items, then narrowed the topic until they found their answer.
By the way, a great exercise as a designer is to play a game and think about *how* and *why* players make their decisions.

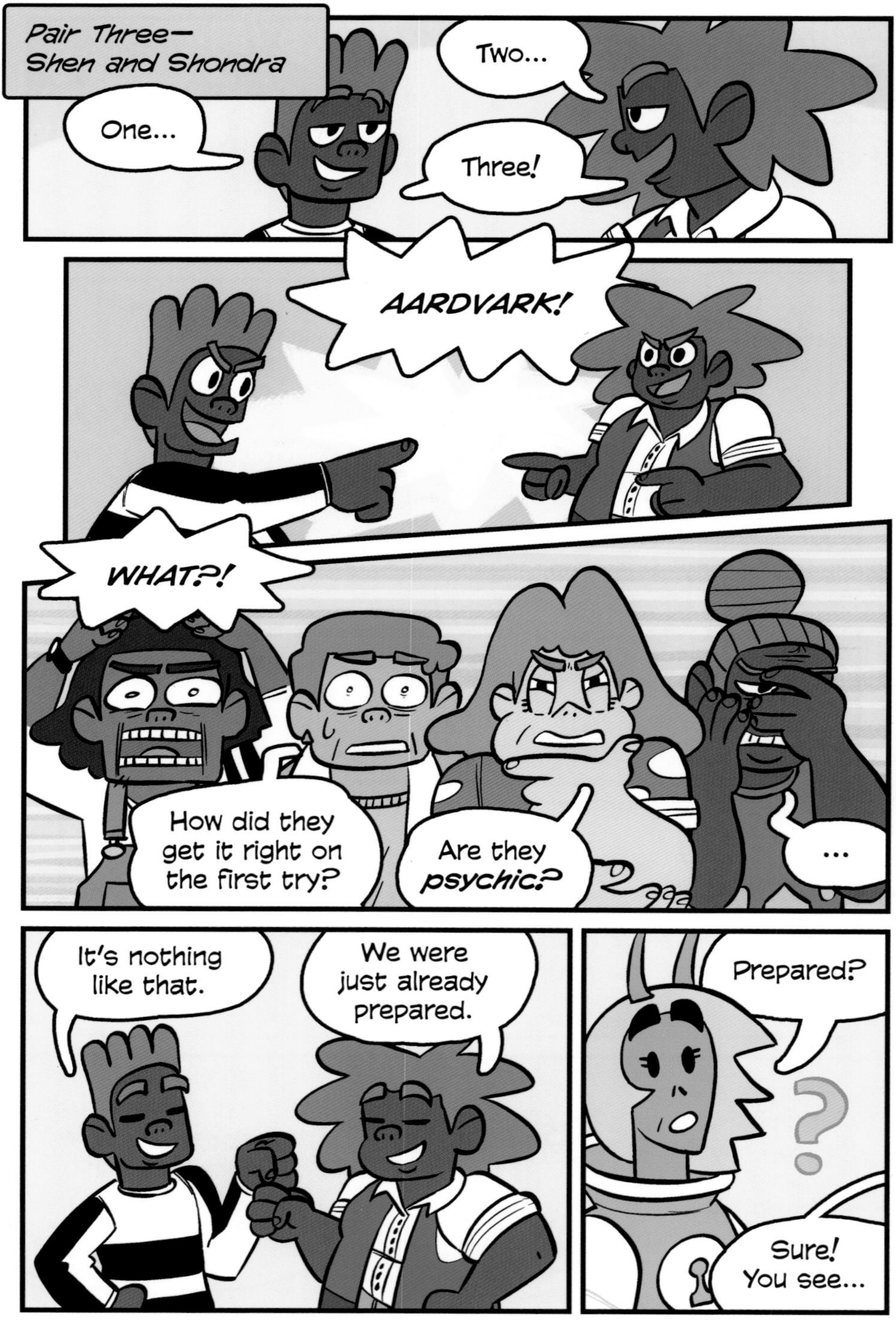
Pair Three—
Shen and Shondra
One...
Two...
Three!
AARDVARK!
WHAT?!
How did they get it right on the first try?
Are they *psychic?*
...
It's nothing like that.
We were just already prepared.
Prepared?
Sure! You see...

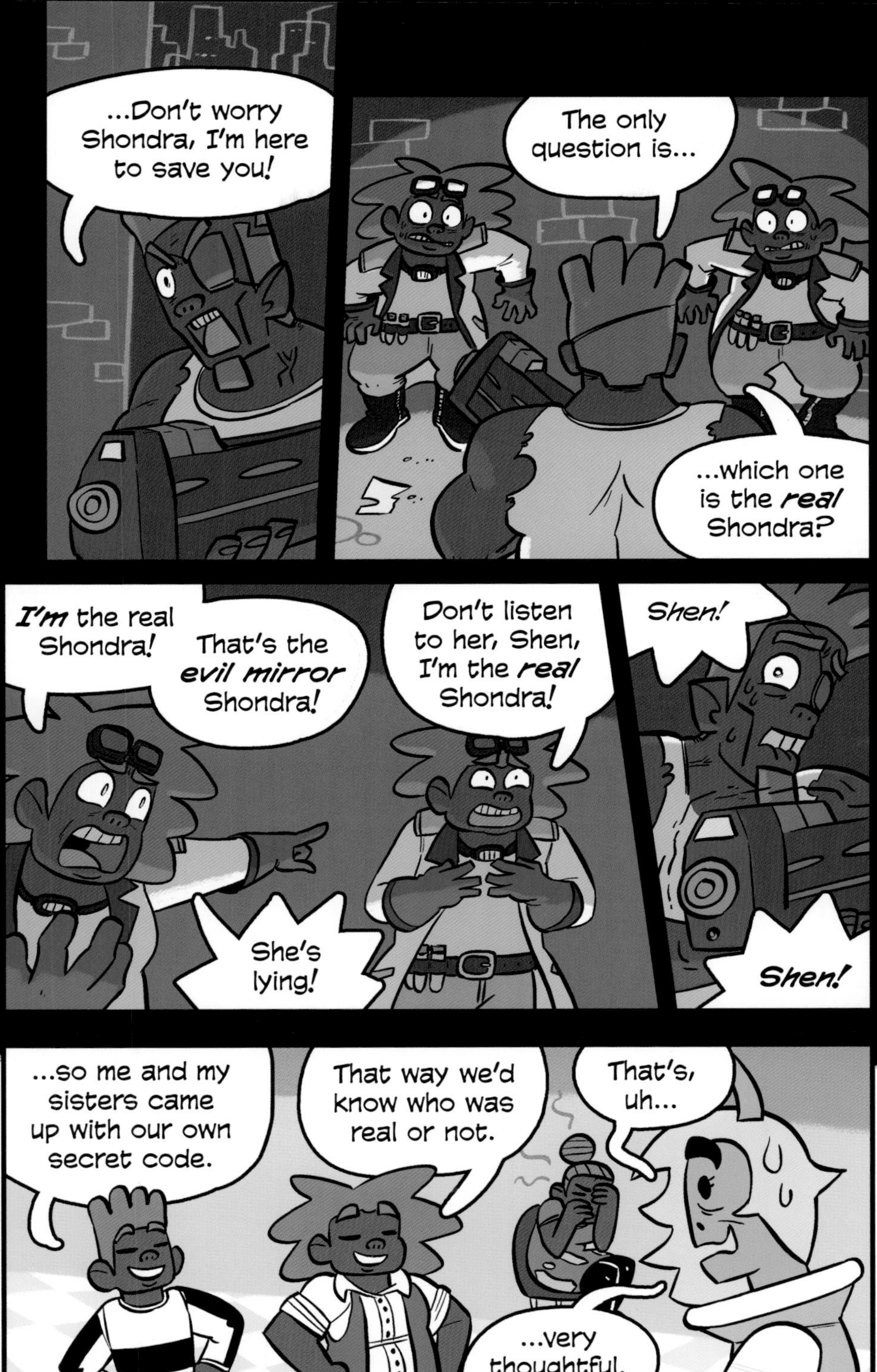

...Don't worry Shondra, I'm here to save you!
The only question is...
...which one is the *real* Shondra?
I'm the real Shondra!
That's the *evil mirror* Shondra!
She's lying!
Don't listen to her, Shen, I'm the *real* Shondra!
Shen!
Shen!
...so me and my sisters came up with our own secret code.
That way we'd know who was real or not.
That's, uh...
...very thoughtful.

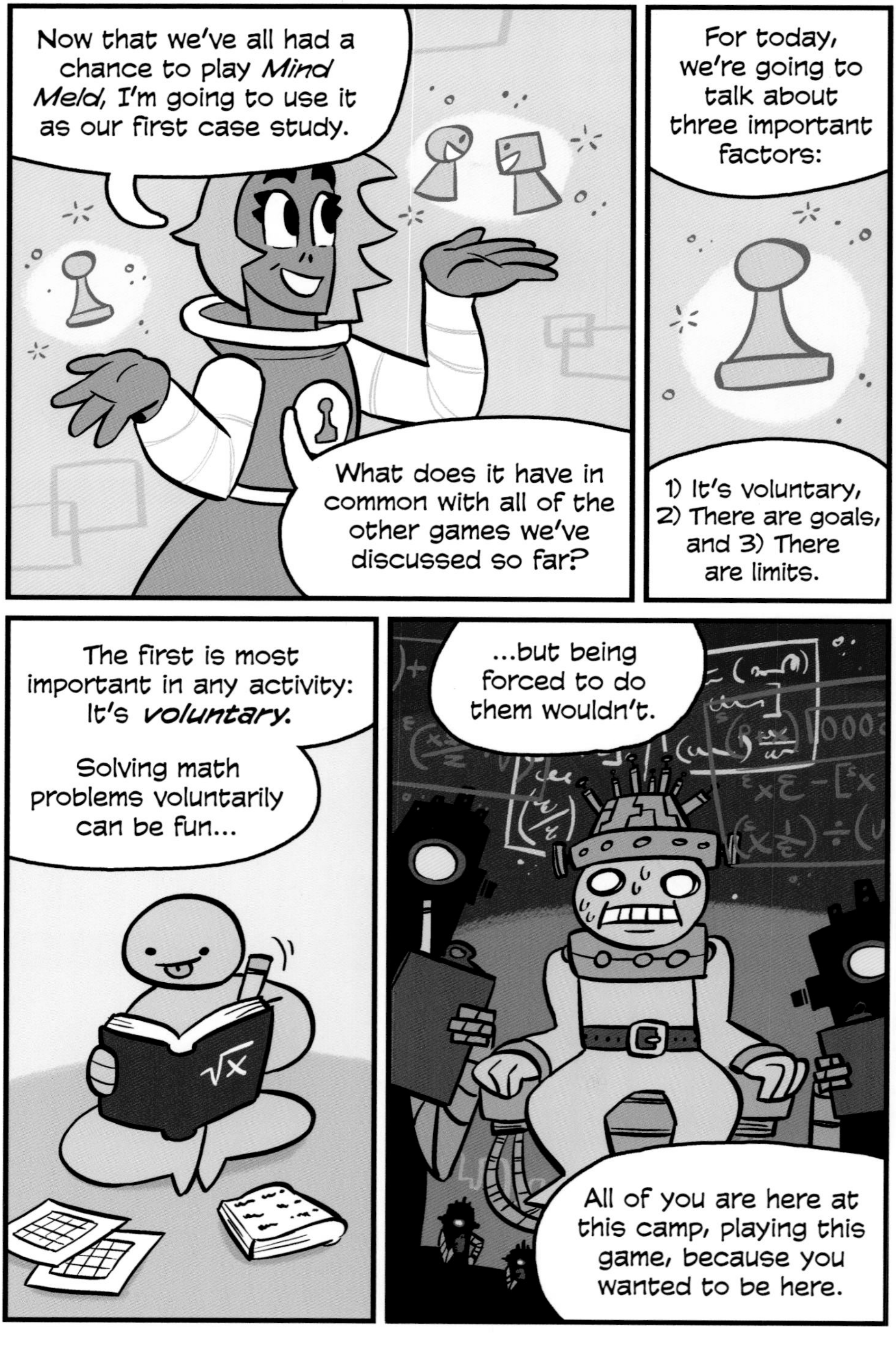
Now that we've all had a chance to play *Mind Meld*, I'm going to use it as our first case study.
What does it have in common with all of the other games we've discussed so far?
For today, we're going to talk about three important factors:
1) It's voluntary, 2) There are goals, and 3) There are limits.
The first is most important in any activity: It's ***voluntary.***
Solving math problems voluntarily can be fun...
...but being forced to do them wouldn't.
All of you are here at this camp, playing this game, because you wanted to be here.

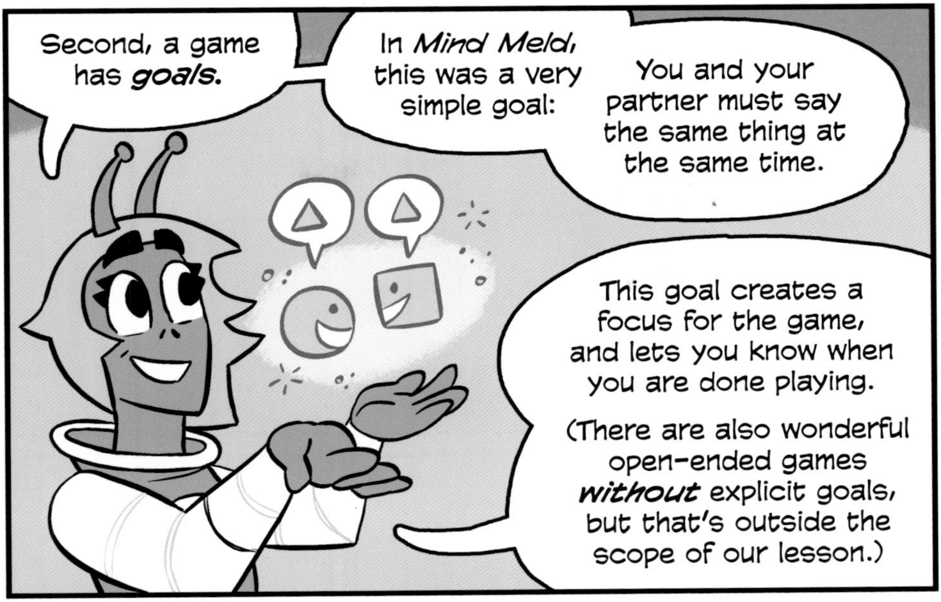
Second, a game has *goals.*
In *Mind Meld,* this was a very simple goal:
You and your partner must say the same thing at the same time.
This goal creates a focus for the game, and lets you know when you are done playing.
(There are also wonderful open-ended games *without* explicit goals, but that's outside the scope of our lesson.)

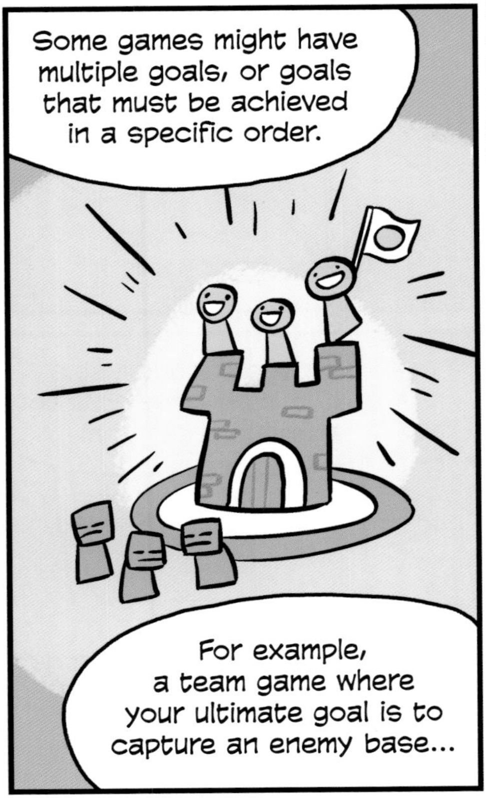
Some games might have multiple goals, or goals that must be achieved in a specific order.
For example, a team game where your ultimate goal is to capture an enemy base...

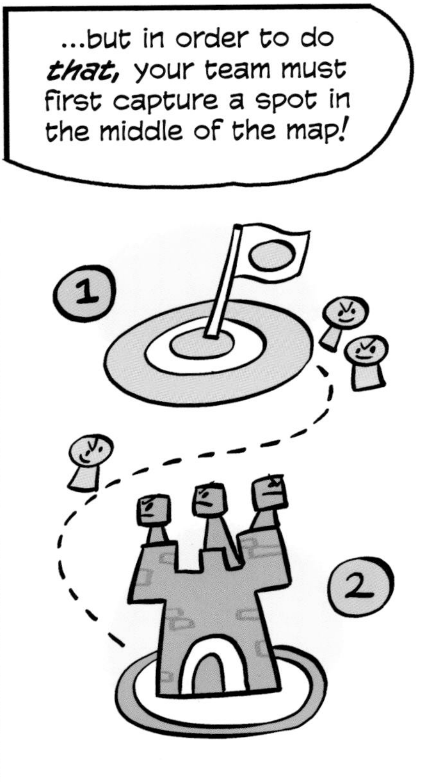
...but in order to do *that,* your team must first capture a spot in the middle of the map!
1
2

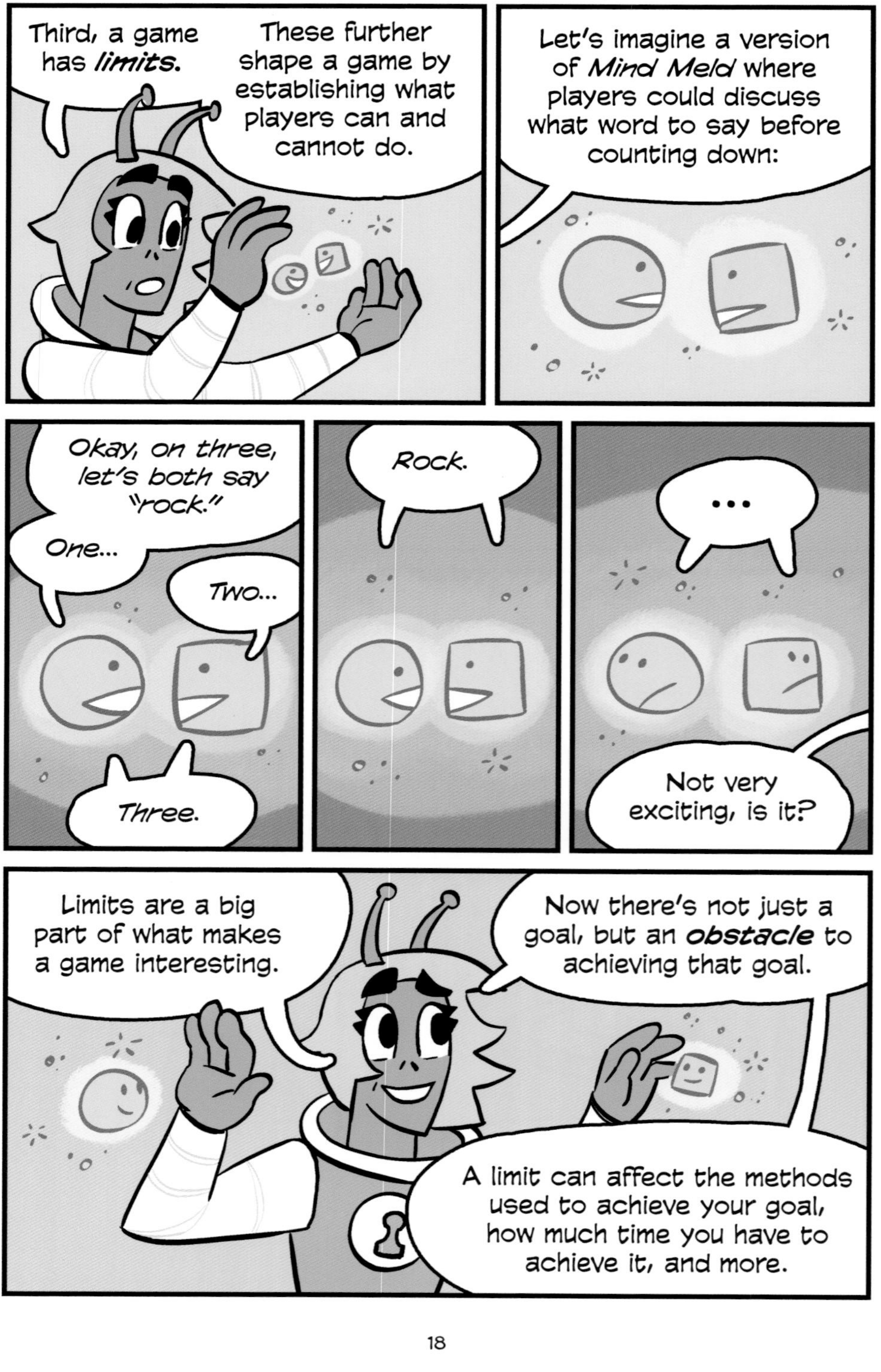

Third, a game has *limits.*
These further shape a game by establishing what players can and cannot do.
Let's imagine a version of *Mind Meld* where players could discuss what word to say before counting down:
Okay, on three, let's both say "rock."
One...
Two...
Three.
Rock.
...
Not very exciting, is it?
Limits are a big part of what makes a game interesting.
Now there's not just a goal, but an ***obstacle*** to achieving that goal.
A limit can affect the methods used to achieve your goal, how much time you have to achieve it, and more.

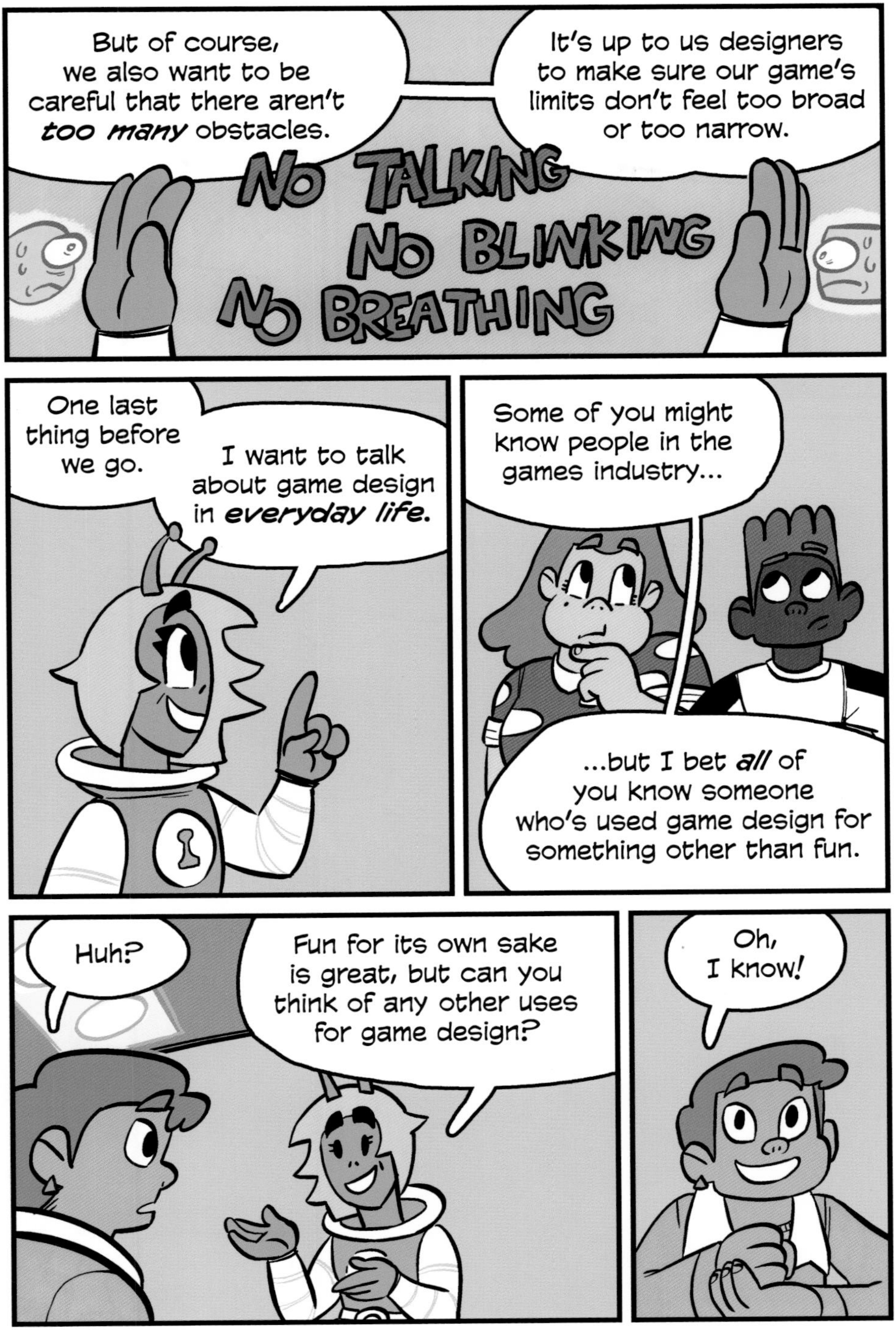
But of course, we also want to be careful that there aren't *too many* obstacles.
It's up to us designers to make sure our game's limits don't feel too broad or too narrow.
NO TALKING
NO BLINKING
NO BREATHING
One last thing before we go.
I want to talk about game design in *everyday life.*
Some of you might know people in the games industry...
...but I bet *all* of you know someone who's used game design for something other than fun.
Huh?
Fun for its own sake is great, but can you think of any other uses for game design?
Oh, I know!

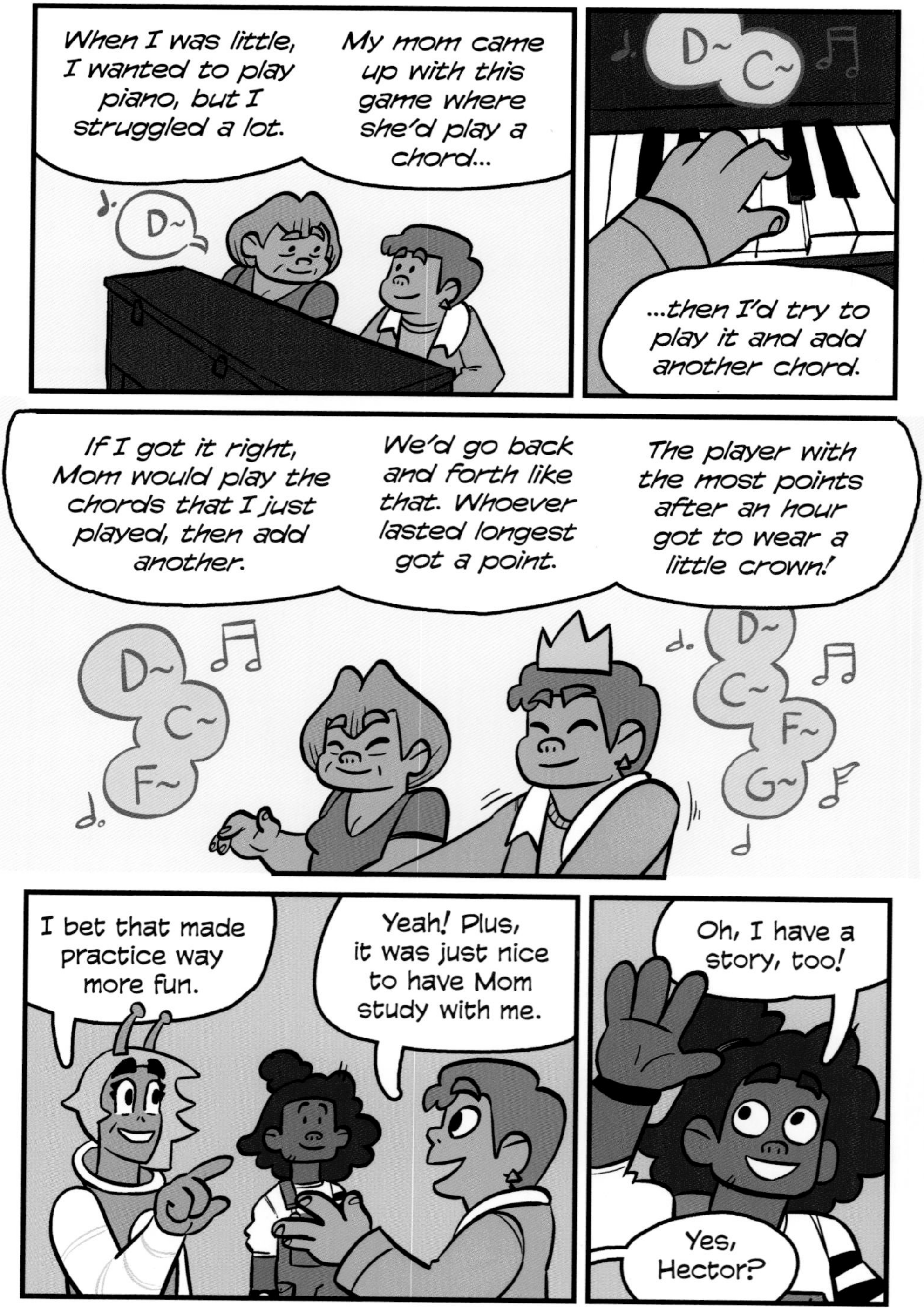
When I was little, I wanted to play piano, but I struggled a lot.
My mom came up with this game where she'd play a chord...
D~
D~
C~
...then I'd try to play it and add another chord.
If I got it right, Mom would play the chords that I just played, then add another.
We'd go back and forth like that. Whoever lasted longest got a point.
The player with the most points after an hour got to wear a little crown!
D~
C~
F~
D~
C~
F~
G~
I bet that made practice way more fun.
Yeah! Plus, it was just nice to have Mom study with me.
Oh, I have a story, too!
Yes, Hector?

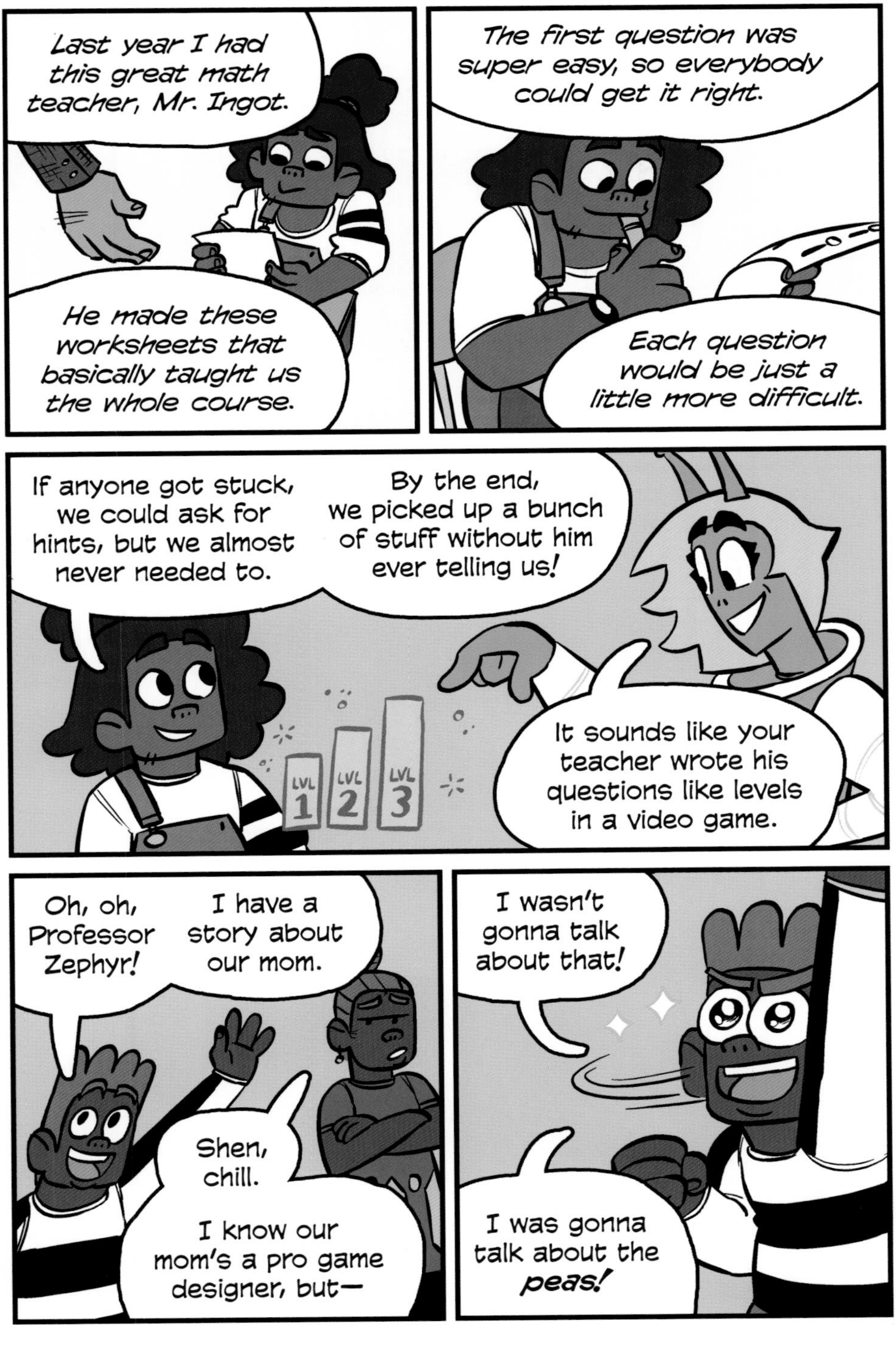
Last year I had this great math teacher, Mr. Ingot.
He made these worksheets that basically taught us the whole course.
The first question was super easy, so everybody could get it right.
Each question would be just a little more difficult.
If anyone got stuck, we could ask for hints, but we almost never needed to.
By the end, we picked up a bunch of stuff without him ever telling us!
LVL 1
LVL 2
LVL 3
It sounds like your teacher wrote his questions like levels in a video game.
Oh, oh, Professor Zephyr!
I have a story about our mom.
Shen, chill.
I know our mom's a pro game designer, but—
I wasn't gonna talk about that!
I was gonna talk about the *peas!*

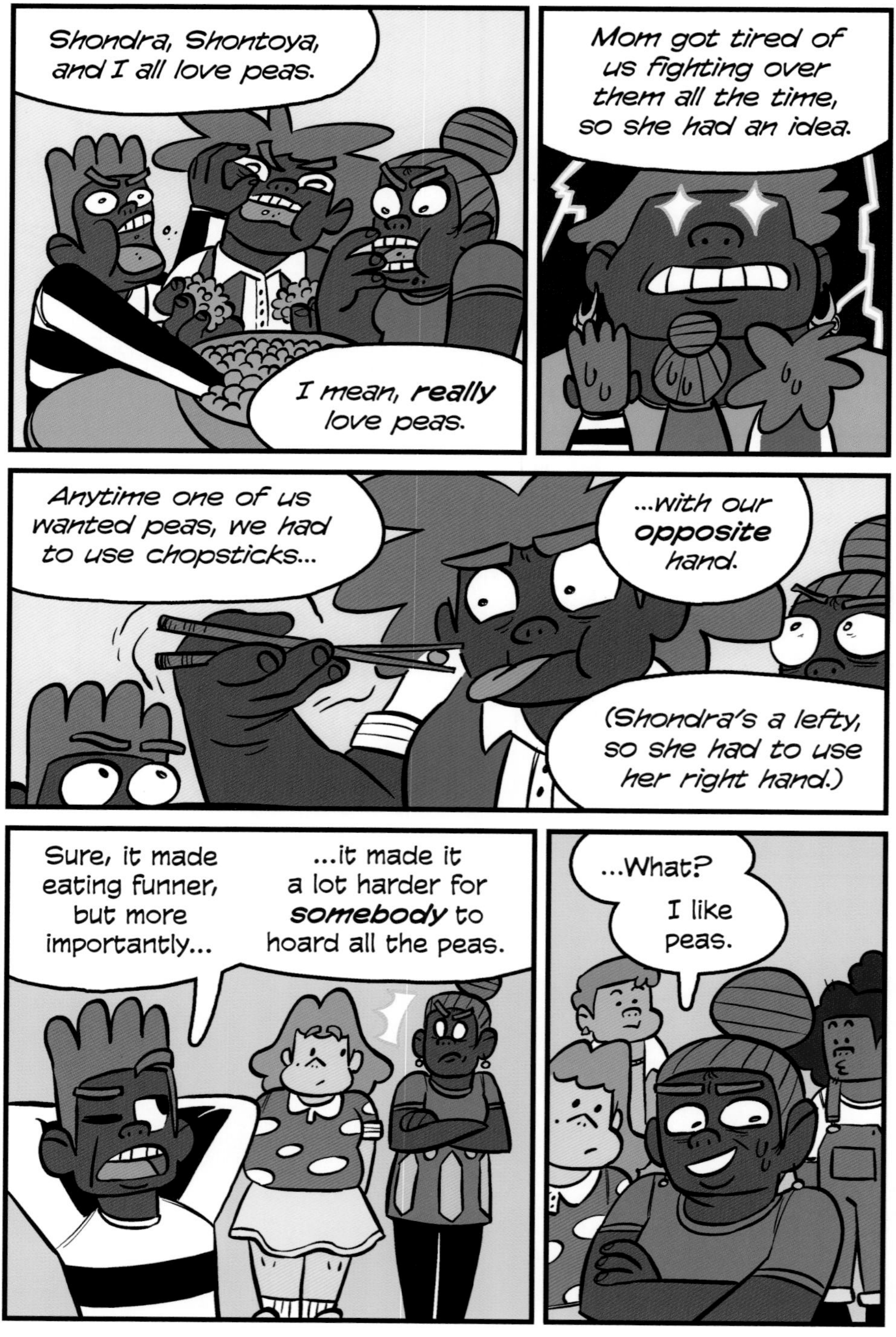
Shondra, Shontoya, and I all love peas.
I mean, **really** love peas.
Mom got tired of us fighting over them all the time, so she had an idea.
Anytime one of us wanted peas, we had to use chopsticks...
...with our **opposite** hand.
(Shondra's a lefty, so she had to use her right hand.)
Sure, it made eating funner, but more importantly...
...it made it a lot harder for ***somebody*** to hoard all the peas.
...What?
I like peas.

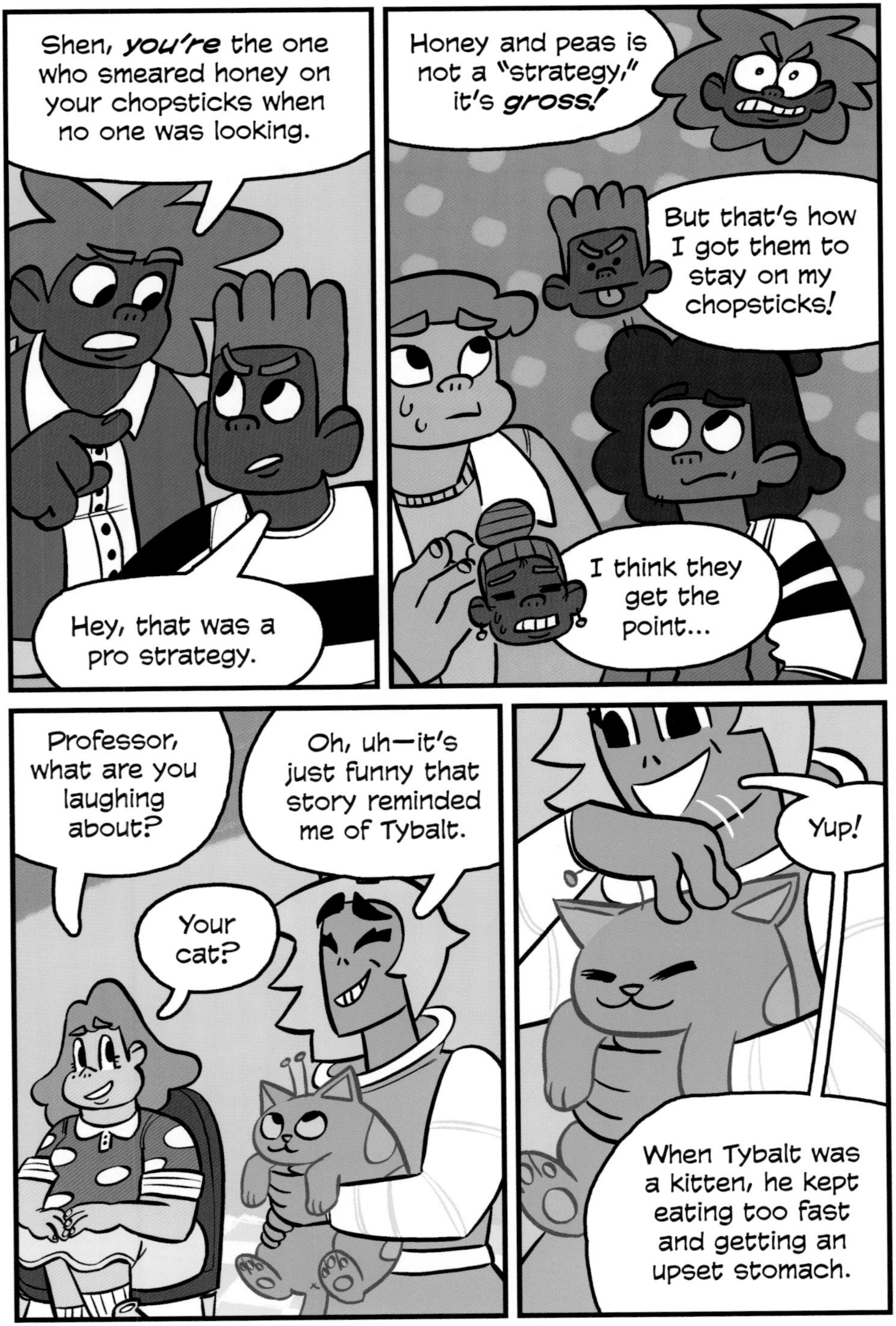
Shen, *you're* the one who smeared honey on your chopsticks when no one was looking.
Hey, that was a pro strategy.
Honey and peas is not a "strategy," it's *gross!*
But that's how I got them to stay on my chopsticks!
I think they get the point...
Professor, what are you laughing about?
Oh, uh—it's just funny that story reminded me of Tybalt.
Your cat?
Yup!
When Tybalt was a kitten, he kept eating too fast and getting an upset stomach.

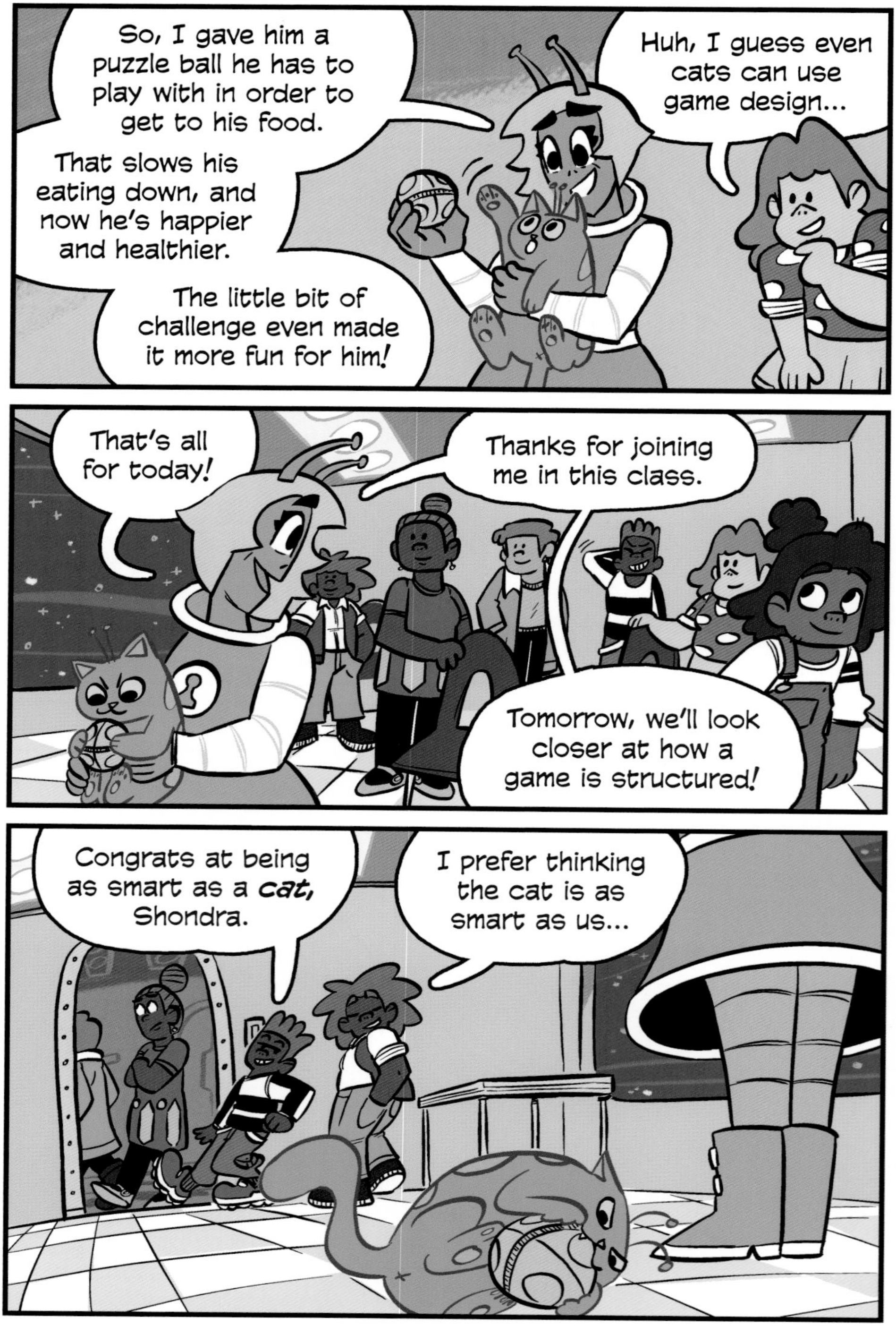
So, I gave him a puzzle ball he has to play with in order to get to his food.
That slows his eating down, and now he's happier and healthier.
The little bit of challenge even made it more fun for him!
Huh, I guess even cats can use game design...
That's all for today!
Thanks for joining me in this class.
Tomorrow, we'll look closer at how a game is structured!
Congrats at being as smart as a *cat,* Shondra.
I prefer thinking the cat is as smart as us...

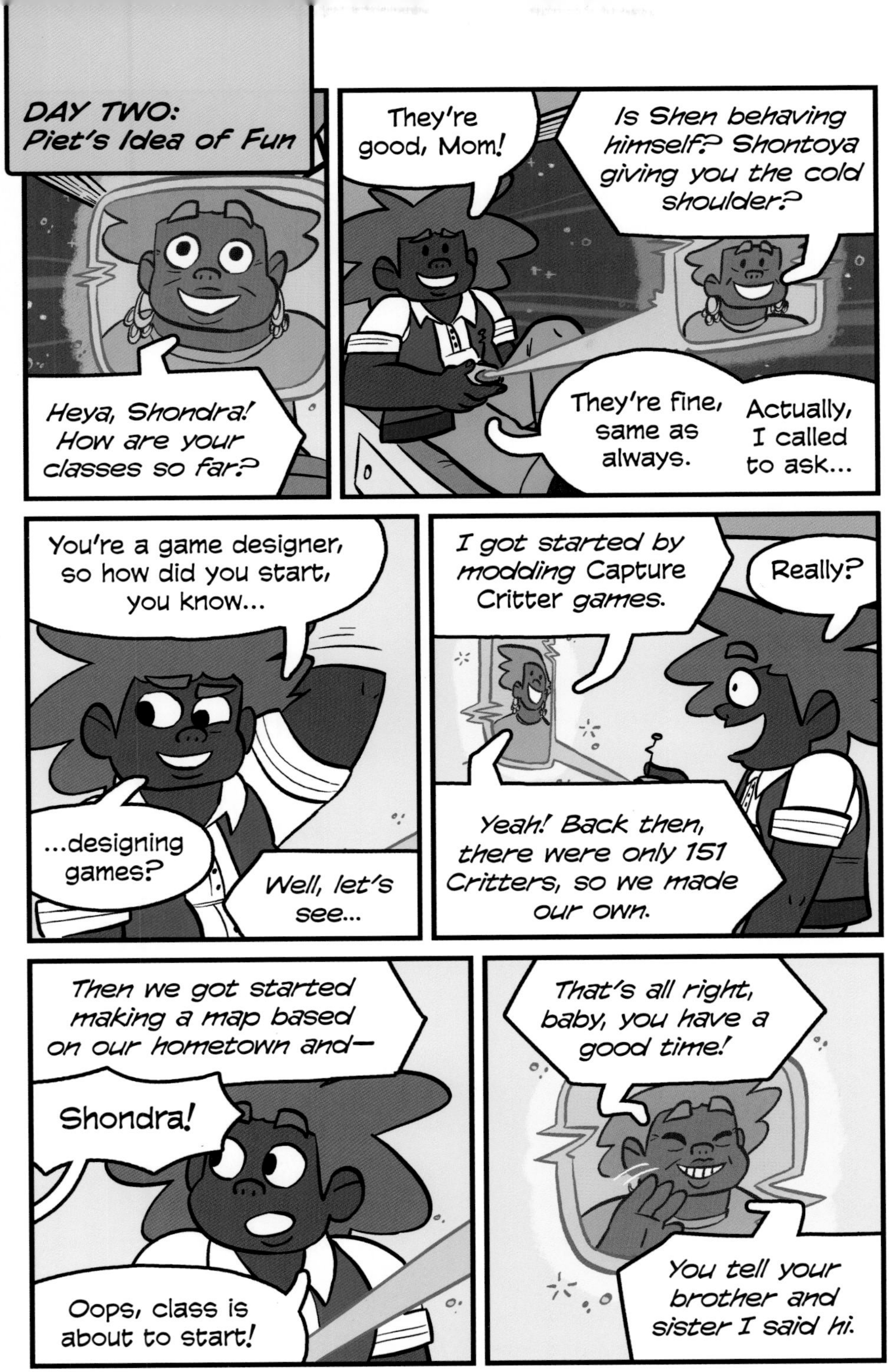

DAY TWO: Piet's Idea of Fun
Heya, Shondra! How are your classes so far?
They're good, Mom!
Is Shen behaving himself? Shontoya giving you the cold shoulder?
They're fine, same as always.
Actually, I called to ask...
You're a game designer, so how did you start, you know...
...designing games?
Well, let's see...
I got started by modding Capture Critter games.
Really?
Yeah! Back then, there were only 151 Critters, so we made our own.
Then we got started making a map based on our hometown and—
Shondra!
Oops, class is about to start!
That's all right, baby, you have a good time!
You tell your brother and sister I said hi.

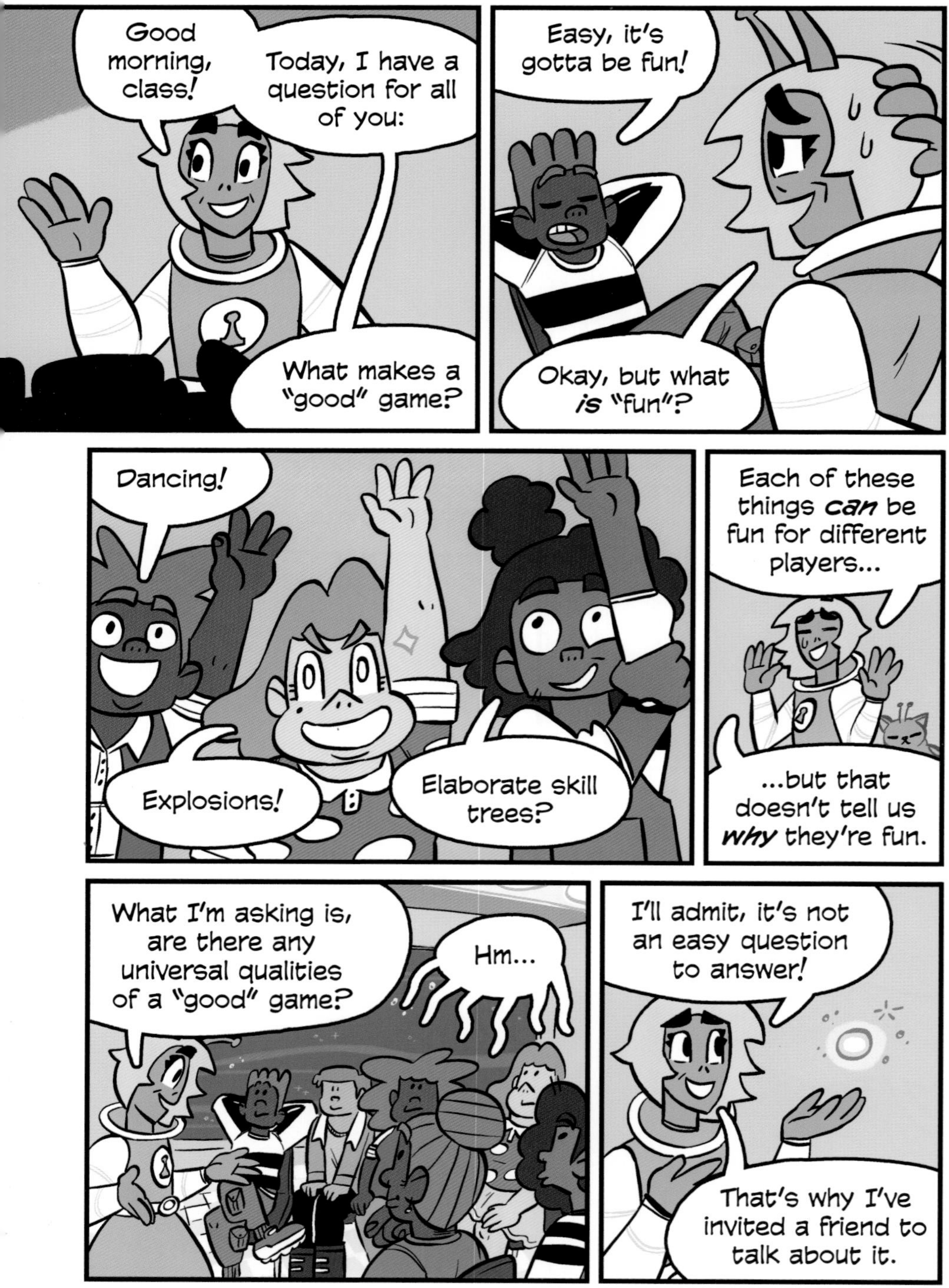
Good morning, class!
Today, I have a question for all of you:
What makes a "good" game?
Easy, it's gotta be fun!
Okay, but what *is* "fun"?
Dancing!
Explosions!
Elaborate skill trees?
Each of these things *can* be fun for different players...
...but that doesn't tell us *why* they're fun.
What I'm asking is, are there any universal qualities of a "good" game?
Hm...
I'll admit, it's not an easy question to answer!
That's why I've invited a friend to talk about it.

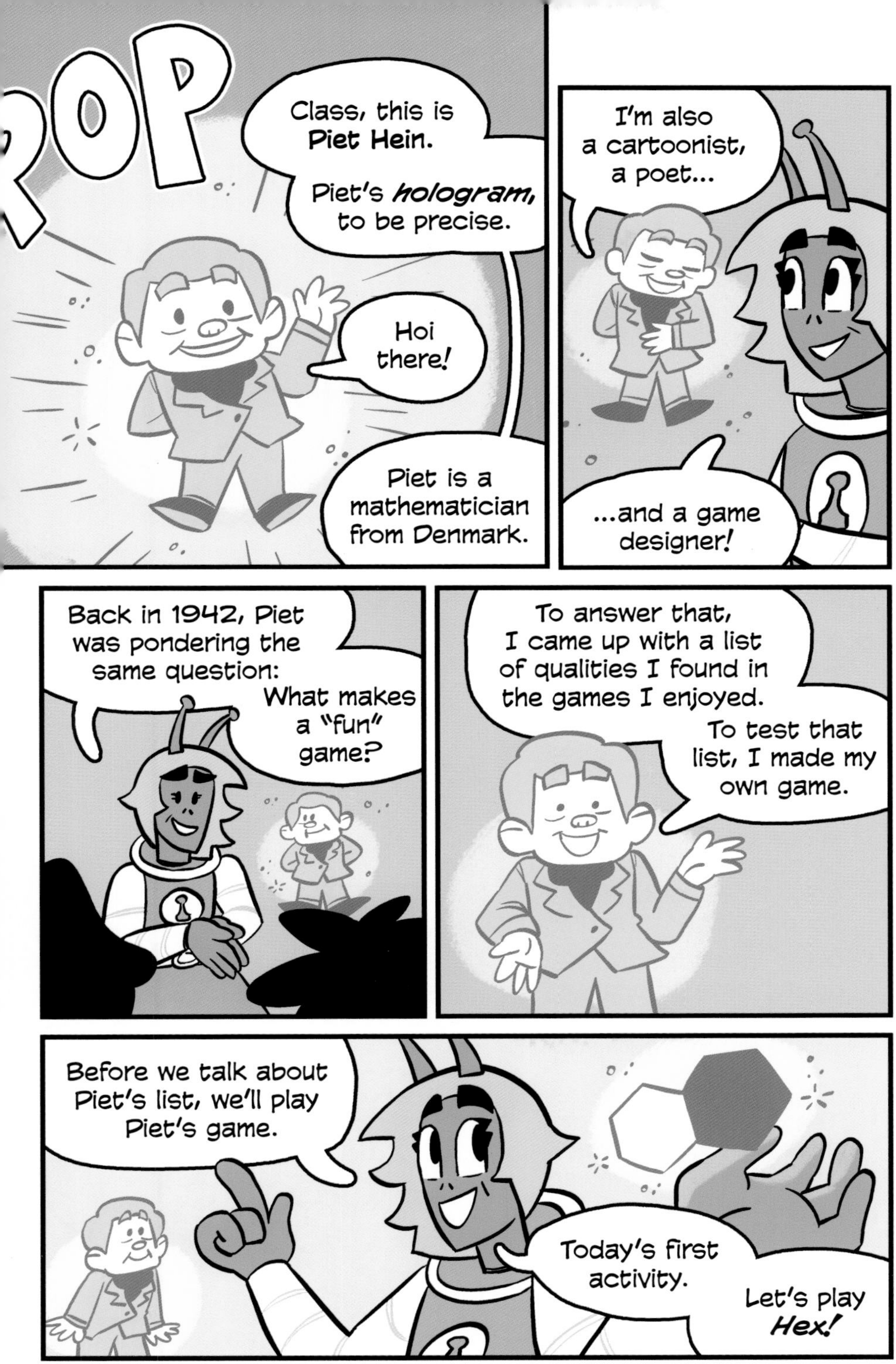
POP
Class, this is **Piet Hein.**
Piet's ***hologram,*** to be precise.
Hoi there!
Piet is a mathematician from Denmark.
I'm also a cartoonist, a poet...
...and a game designer!
Back in 1942, Piet was pondering the same question:
What makes a "fun" game?
To answer that, I came up with a list of qualities I found in the games I enjoyed.
To test that list, I made my own game.
Before we talk about Piet's list, we'll play Piet's game.
Today's first activity.
Let's play ***Hex!***

Let's Play *Hex!*

Players:	Materials:	Time to play:
2	2 different colored pencils, printout of *Hex* game board	5–10 minutes

1. Copy and print the *Hex* template on page 122 to make your game board! Each player colors two opposite sides of the board with their pencil.

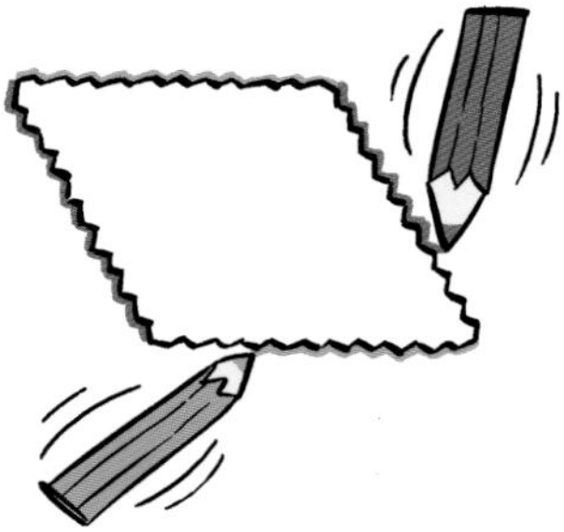

2. Flip a coin or play *rock-paper-scissors* to decide who goes first.

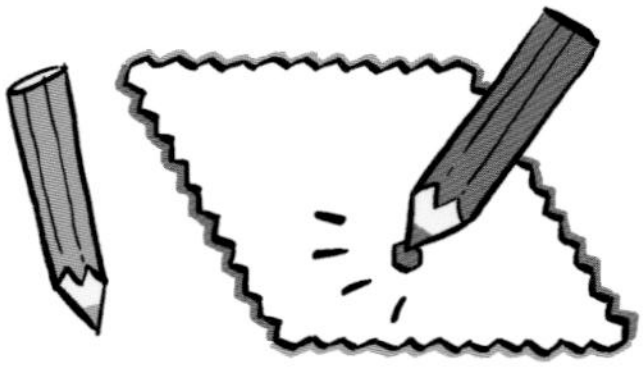

3. Players take turns coloring in one empty space on the board to claim it. When you color in a space, it becomes your territory!

   (Keep in mind that you do not have to choose spaces near ones you've already claimed!)

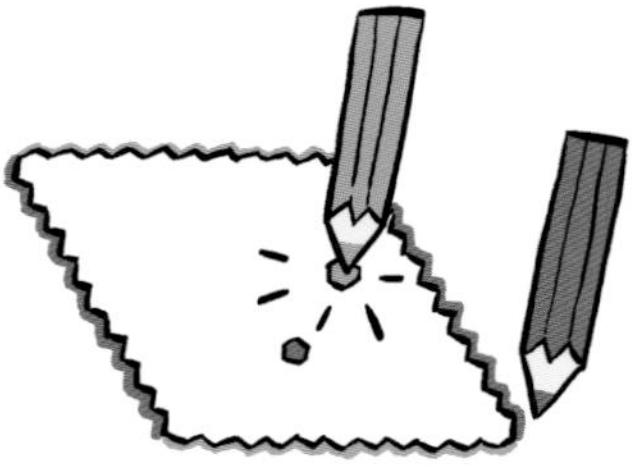

4. The first player to color a line connecting their two sides is the winner!

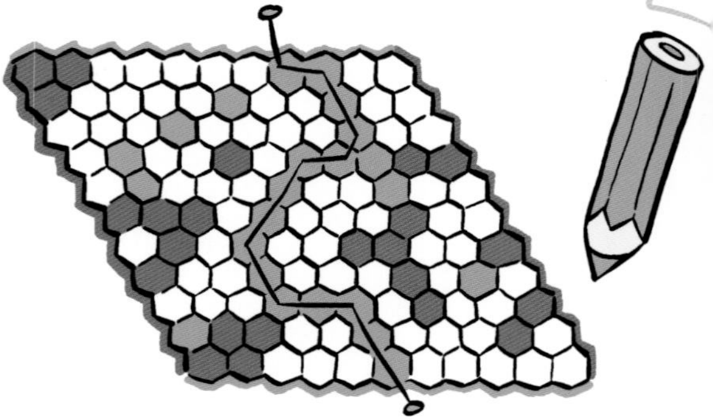

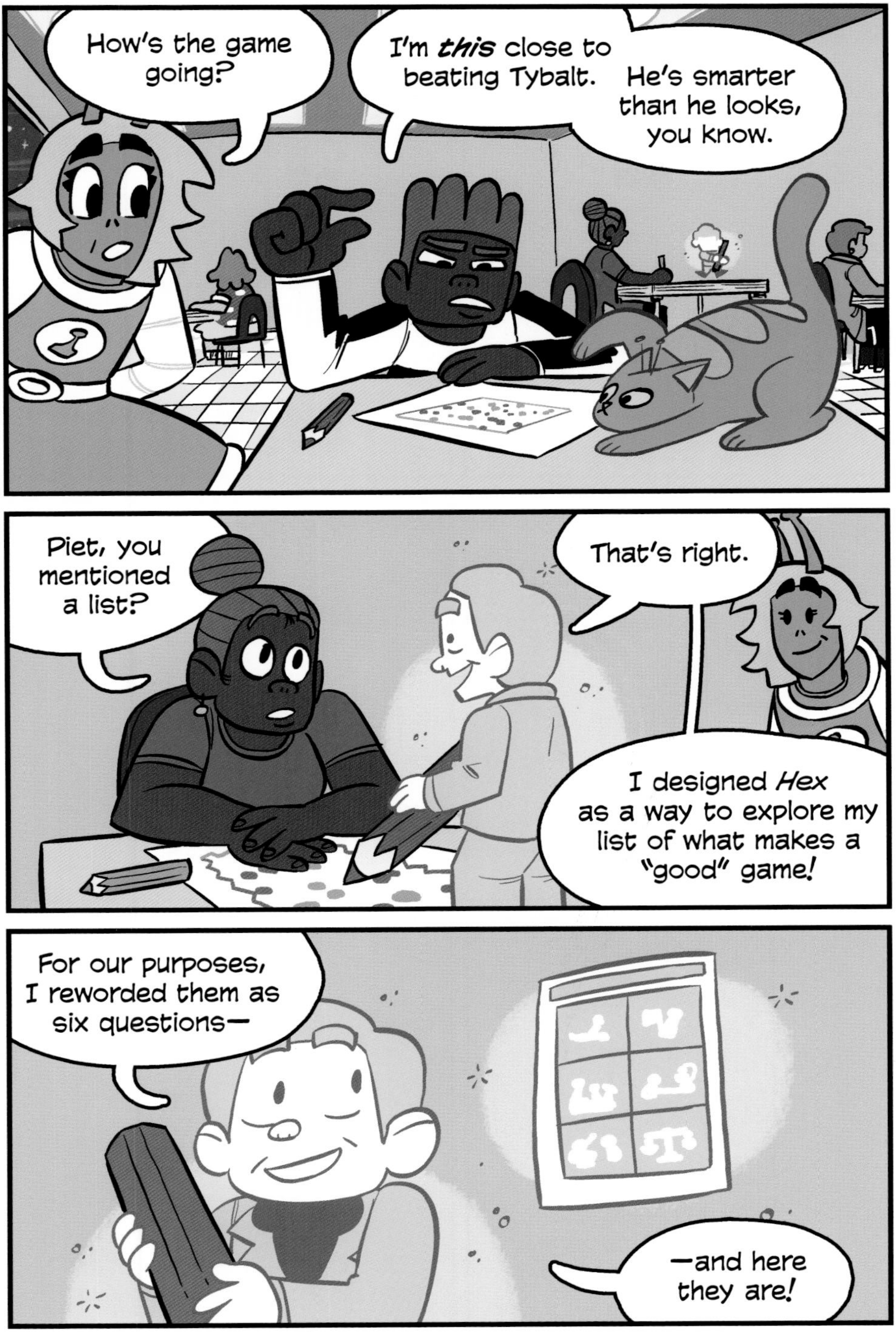
How's the game going?
I'm *this* close to beating Tybalt.
He's smarter than he looks, you know.
Piet, you mentioned a list?
That's right.
I designed *Hex* as a way to explore my list of what makes a "good" game!
For our purposes, I reworded them as six questions—
—and here they are!

Hein's Questions for Games:
"Is this game..."

1) Progressive?

Does the game feel like it's moving forward, or is it just going in circles?

2) Final?

Can we see the "finish line"? Is it clear when we cross it?

3) Decisive?

Is there (usually) a clear winner? How do we know who won?

4) Strategic?

Do we get to make interesting choices? As we improve, can we see further into the game?

5) Emergent?

Can we surprise each other with our strategies? Can we even surprise the game designers?

6) Fair?

Do all of the players start with an equal chance to win?

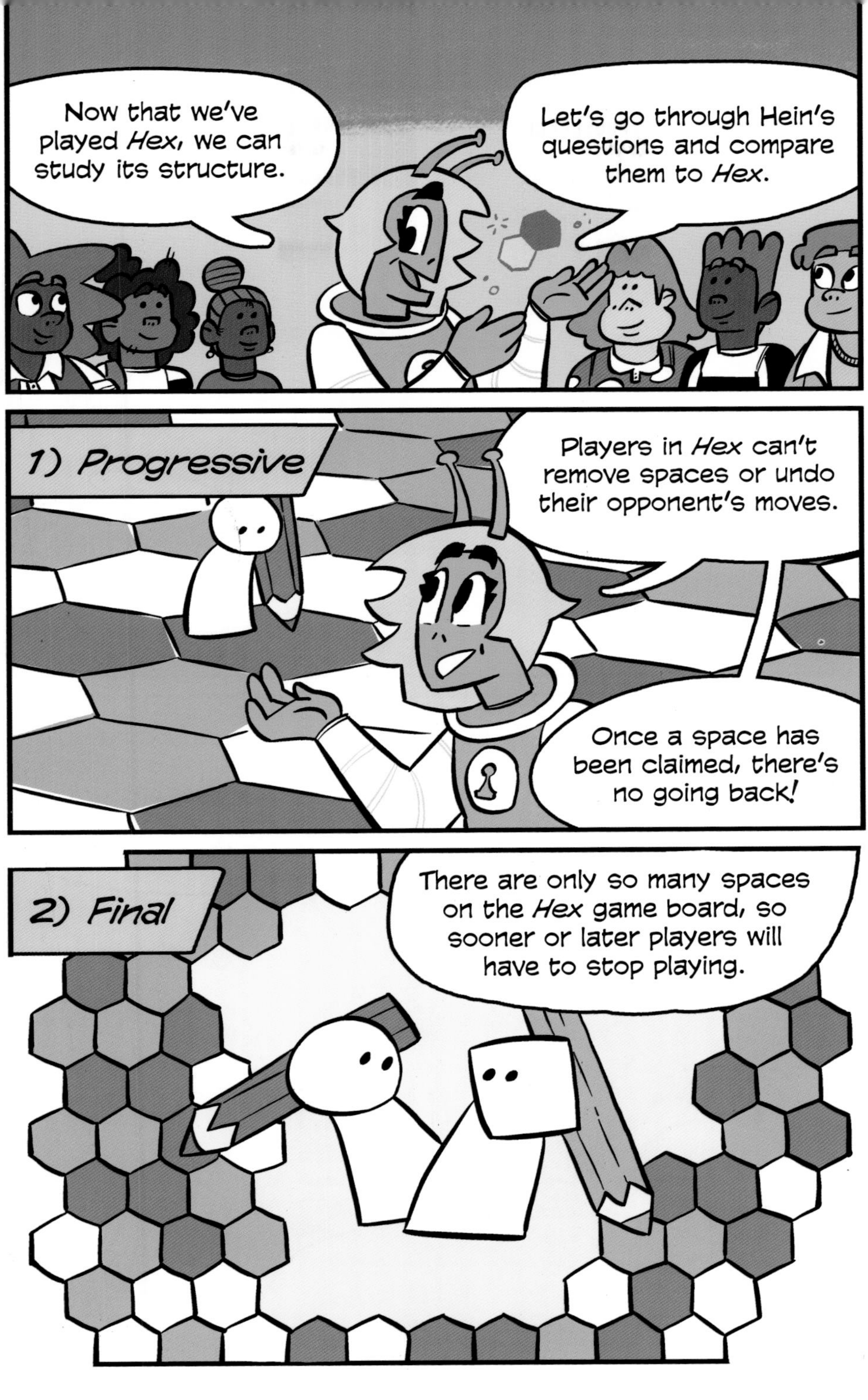

Now that we've played *Hex*, we can study its structure.
Let's go through Hein's questions and compare them to *Hex*.
1) Progressive
Players in *Hex* can't remove spaces or undo their opponent's moves.
Once a space has been claimed, there's no going back!
2) Final
There are only so many spaces on the *Hex* game board, so sooner or later players will have to stop playing.

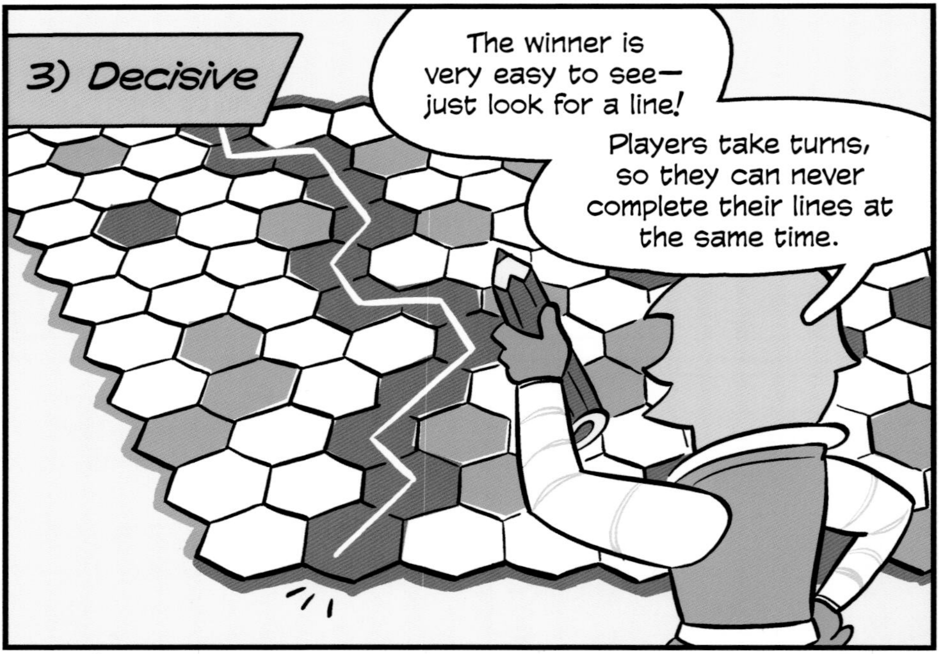
3) Decisive
The winner is very easy to see—just look for a line!
Players take turns, so they can never complete their lines at the same time.

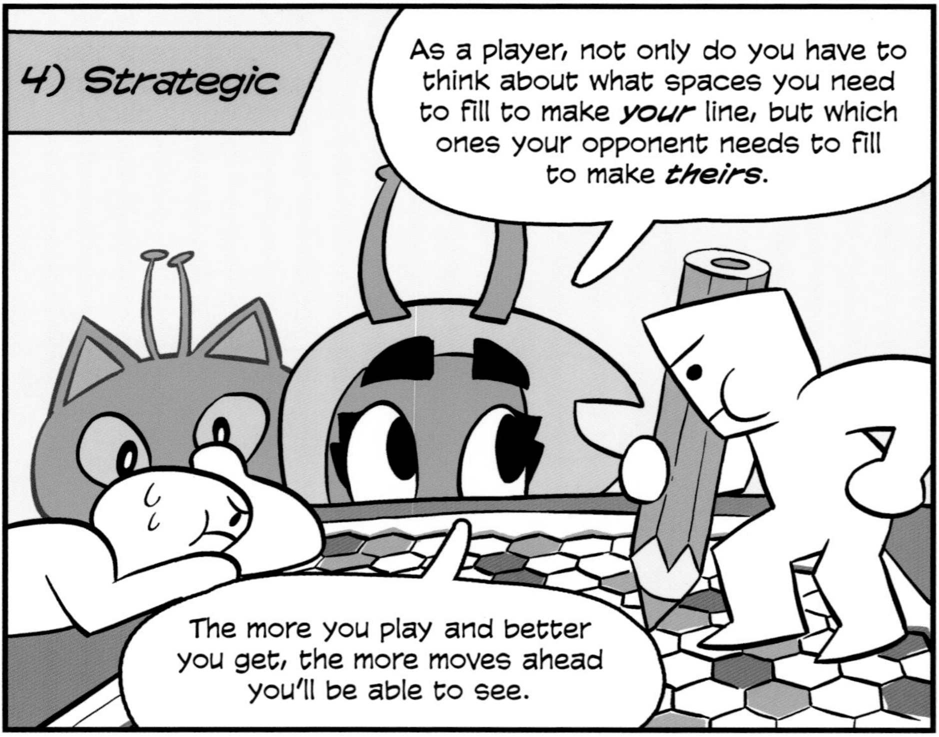
4) Strategic
As a player, not only do you have to think about what spaces you need to fill to make *your* line, but which ones your opponent needs to fill to make *theirs*.
The more you play and better you get, the more moves ahead you'll be able to see.

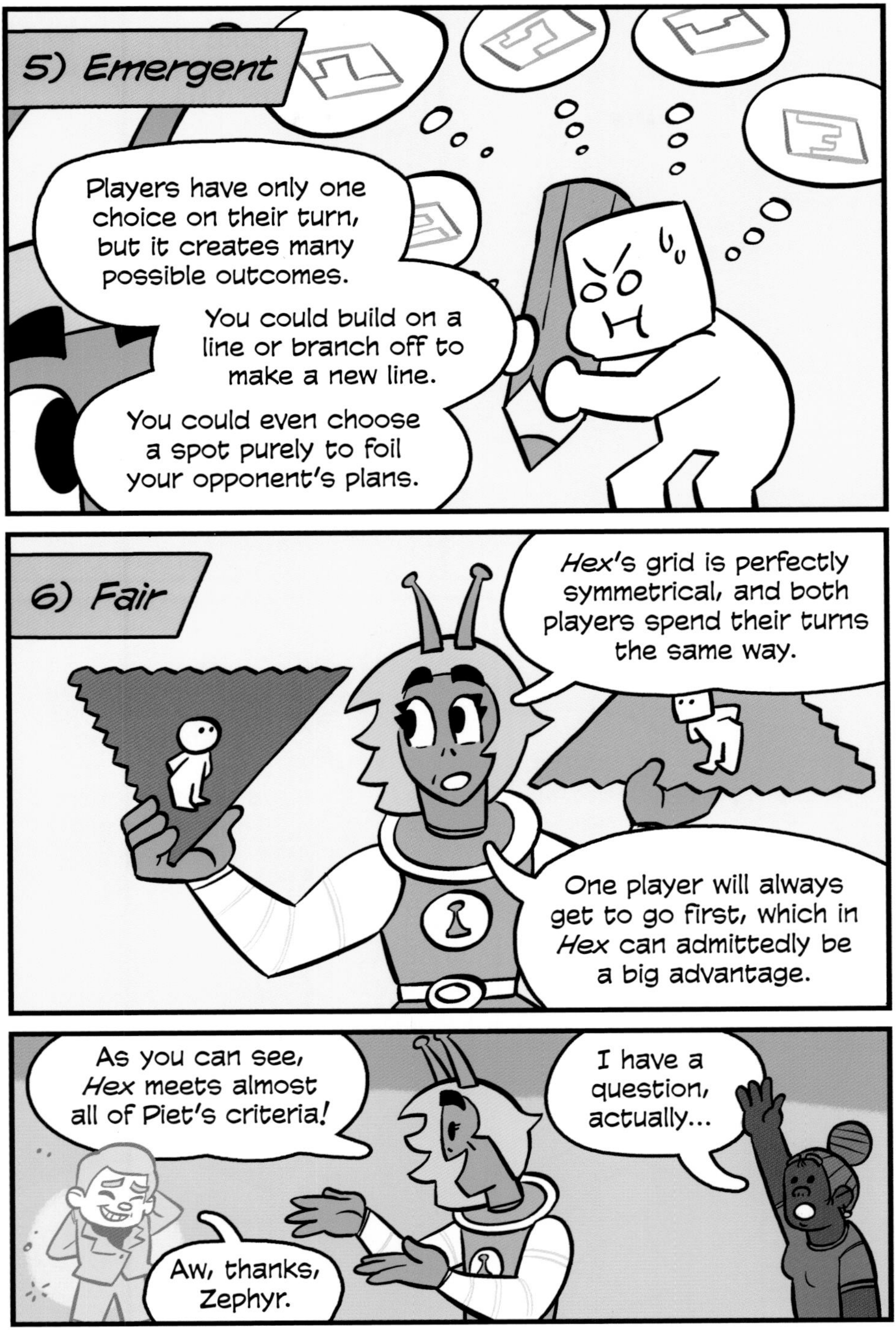
5) Emergent
Players have only one choice on their turn, but it creates many possible outcomes.
You could build on a line or branch off to make a new line.
You could even choose a spot purely to foil your opponent's plans.
6) Fair
Hex's grid is perfectly symmetrical, and both players spend their turns the same way.
One player will always get to go first, which in *Hex* can admittedly be a big advantage.
As you can see, *Hex* meets almost all of Piet's criteria!
I have a question, actually...
Aw, thanks, Zephyr.

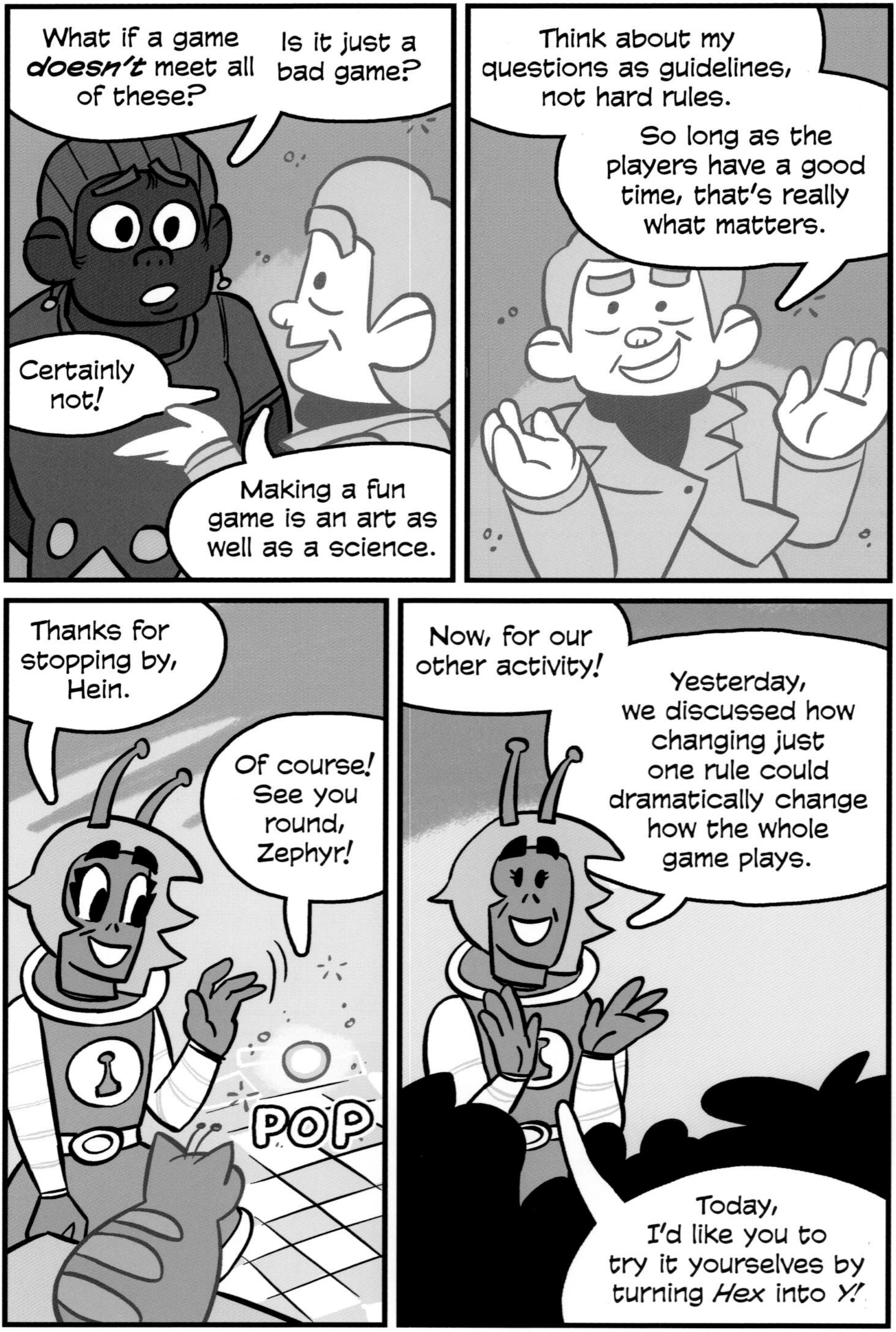

What if a game *doesn't* meet all of these?
Is it just a bad game?
Certainly not!
Making a fun game is an art as well as a science.
Think about my questions as guidelines, not hard rules.
So long as the players have a good time, that's really what matters.
Thanks for stopping by, Hein.
Of course! See you round, Zephyr!
POP
Now, for our other activity!
Yesterday, we discussed how changing just one rule could dramatically change how the whole game plays.
Today, I'd like you to try it yourselves by turning *Hex* into *Y*!

Craige Schensted and Charles Titus created Y, a game that was derived from Hex.

Make a New Game from *Hex!*

1. Create a *Y* board. (Actually, two!) Take a copy of the board on page 122 and cut it in half as shown.

2. To win a game of *Y*, a player must connect all three sides of the board. (A corner space can count as either side.) Play a few games. How does it feel compared to *Hex?*

3. Play a game of *Hex* or *Y* with any one of these rule changes:

a. Players can only choose a space next to one they have already claimed.

b. There are spaces that nobody can use.

c. Certain spaces allow you to claim an extra space on that turn.

d. Play a "loser wins" variant: you only win if your *opponent* connects their sides.

You can also come up with your own!

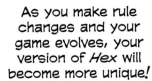

As you make rule changes and your game evolves, your version of *Hex* will become more unique!

BONUS!
Try another person's custom *Hex* game. How does it feel playing this compared to yours or to the normal *Hex* game?

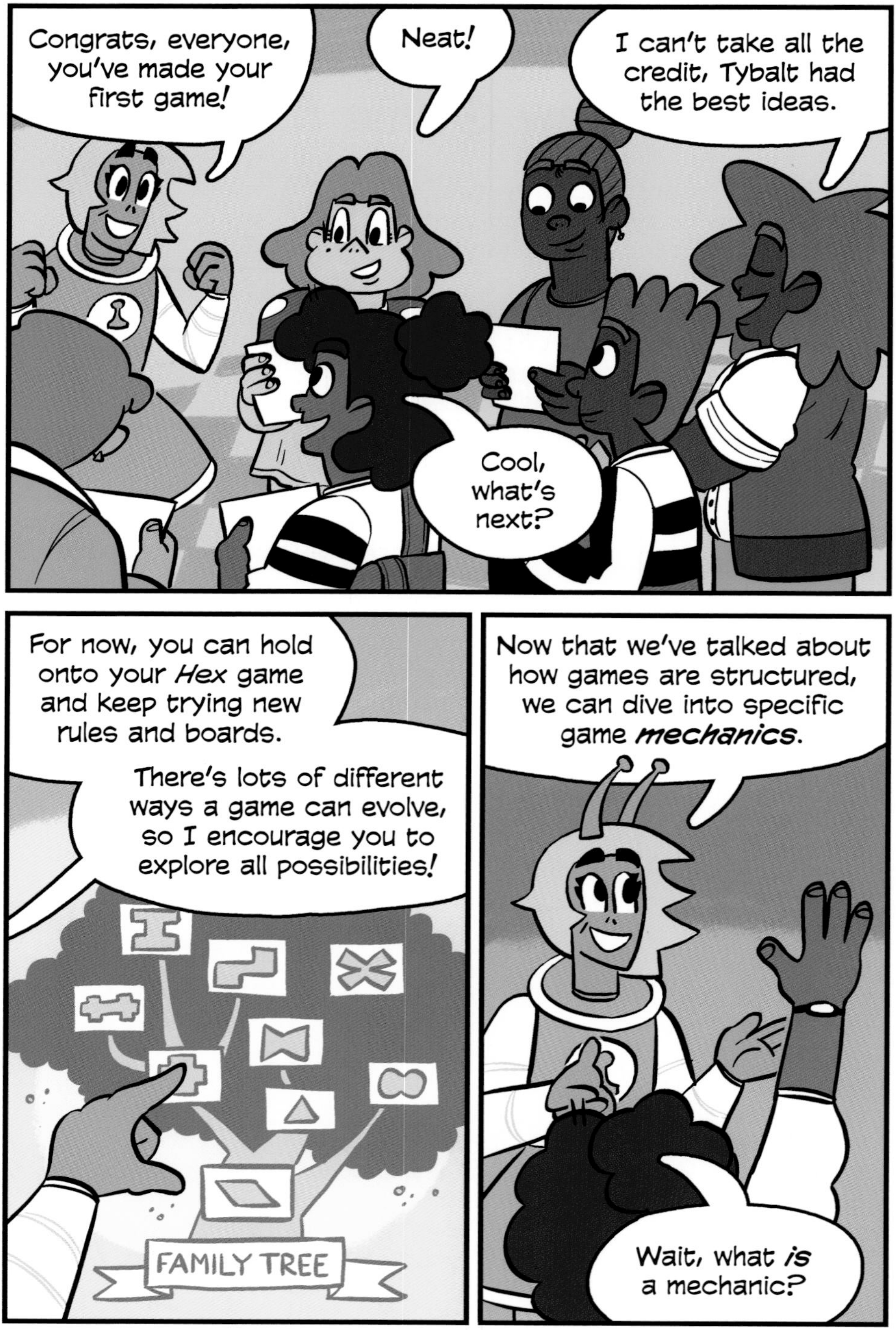
Congrats, everyone, you've made your first game!
Neat!
I can't take all the credit, Tybalt had the best ideas.
Cool, what's next?
For now, you can hold onto your *Hex* game and keep trying new rules and boards.
There's lots of different ways a game can evolve, so I encourage you to explore all possibilities!
FAMILY TREE
Now that we've talked about how games are structured, we can dive into specific game ***mechanics***.
Wait, what *is* a mechanic?

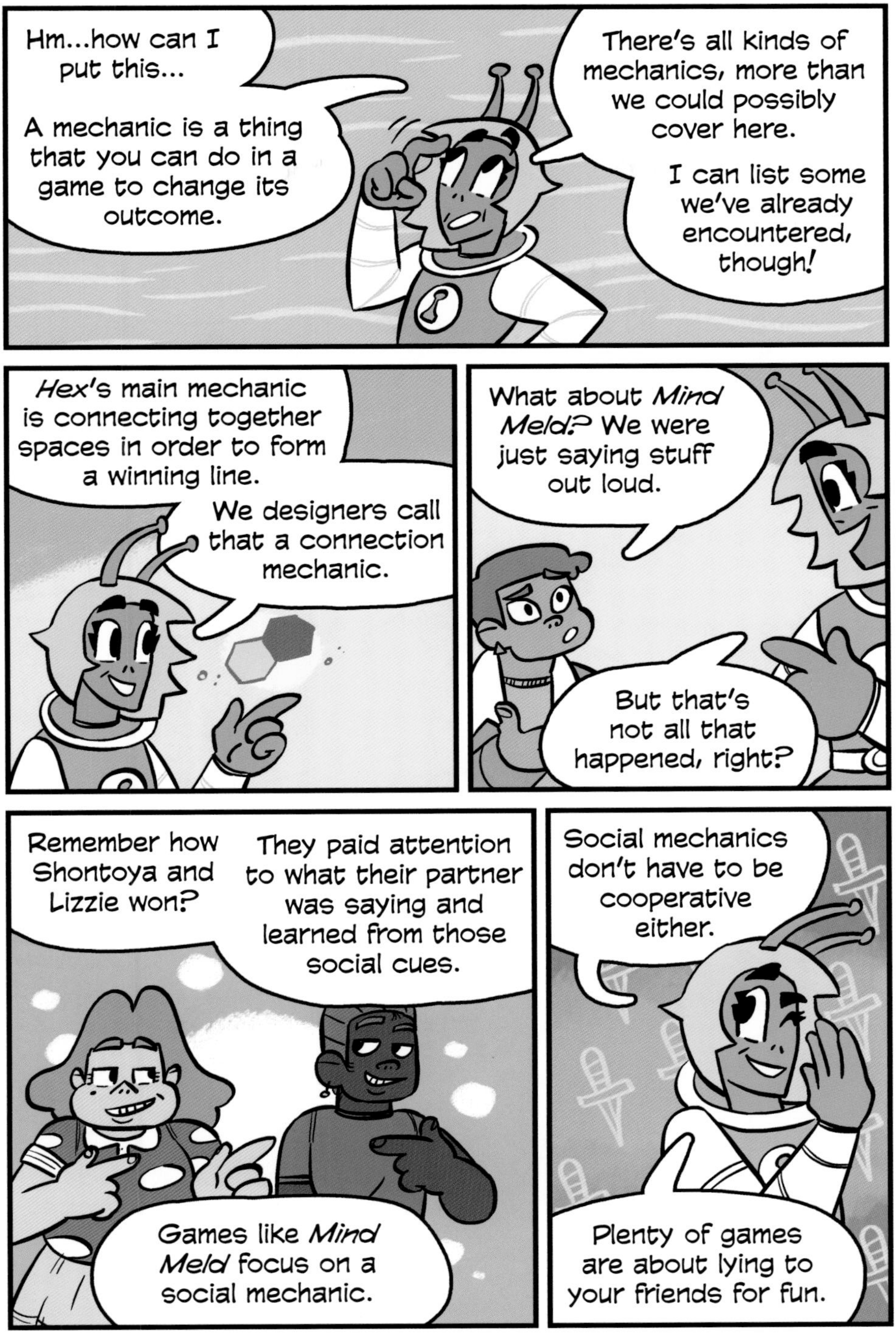

Hm...how can I put this...
A mechanic is a thing that you can do in a game to change its outcome.
There's all kinds of mechanics, more than we could possibly cover here.
I can list some we've already encountered, though!
Hex's main mechanic is connecting together spaces in order to form a winning line.
We designers call that a connection mechanic.
What about *Mind Meld?* We were just saying stuff out loud.
But that's not all that happened, right?
Remember how Shontoya and Lizzie won?
They paid attention to what their partner was saying and learned from those social cues.
Games like *Mind Meld* focus on a social mechanic.
Social mechanics don't have to be cooperative either.
Plenty of games are about lying to your friends for fun.

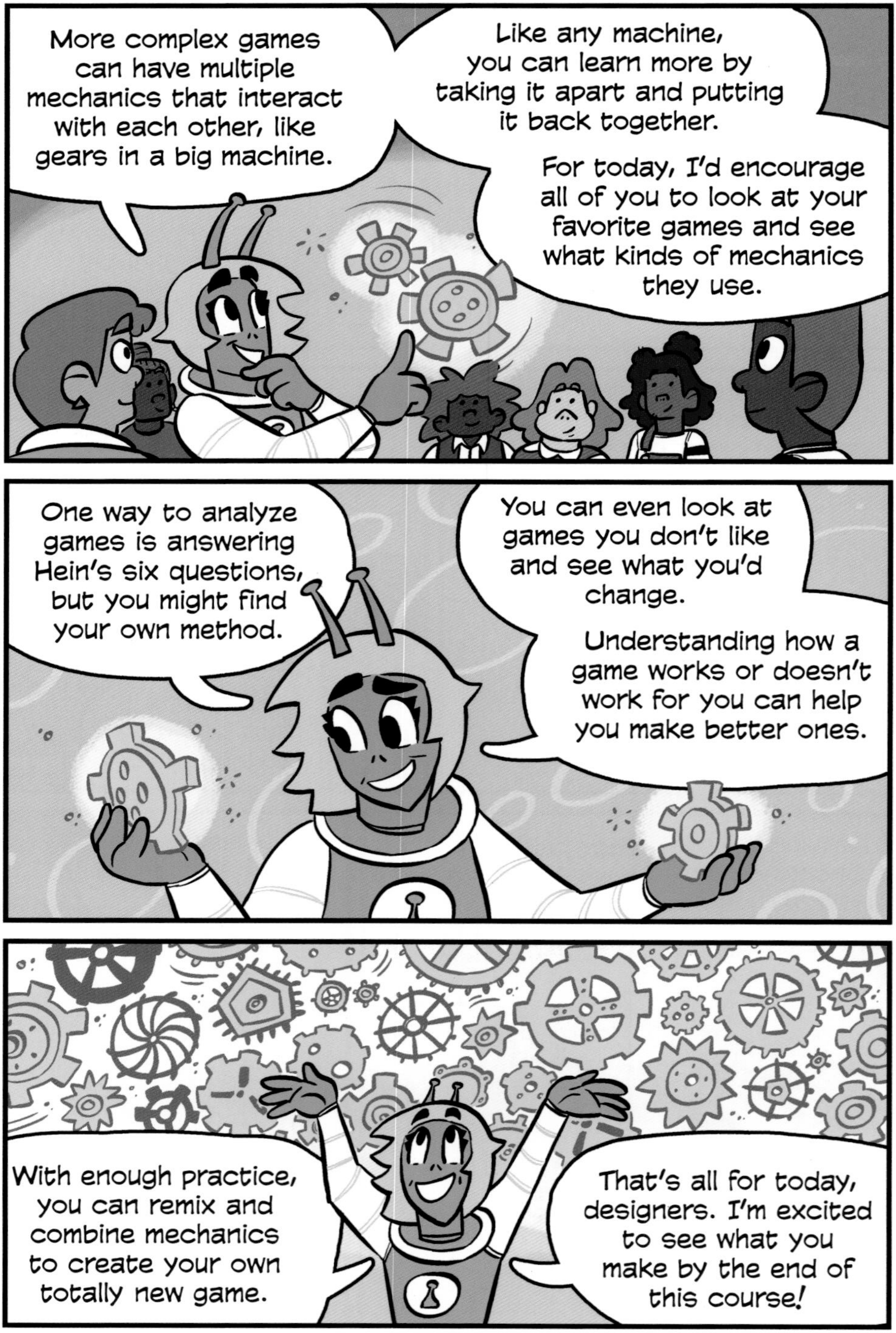
More complex games can have multiple mechanics that interact with each other, like gears in a big machine.
Like any machine, you can learn more by taking it apart and putting it back together.
For today, I'd encourage all of you to look at your favorite games and see what kinds of mechanics they use.
One way to analyze games is answering Hein's six questions, but you might find your own method.
You can even look at games you don't like and see what you'd change.
Understanding how a game works or doesn't work for you can help you make better ones.
With enough practice, you can remix and combine mechanics to create your own totally new game.
That's all for today, designers. I'm excited to see what you make by the end of this course!

DAY THREE: Chance and Memory

...Well? Have you decided yet?

If you can guess which one is the real list...

```
TTHHTT      HHHTHTH
THTTHH      HTTTTTT
TTHTHTH     HHTHTHH
TTHHTTT     TTHTHTH
HHTTHHT     TTHHHTH
TTHTHTH     HTHHTTT
TTHHHTT     HTHTHTT
```

...the whole class will get an ice cream party.

If you don't...

...only those two will get ice cream.

Who's feeling lucky?

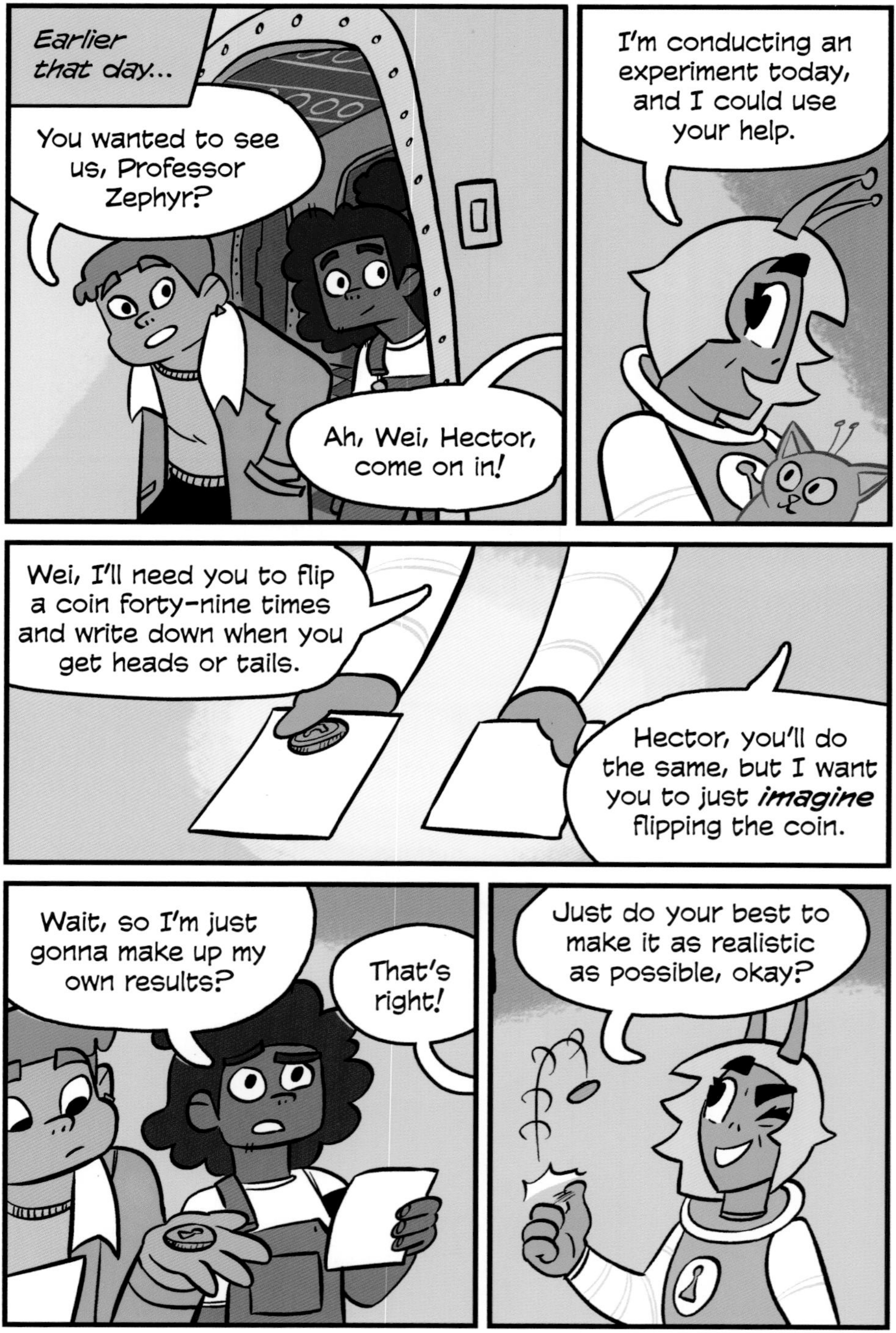
Earlier that day...
You wanted to see us, Professor Zephyr?
Ah, Wei, Hector, come on in!
I'm conducting an experiment today, and I could use your help.
Wei, I'll need you to flip a coin forty-nine times and write down when you get heads or tails.
Hector, you'll do the same, but I want you to just *imagine* flipping the coin.
Wait, so I'm just gonna make up my own results?
That's right!
Just do your best to make it as realistic as possible, okay?

...So, which is the real deal?

Hrngh...

Aha!

It's this one!

I see! Why that one?

HTTHHTTT
HTHTHTTHH
TTHTHTH
TTHHTTT
HTTTAHT
TTHTTT
TTHHHTT

HHHTHTH
HTTTTTT
HHTHTHHA
TTTHHTT
TTHHHTH
HTHTHT

The other one has a bunch of tails in a row. There's no way anyone would flip a coin like that!

HHTT
TTHH
ATHTH
TTHHTTT
HHTTAHT
TTTHTTH
TTHHHTT

That's very clever, Lizzie!

...Unfortunately, it's wrong.

...Eh?

41

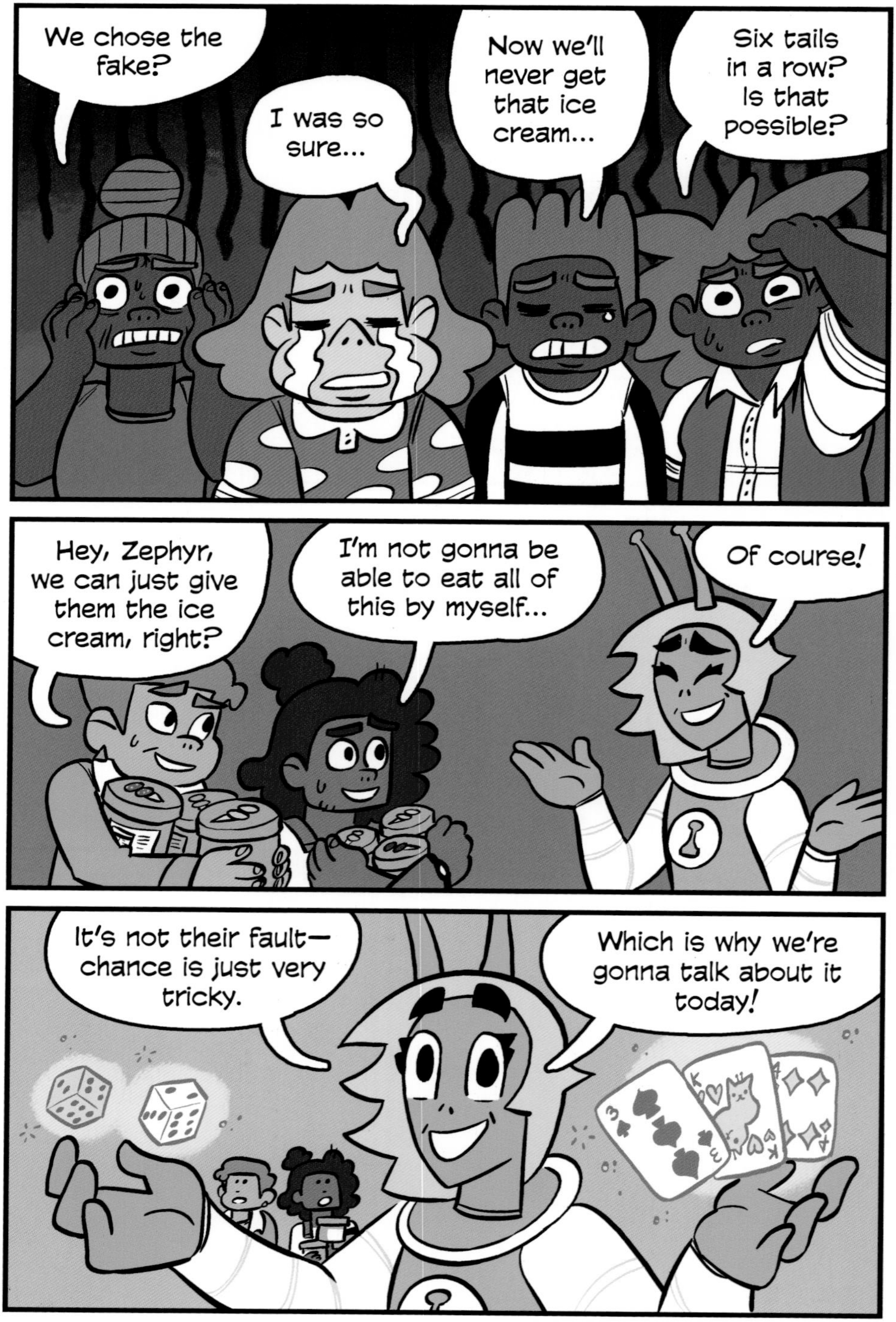
We chose the fake?
I was so sure...
Now we'll never get that ice cream...
Six tails in a row? Is that possible?
Hey, Zephyr, we can just give them the ice cream, right?
I'm not gonna be able to eat all of this by myself...
Of course!
It's not their fault—chance is just very tricky.
Which is why we're gonna talk about it today!

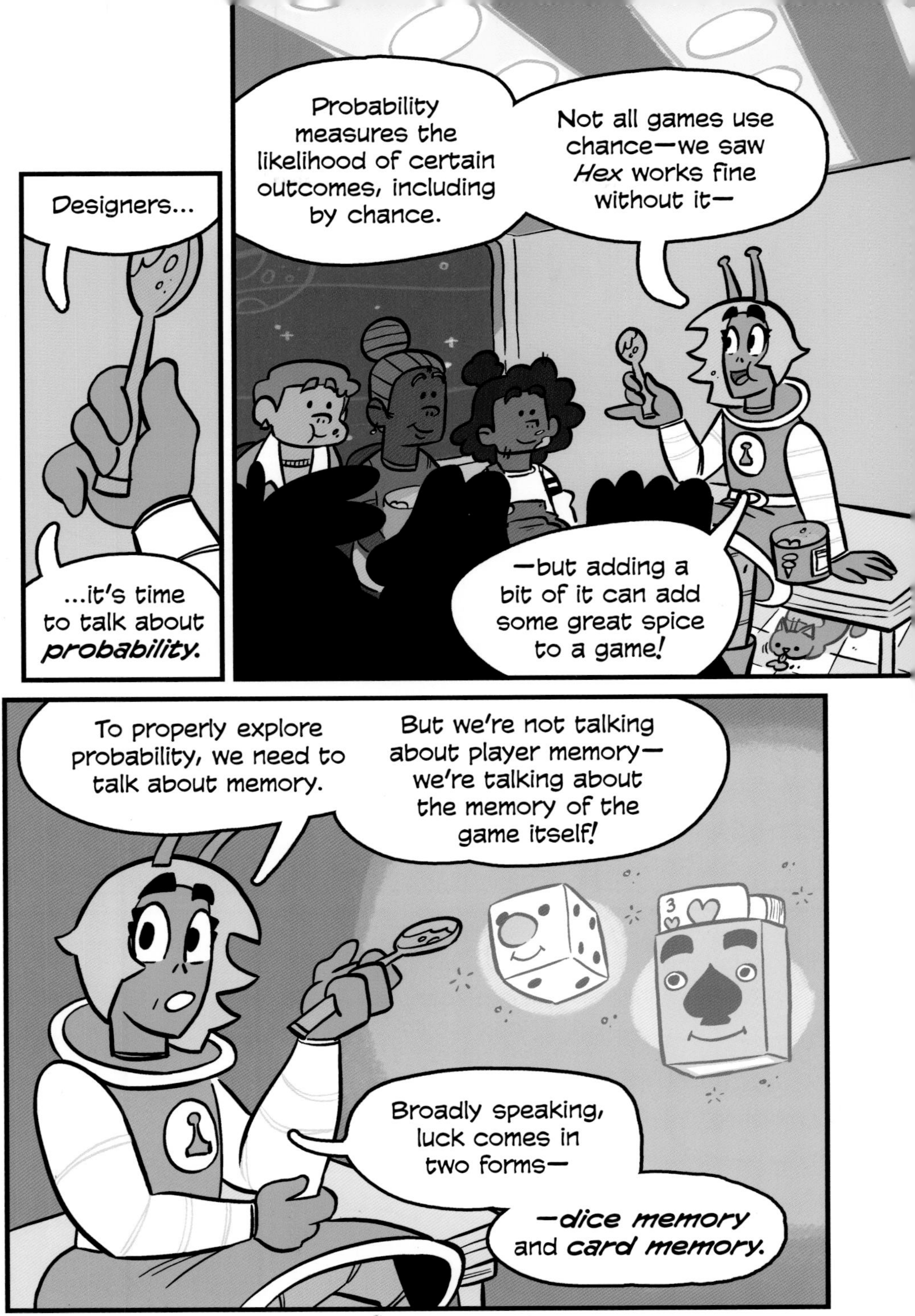
Designers...
...it's time to talk about ***probability.***
Probability measures the likelihood of certain outcomes, including by chance.
Not all games use chance—we saw *Hex* works fine without it—
—but adding a bit of it can add some great spice to a game!
To properly explore probability, we need to talk about memory.
But we're not talking about player memory—we're talking about the memory of the game itself!
Broadly speaking, luck comes in two forms—
—***dice memory*** and ***card memory.***

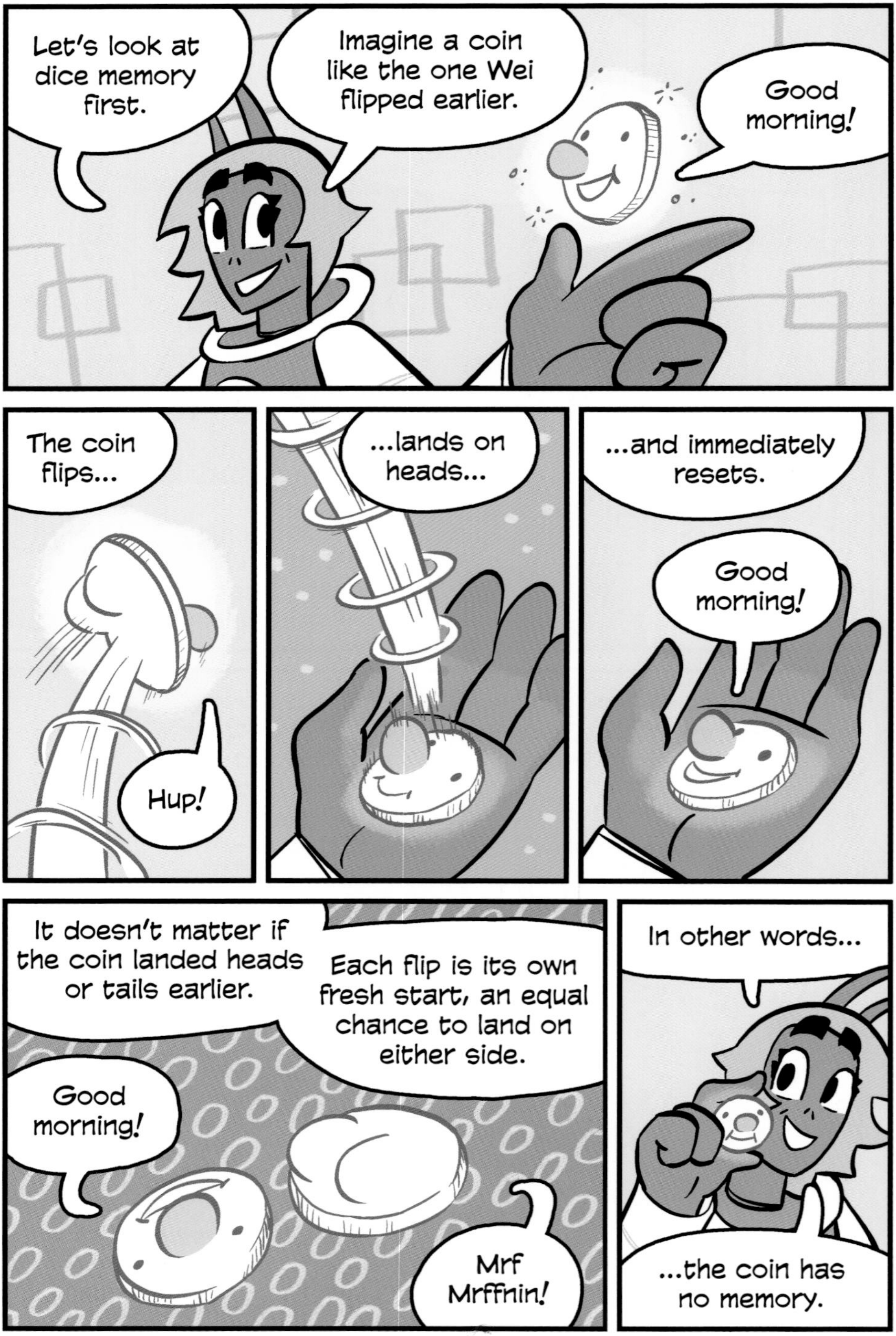
Let's look at dice memory first.
Imagine a coin like the one Wei flipped earlier.
Good morning!
The coin flips...
Hup!
...lands on heads...
...and immediately resets.
Good morning!
It doesn't matter if the coin landed heads or tails earlier.
Each flip is its own fresh start, an equal chance to land on either side.
Good morning!
Mrf Mrffnin!
In other words...
...the coin has no memory.

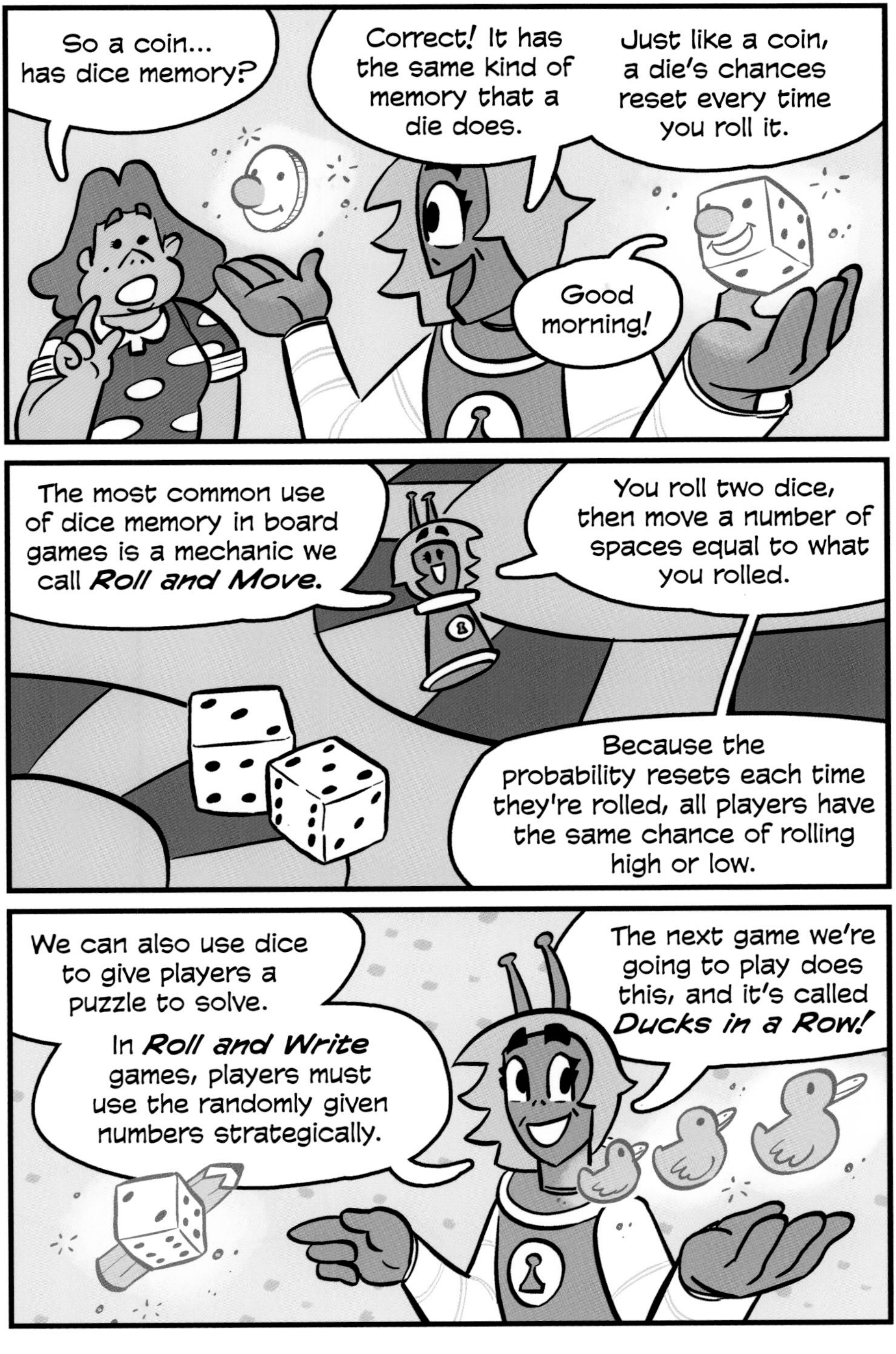
So a coin... has dice memory?
Correct! It has the same kind of memory that a die does.
Just like a coin, a die's chances reset every time you roll it.
Good morning!
The most common use of dice memory in board games is a mechanic we call ***Roll and Move.***
You roll two dice, then move a number of spaces equal to what you rolled.
Because the probability resets each time they're rolled, all players have the same chance of rolling high or low.
We can also use dice to give players a puzzle to solve.
In ***Roll and Write*** games, players must use the randomly given numbers strategically.
The next game we're going to play does this, and it's called ***Ducks in a Row!***

 # Ducks in a Row

Players: 1+	Materials: 2 x 6-sided dice, paper, pencil	Time to play: 15+ minutes

1. Each player draws a row of thirteen boxes or dashes on a sheet of paper.

2. Each turn, one player will roll two dice and call out the sum. All players write this number in one of the boxes on their row. Players can write the called number in any box, as long as it's bigger than (or equal to) every number already written to its left, and smaller than (or equal to) every number already written to its right. Once a box is filled, it cannot be erased.

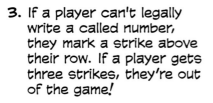

3. If a player can't legally write a called number, they mark a strike above their row. If a player gets three strikes, they're out of the game!

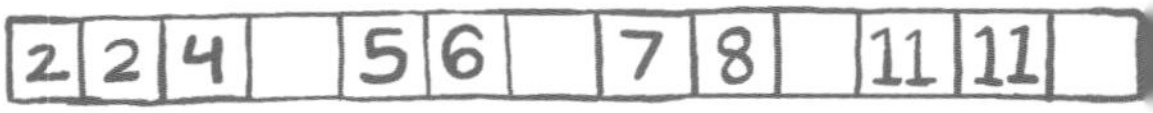

| 2 | 2 | 4 | | 5 | | | | 8 | | 11 | |

4. The winner is the first player to completely fill their row, or the last player eliminated. (Either way can result in a tie.) In a solo game, you can only win by completely filling your row. If you can't legally place a number, that's a strike. Three strikes and you're out.

| 2 | 2 | 4 | | 5 | 6 | | 7 | 8 | | 11 | 11 |

―BONUS!―

Try playing with different types of dice, and/or more dice per roll. For some truly wild results, use the product of the dice instead of the sum!

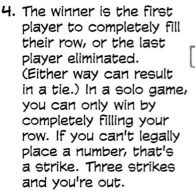

When designing a mechanic with chance, it helps to look at its probability range.

This graphs the likelihood of specific outcomes from a specific random input.

We'll start with a single six-sided die.

Notice that it's perfectly flat.

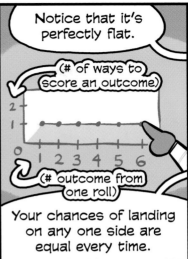

(# of ways to score an outcome)

(# outcome from one roll)

Your chances of landing on any one side are equal every time.

Now let's chart the range for a single turn of *Ducks in a Row*.

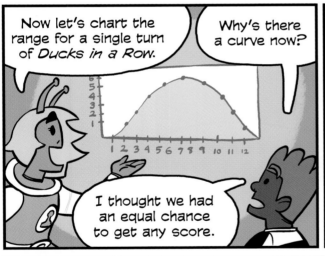

Why's there a curve now?

I thought we had an equal chance to get any score.

For one die, yes. But now we're using *two*.

Some scores are going to be easier or harder to get.

We have many ways to score seven points...

① ④
② ⑤
③ ⑥

...but only one way to score twelve.

Still, dice aren't the only way to add chance to our games!

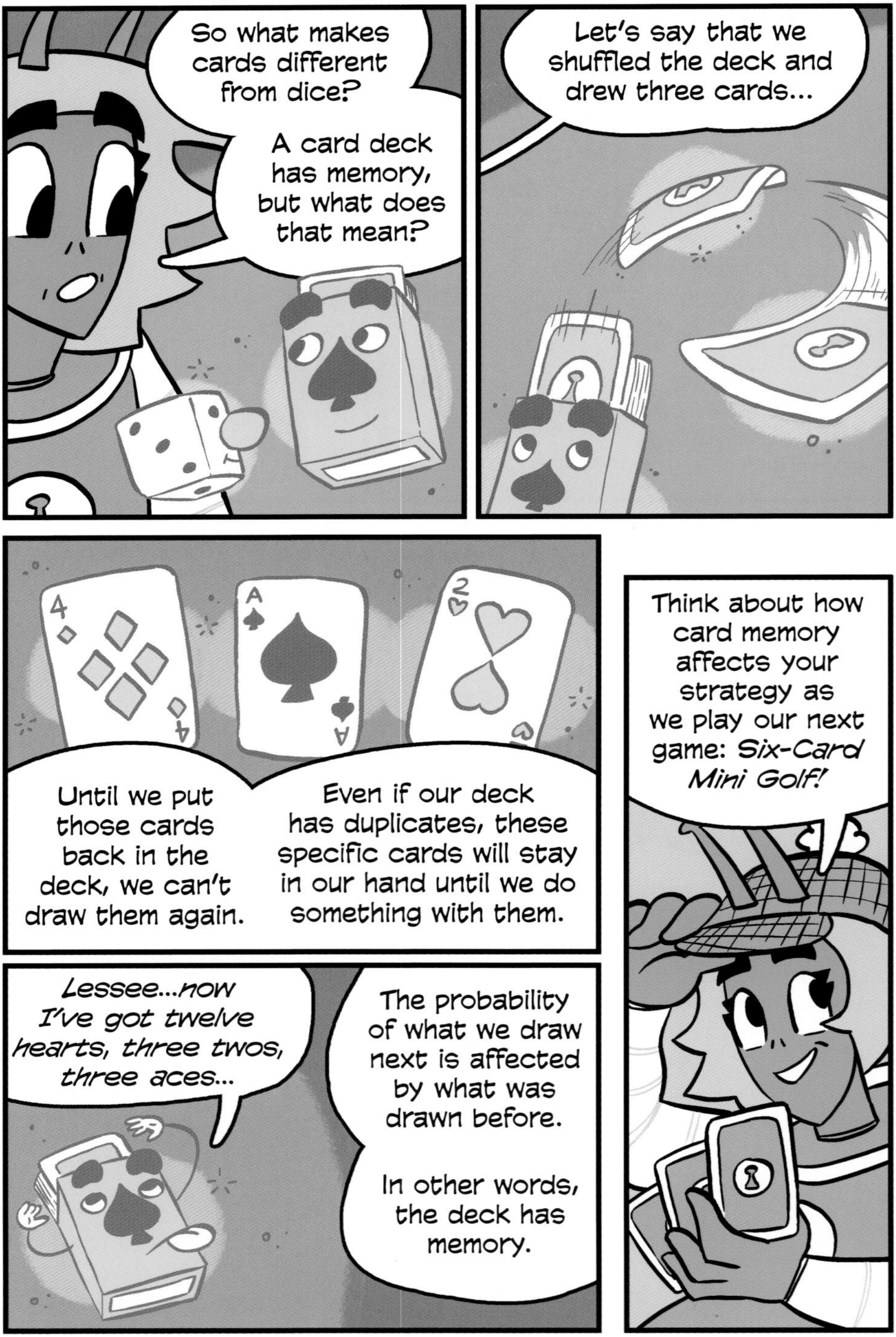

So what makes cards different from dice?
A card deck has memory, but what does that mean?
Let's say that we shuffled the deck and drew three cards...
4
A
2
Until we put those cards back in the deck, we can't draw them again.
Even if our deck has duplicates, these specific cards will stay in our hand until we do something with them.
Think about how card memory affects your strategy as we play our next game: *Six-Card Mini Golf!*
Lessee...now I've got twelve hearts, three twos, three aces...
The probability of what we draw next is affected by what was drawn before.
In other words, the deck has memory.

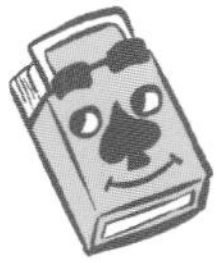

Six-Card Mini Golf

Players:	Materials:	Time to play:
2	deck of playing cards, pencil, paper	20+ minutes

1. Use a sheet of paper to record the scores. Choose one player to be the dealer. Remove diamonds, spades, and jokers from the deck—they won't be used. Shuffle the deck and deal each player six cards facedown. Do not look at these!

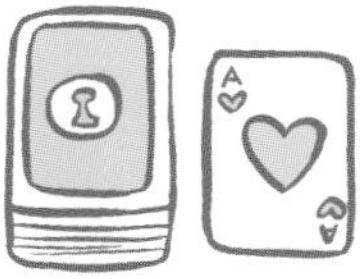

Deck and discard pile

2. Place the deck in the center. Turn its top card faceup and place it next to the deck to start the discard pile.

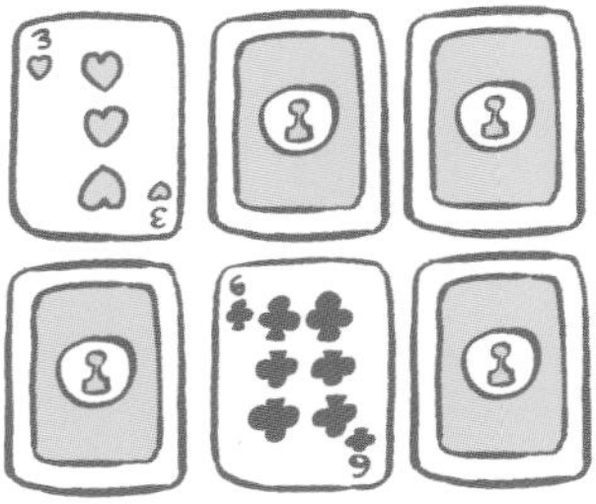

Turf example

3. Players arrange their cards in two rows of three, then flip any two of their cards faceup. This area will be called the player's turf. Players cannot look at any facedown cards, even their own.

4. Players want to have the ***lowest*** scoring turf by the end of the round (also called the "hole"). See the scoring guide on the next page for more information.

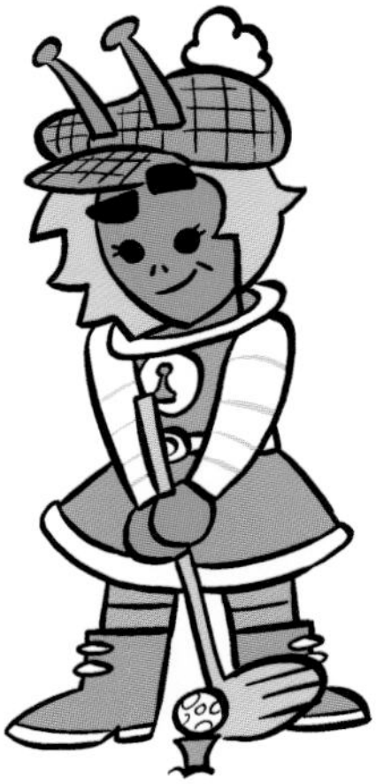

5. Beginning with the non-dealer, take turns. On your turn, draw the top card from the deck or discard pile. Either discard the drawn card or replace any card in your turf with it, discarding the replaced card. Cards are always drawn, played, and discarded face-up.

Cont. on next page

6. If there are no cards left in the deck at the start of your turn, shuffle the discard pile and create a new deck.

7. The hole immediately ends when a player's turf is completely faceup. Flip the other turf faceup. Calculate each player's scores and write them on the scoresheet. Reshuffle all of the cards and begin a new hole.

Scoring Guide

Ace	1 pt each
2	-2 pts each
3-10	= face value
Jack/Queen	10 pts each
King	0 pts each

SPECIAL! A pair of equal cards in the same column scores zero points for the column (even if the equal cards are twos).

8. A full game is nine holes. The player with the lowest total score after the ninth hole is the winner.

Scoring Example

In this example, the player earned a total of 7 points.

Because the two fives are in a column together, they score 0 points instead of 10.

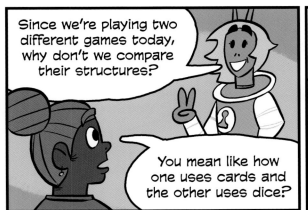

Since we're playing two different games today, why don't we compare their structures?

You mean like how one uses cards and the other uses dice?

That too, but I'd like to highlight their differences in *player interaction!*

Ducks in a Row is what we would call a "low interaction" game.

You're racing against other players to complete your sheet first, but are otherwise free from their influence.

This can make a game feel more relaxed and casual.

Six-Card Golf has a bit more interaction, since what a player chooses to draw or discard can affect your next turn.

And in a strategy game like *Hex*, you are directly competing with another player in the same space...

...making that a "high interaction" game.

Look at your favorite games and think about not only how you interact with the game, but with *other players*.

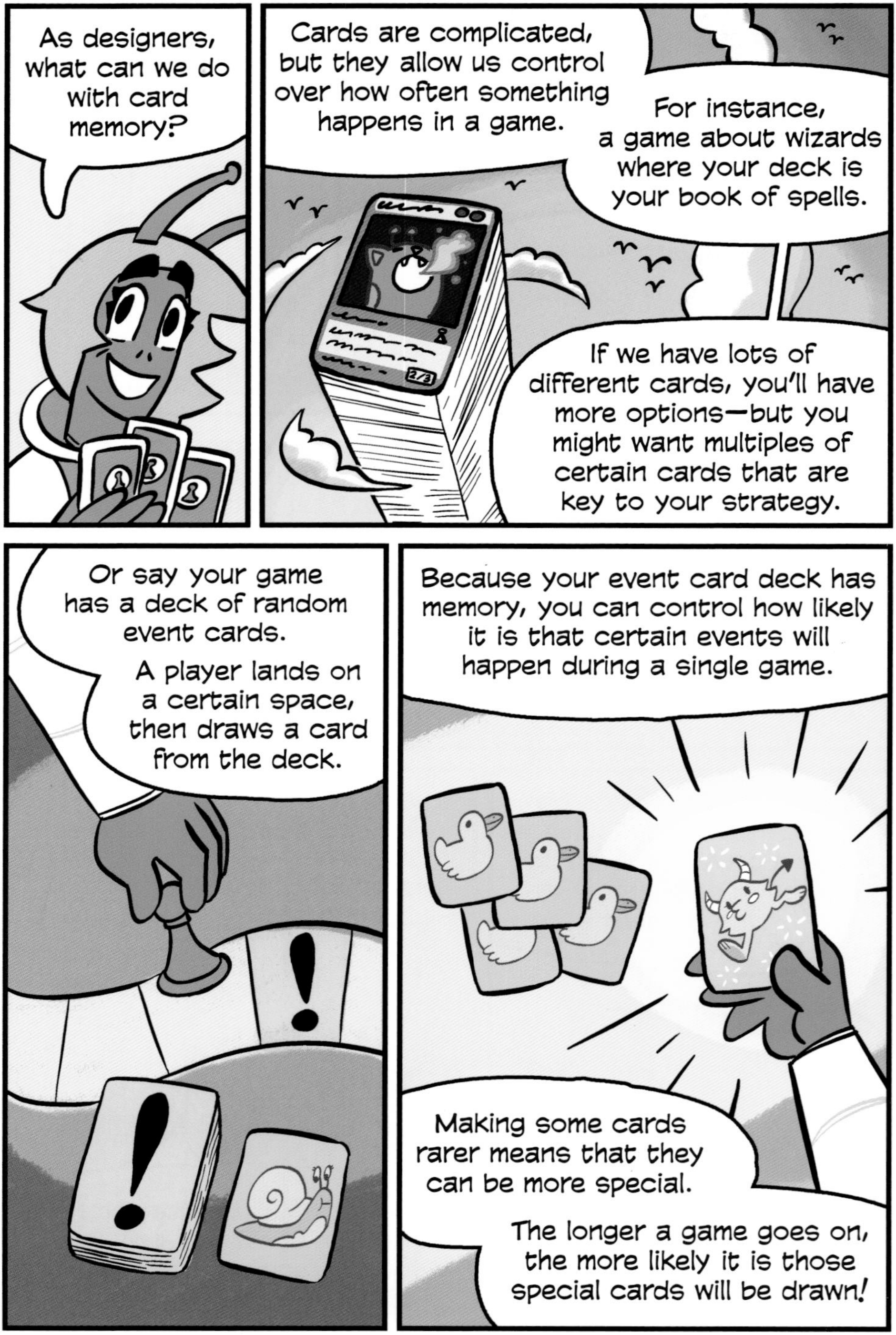
As designers, what can we do with card memory?
Cards are complicated, but they allow us control over how often something happens in a game.
For instance, a game about wizards where your deck is your book of spells.
If we have lots of different cards, you'll have more options—but you might want multiples of certain cards that are key to your strategy.
Or say your game has a deck of random event cards.
A player lands on a certain space, then draws a card from the deck.
Because your event card deck has memory, you can control how likely it is that certain events will happen during a single game.
Making some cards rarer means that they can be more special.
The longer a game goes on, the more likely it is those special cards will be drawn!

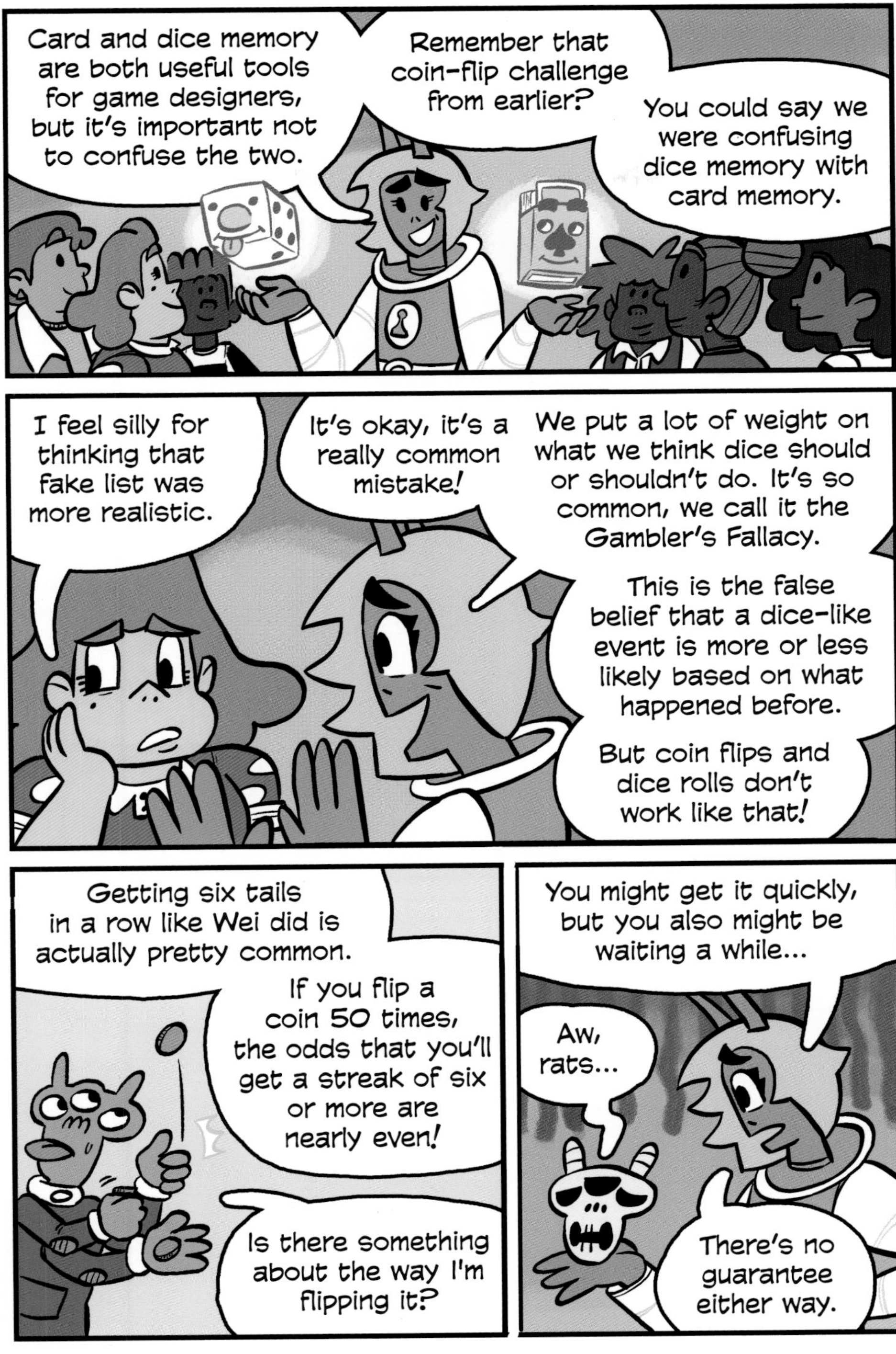

Card and dice memory are both useful tools for game designers, but it's important not to confuse the two.
Remember that coin-flip challenge from earlier?
You could say we were confusing dice memory with card memory.
I feel silly for thinking that fake list was more realistic.
It's okay, it's a really common mistake!
We put a lot of weight on what we think dice should or shouldn't do. It's so common, we call it the Gambler's Fallacy.
This is the false belief that a dice-like event is more or less likely based on what happened before.
But coin flips and dice rolls don't work like that!
Getting six tails in a row like Wei did is actually pretty common.
If you flip a coin 50 times, the odds that you'll get a streak of six or more are nearly even!
Is there something about the way I'm flipping it?
You might get it quickly, but you also might be waiting a while...
Aw, rats...
There's no guarantee either way.

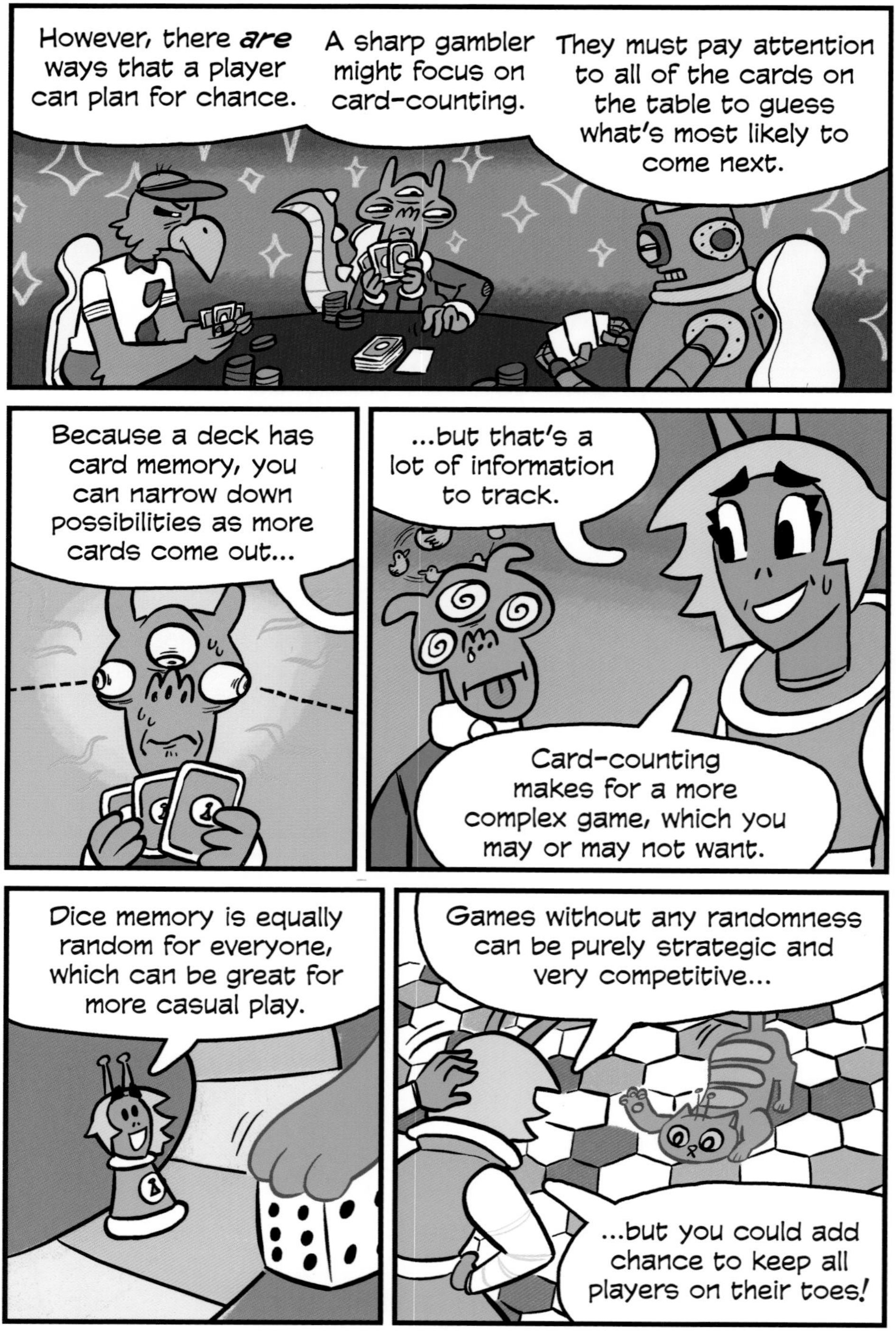
However, there *are* ways that a player can plan for chance.
A sharp gambler might focus on card-counting.
They must pay attention to all of the cards on the table to guess what's most likely to come next.
Because a deck has card memory, you can narrow down possibilities as more cards come out...
...but that's a lot of information to track.
Card-counting makes for a more complex game, which you may or may not want.
Dice memory is equally random for everyone, which can be great for more casual play.
Games without any randomness can be purely strategic and very competitive...
...but you could add chance to keep all players on their toes!

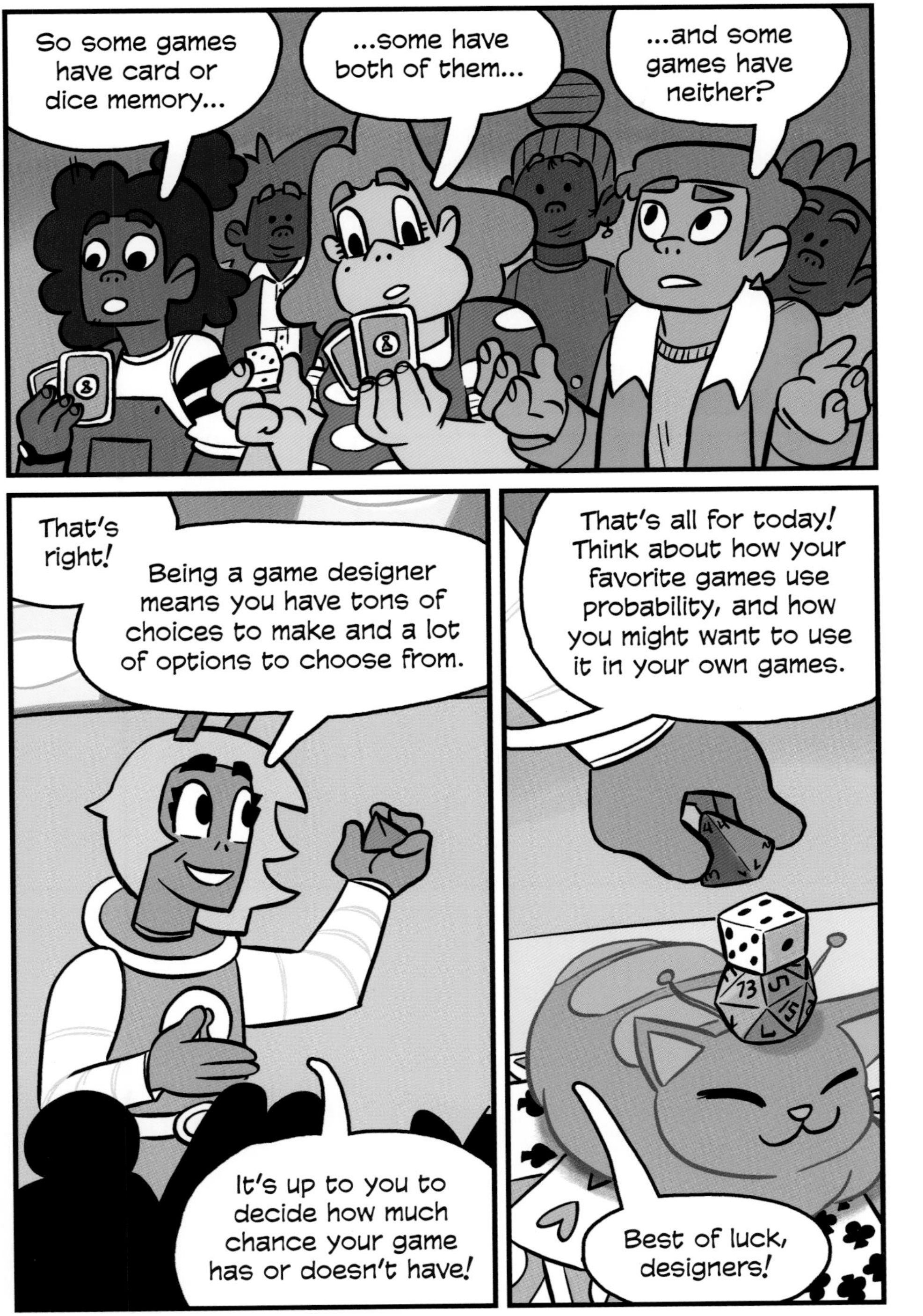
So some games have card or dice memory...
...some have both of them...
...and some games have neither?
That's right!
Being a game designer means you have tons of choices to make and a lot of options to choose from.
It's up to you to decide how much chance your game has or doesn't have!
That's all for today! Think about how your favorite games use probability, and how you might want to use it in your own games.
Best of luck, designers!

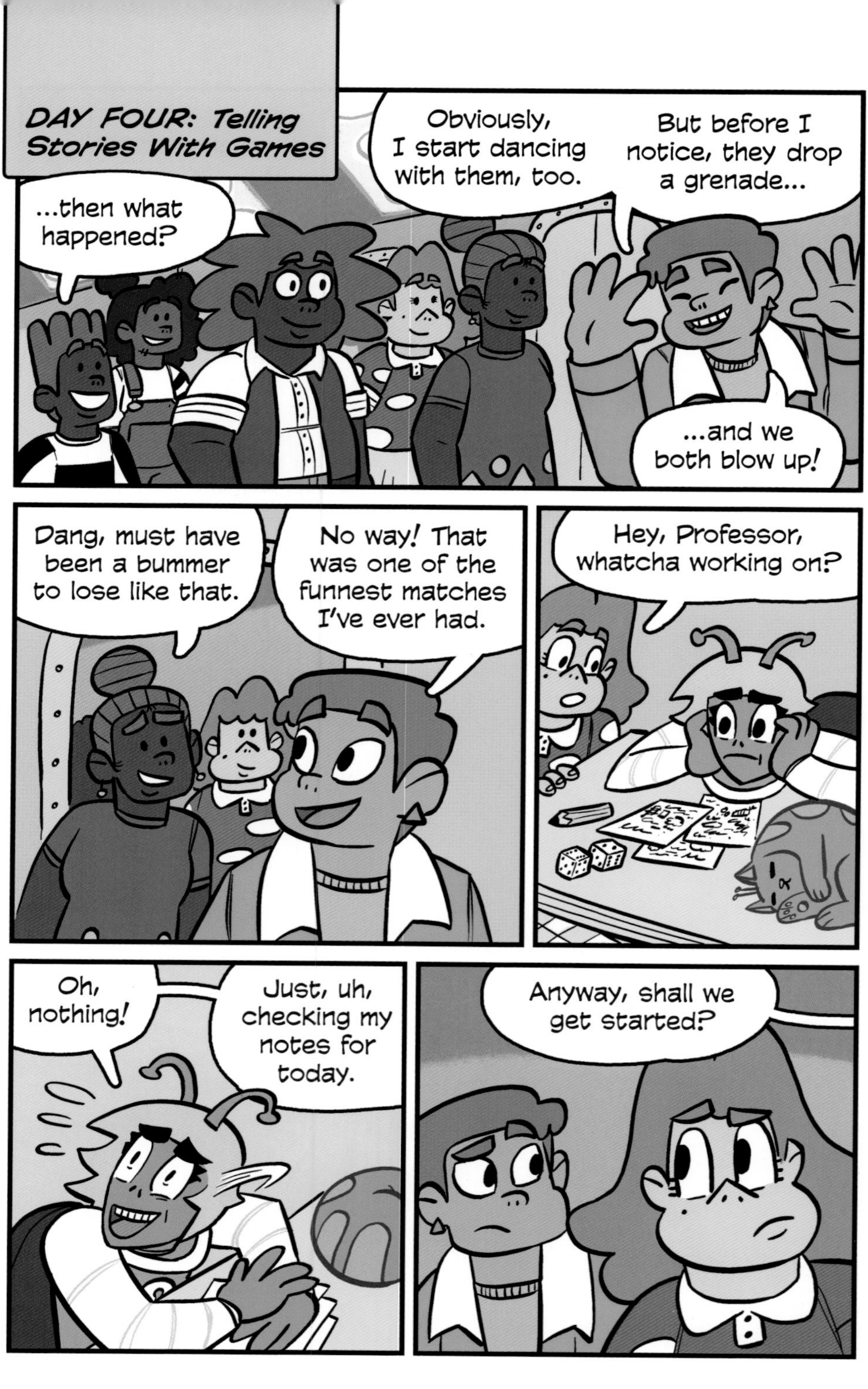
DAY FOUR: Telling Stories With Games
...then what happened?
Obviously, I start dancing with them, too.
But before I notice, they drop a grenade...
...and we both blow up!
Dang, must have been a bummer to lose like that.
No way! That was one of the funnest matches I've ever had.
Hey, Professor, whatcha working on?
Oh, nothing!
Just, uh, checking my notes for today.
Anyway, shall we get started?

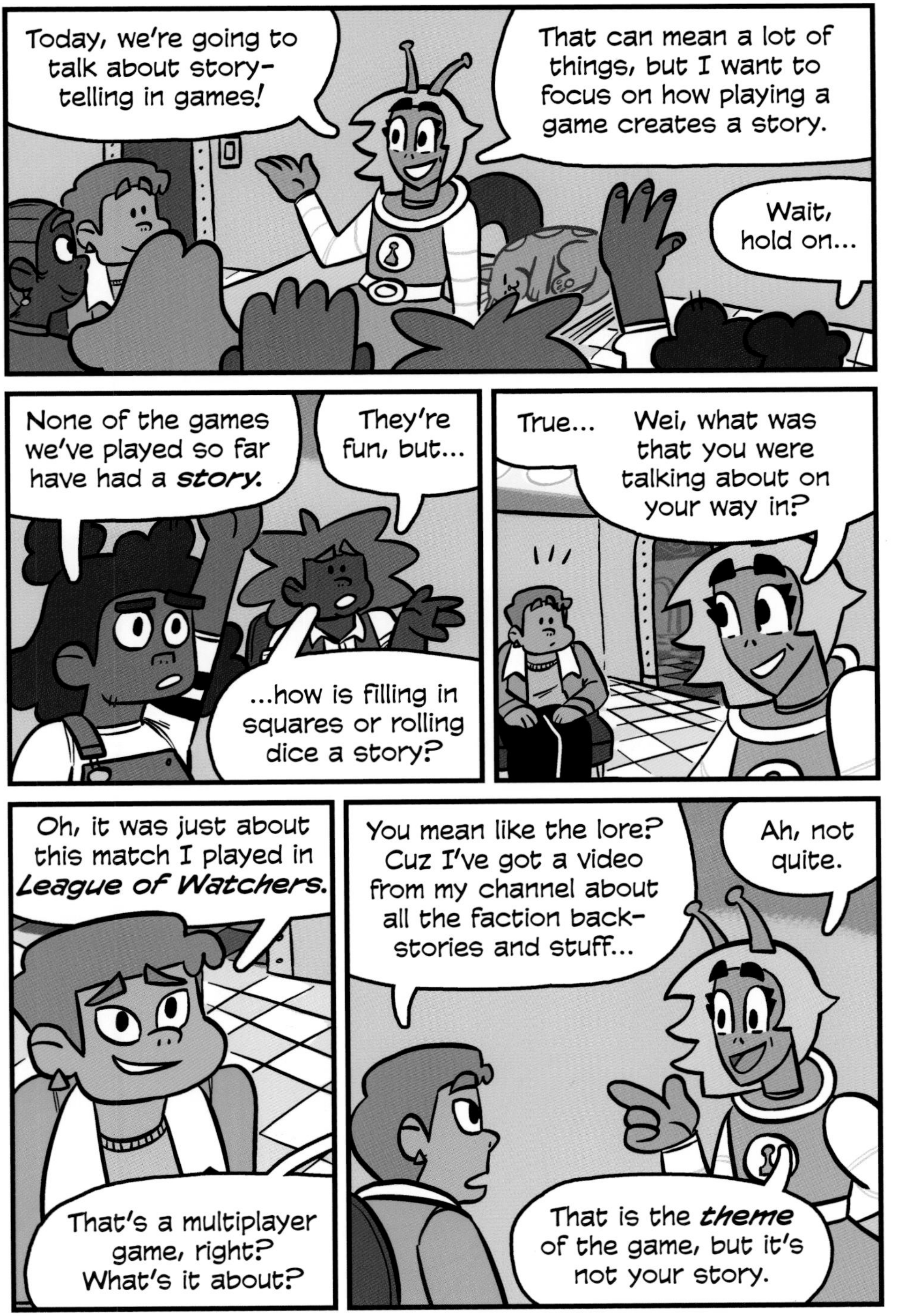
Today, we're going to talk about story-telling in games!
That can mean a lot of things, but I want to focus on how playing a game creates a story.
Wait, hold on...
None of the games we've played so far have had a *story*.
They're fun, but...
...how is filling in squares or rolling dice a story?
True...
Wei, what was that you were talking about on your way in?
Oh, it was just about this match I played in *League of Watchers*.
That's a multiplayer game, right? What's it about?
You mean like the lore? Cuz I've got a video from my channel about all the faction back-stories and stuff...
Ah, not quite.
That is the *theme* of the game, but it's not your story.

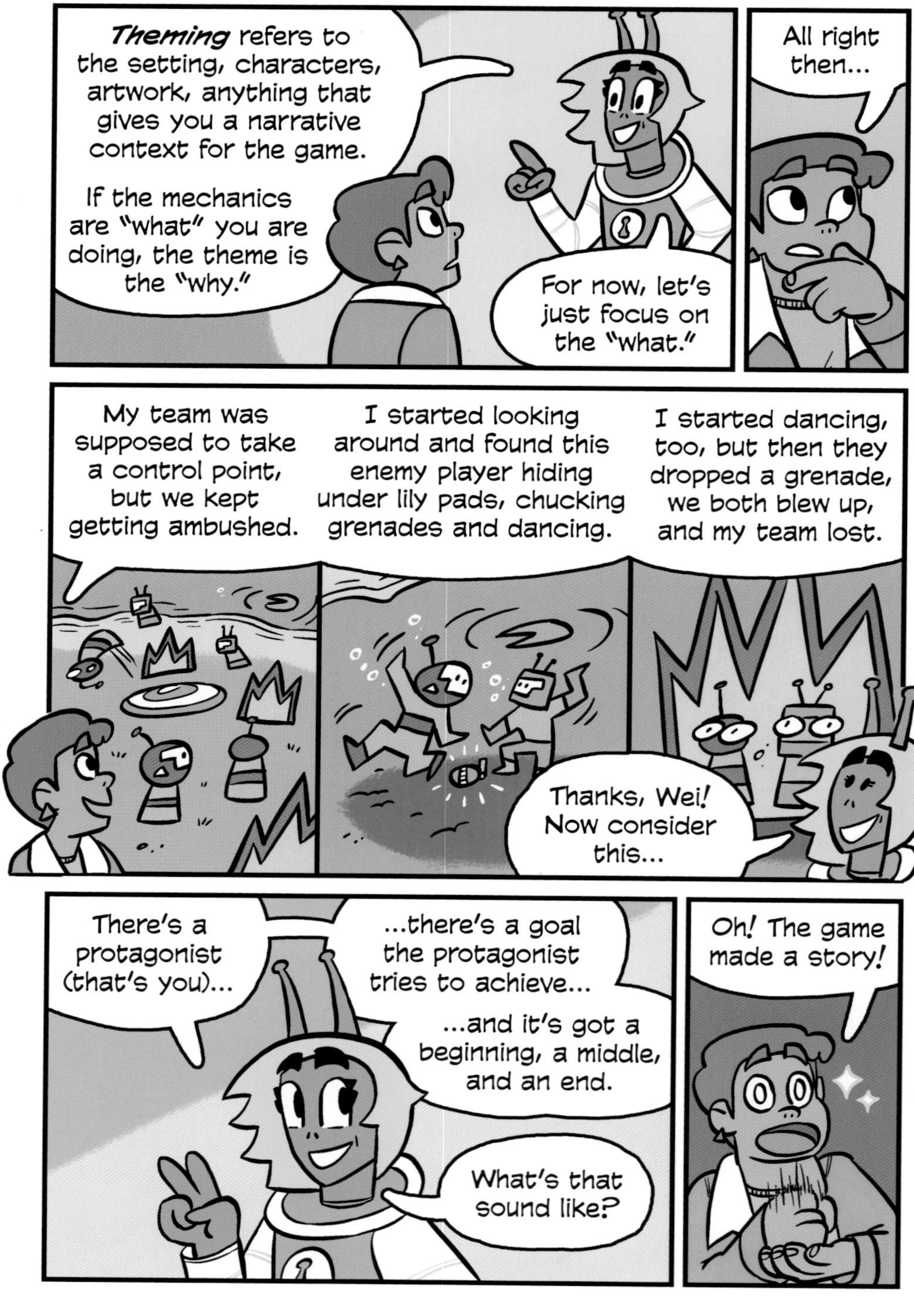
Theming refers to the setting, characters, artwork, anything that gives you a narrative context for the game.
If the mechanics are "what" you are doing, the theme is the "why."
For now, let's just focus on the "what."
All right then...
My team was supposed to take a control point, but we kept getting ambushed.
I started looking around and found this enemy player hiding under lily pads, chucking grenades and dancing.
I started dancing, too, but then they dropped a grenade, we both blew up, and my team lost.
Thanks, Wei! Now consider this...
There's a protagonist (that's you)...
...there's a goal the protagonist tries to achieve...
...and it's got a beginning, a middle, and an end.
What's that sound like?
Oh! The game made a story!

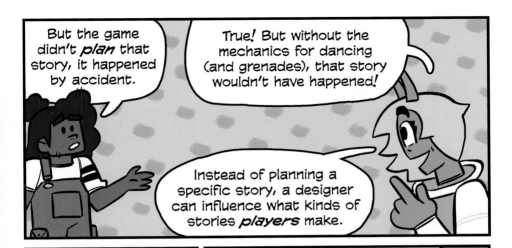

But the game didn't *plan* that story, it happened by accident.

True! But without the mechanics for dancing (and grenades), that story wouldn't have happened!

Instead of planning a specific story, a designer can influence what kinds of stories *players* make.

A movie plays the same each time, right? It's set in stone before you watch it.

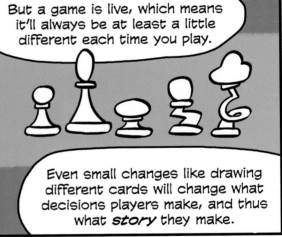

But a game is live, which means it'll always be at least a little different each time you play.

Even small changes like drawing different cards will change what decisions players make, and thus what *story* they make.

Game designers can guide players toward interesting stories, even if they can't control exactly how they'll play out.

Player-created stories about their decisions, influenced by mechanics and theming: *that's* what we're talking about today.

Oh, like when I accidentally dropped a grenade on Wei?

THAT WAS YOU?!

YOOOO! That's so cool!

Games tell stories, got it. Are we gonna do an activity next?

We gotta exchange friend codes!

Er, well...

...I *had* a game planned for today but I'm not happy with it yet.

I can't put my finger on it, but something feels missing...

Hrm...

Oh! Oh! What if me an' Shontoya playtested it for you?

That's a great idea, Shen!

Here are the rules I have so far...

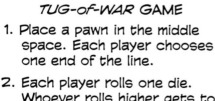

TUG-of-WAR GAME

1. Place a pawn in the middle space. Each player chooses one end of the line.

2. Each player rolls one die. Whoever rolls higher gets to move the pawn one space closer to their end.
If players roll the same, nothing happens.

3. The player who moves the pawn to their end first wins.

Okay, let's do it!

You're on!

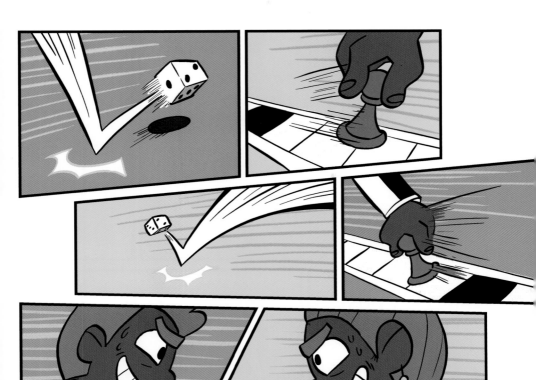

How's it going?

Who won?

After forty turns...

...and dozens of dice rolls...

...*nobody won.*

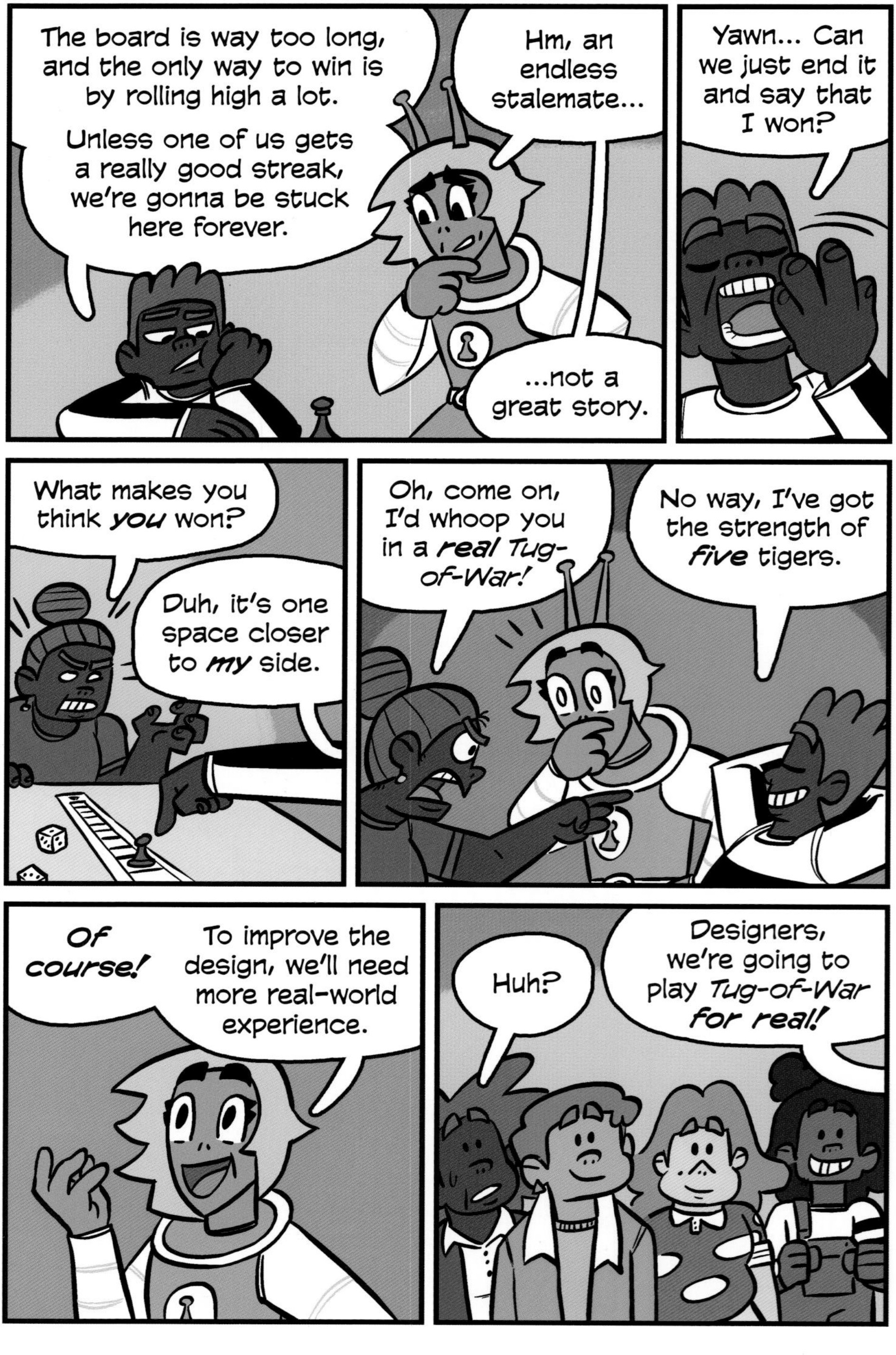
The board is way too long, and the only way to win is by rolling high a lot.
Unless one of us gets a really good streak, we're gonna be stuck here forever.
Hm, an endless stalemate...
...not a great story.
Yawn... Can we just end it and say that I won?
What makes you think *you* won?
Duh, it's one space closer to *my* side.
Oh, come on, I'd whoop you in a *real* Tug-of-War!
No way, I've got the strength of *five* tigers.
Of course!
To improve the design, we'll need more real-world experience.
Huh?
Designers, we're going to play *Tug-of-War for real!*

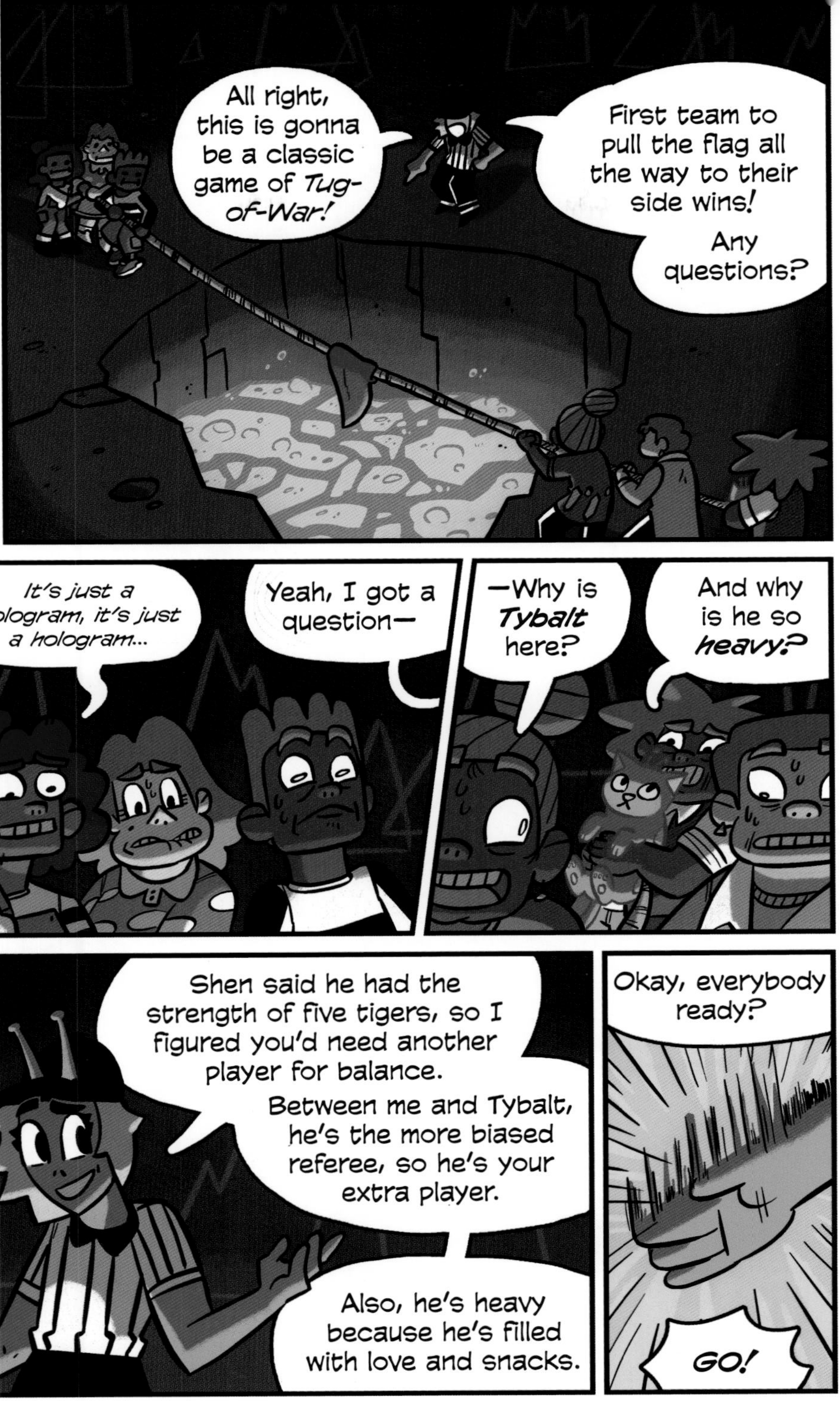
All right, this is gonna be a classic game of *Tug-of-War!*
First team to pull the flag all the way to their side wins!
Any questions?
It's just a hologram, it's just a hologram...
Yeah, I got a question—
—Why is ***Tybalt*** here?
And why is he so ***heavy?***
Shen said he had the strength of five tigers, so I figured you'd need another player for balance.
Between me and Tybalt, he's the more biased referee, so he's your extra player.
Also, he's heavy because he's filled with love and snacks.
Okay, everybody ready?
GO!

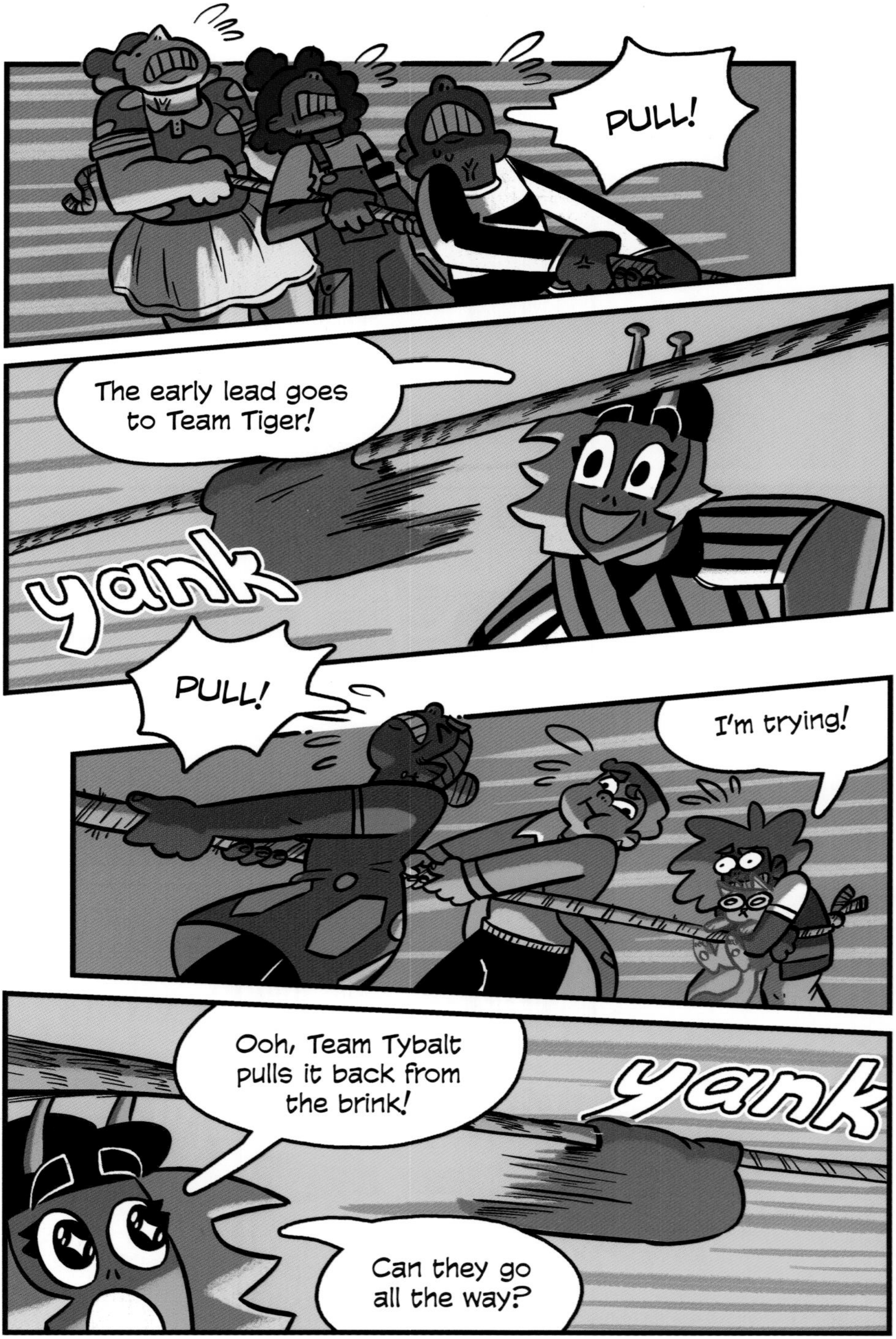
PULL!
The early lead goes to Team Tiger!
yank
PULL!
I'm trying!
Ooh, Team Tybalt pulls it back from the brink!
yank
Can they go all the way?

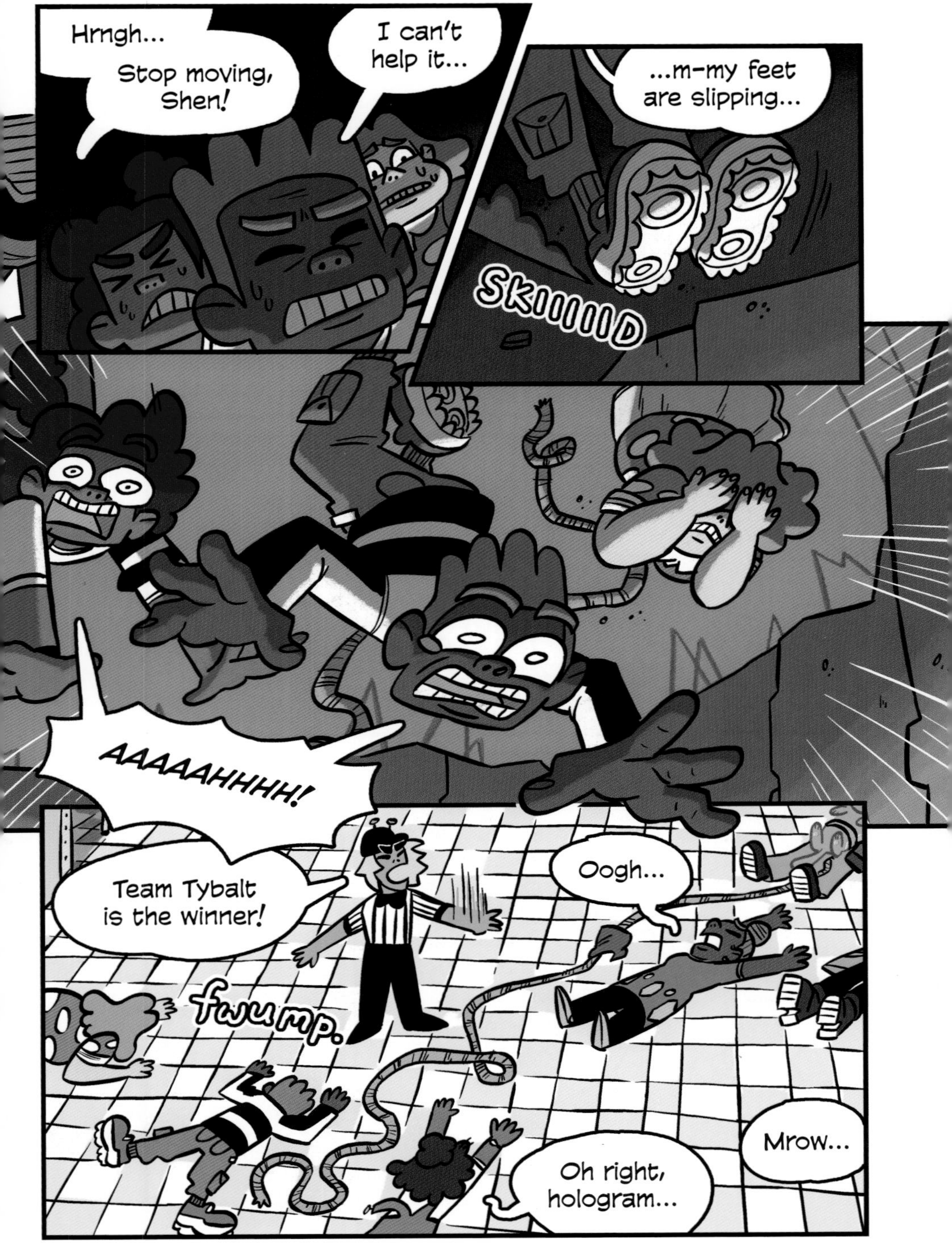
Hrngh...
Stop moving, Shen!
I can't help it...
...m-my feet are slipping...
SKIIIIIID
AAAAAHHHHH!
Team Tybalt is the winner!
Oogh...
fwump.
Mrow...
Oh right, hologram...

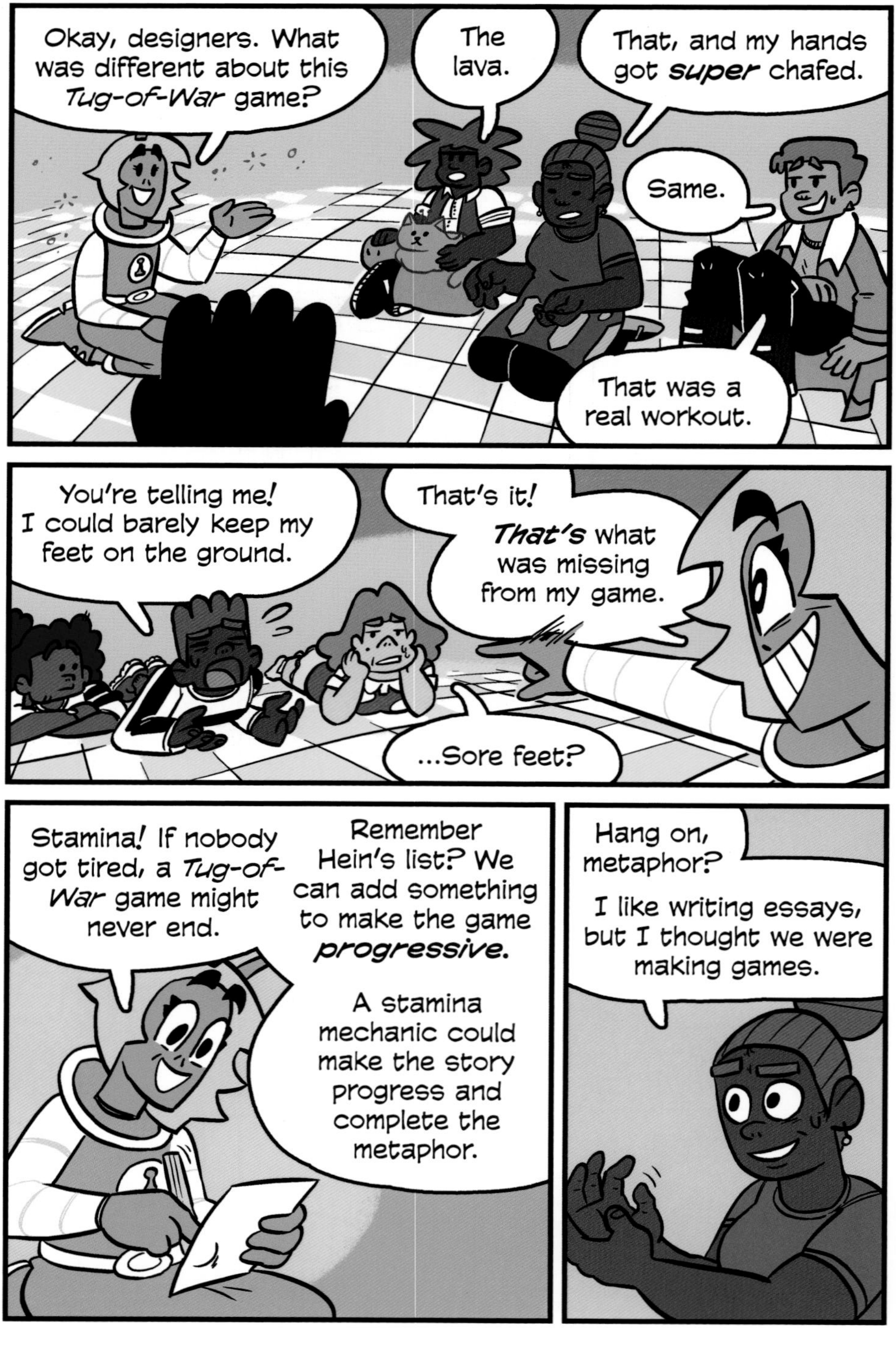
Okay, designers. What was different about this *Tug-of-War* game?
The lava.
That, and my hands got ***super*** chafed.
Same.
That was a real workout.
You're telling me! I could barely keep my feet on the ground.
That's it! ***That's*** what was missing from my game.
...Sore feet?
Stamina! If nobody got tired, a *Tug-of-War* game might never end.
Remember Hein's list? We can add something to make the game ***progressive.***
A stamina mechanic could make the story progress and complete the metaphor.
Hang on, metaphor?
I like writing essays, but I thought we were making games.

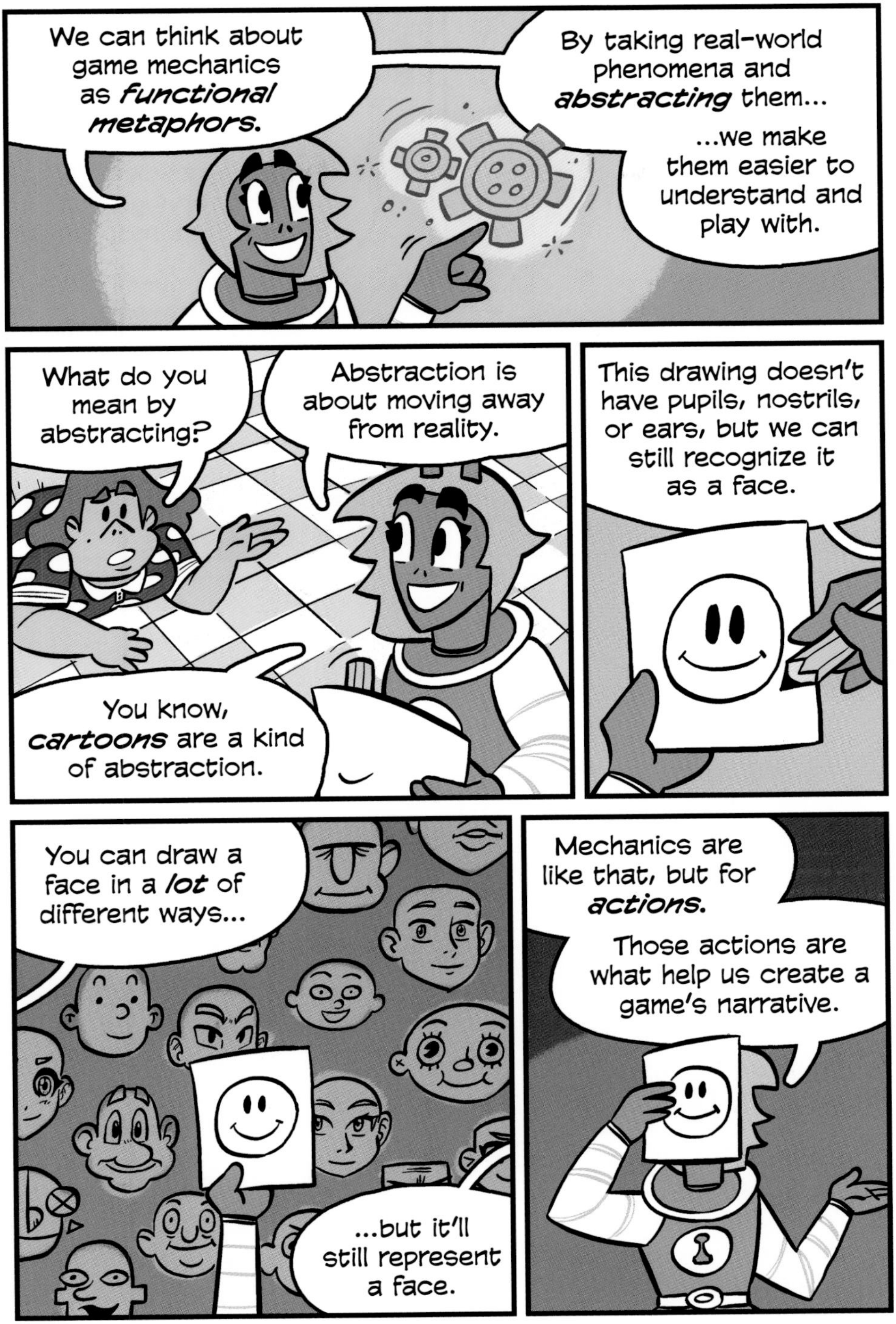
We can think about game mechanics as *functional metaphors.*
By taking real-world phenomena and *abstracting* them...
...we make them easier to understand and play with.
What do you mean by abstracting?
Abstraction is about moving away from reality.
You know, *cartoons* are a kind of abstraction.
This drawing doesn't have pupils, nostrils, or ears, but we can still recognize it as a face.
You can draw a face in a *lot* of different ways...
...but it'll still represent a face.
Mechanics are like that, but for *actions.*
Those actions are what help us create a game's narrative.

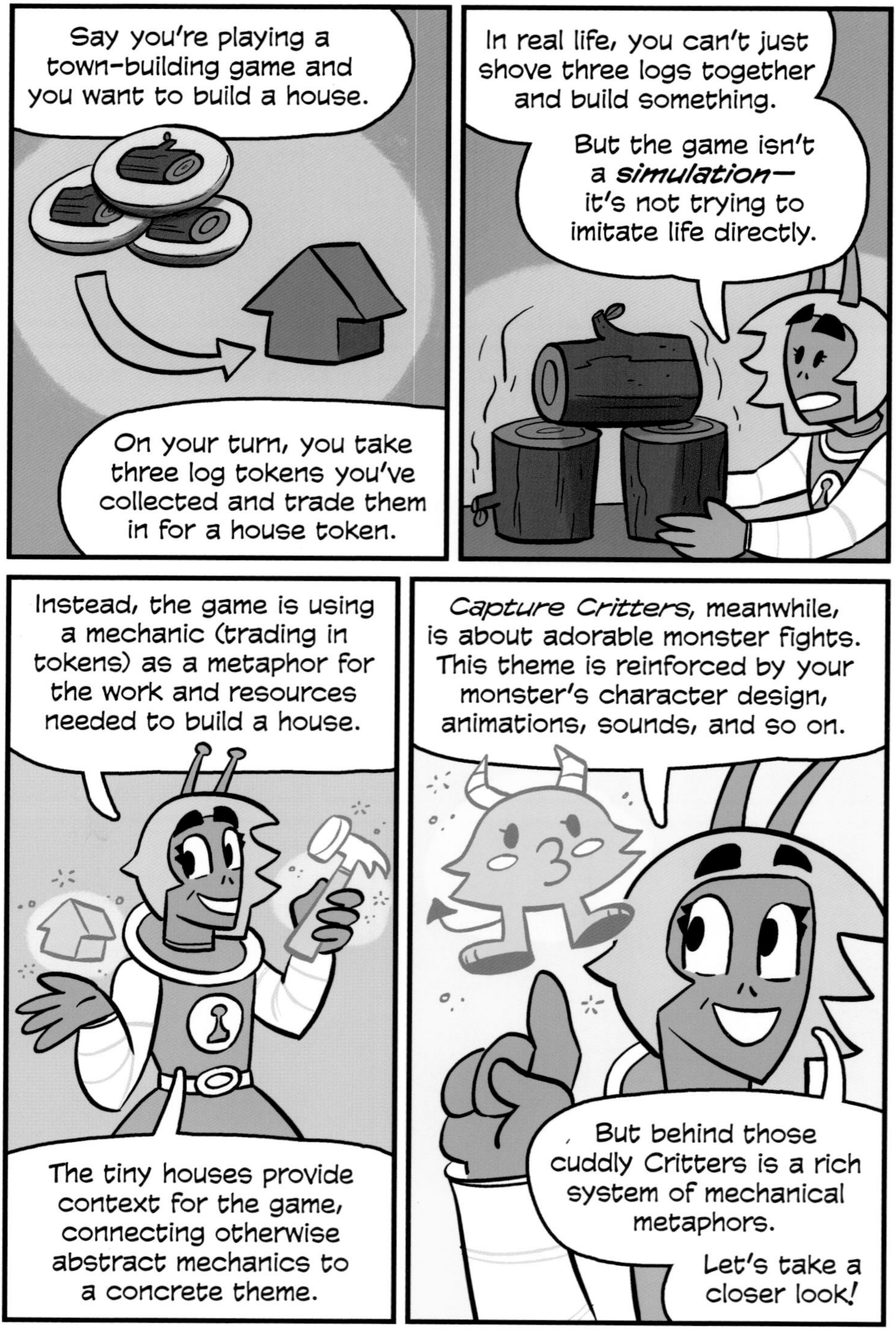

Say you're playing a town-building game and you want to build a house.
On your turn, you take three log tokens you've collected and trade them in for a house token.
In real life, you can't just shove three logs together and build something.
But the game isn't a *simulation*— it's not trying to imitate life directly.
Instead, the game is using a mechanic (trading in tokens) as a metaphor for the work and resources needed to build a house.
The tiny houses provide context for the game, connecting otherwise abstract mechanics to a concrete theme.
Capture Critters, meanwhile, is about adorable monster fights. This theme is reinforced by your monster's character design, animations, sounds, and so on.
But behind those cuddly Critters is a rich system of mechanical metaphors.
Let's take a closer look!

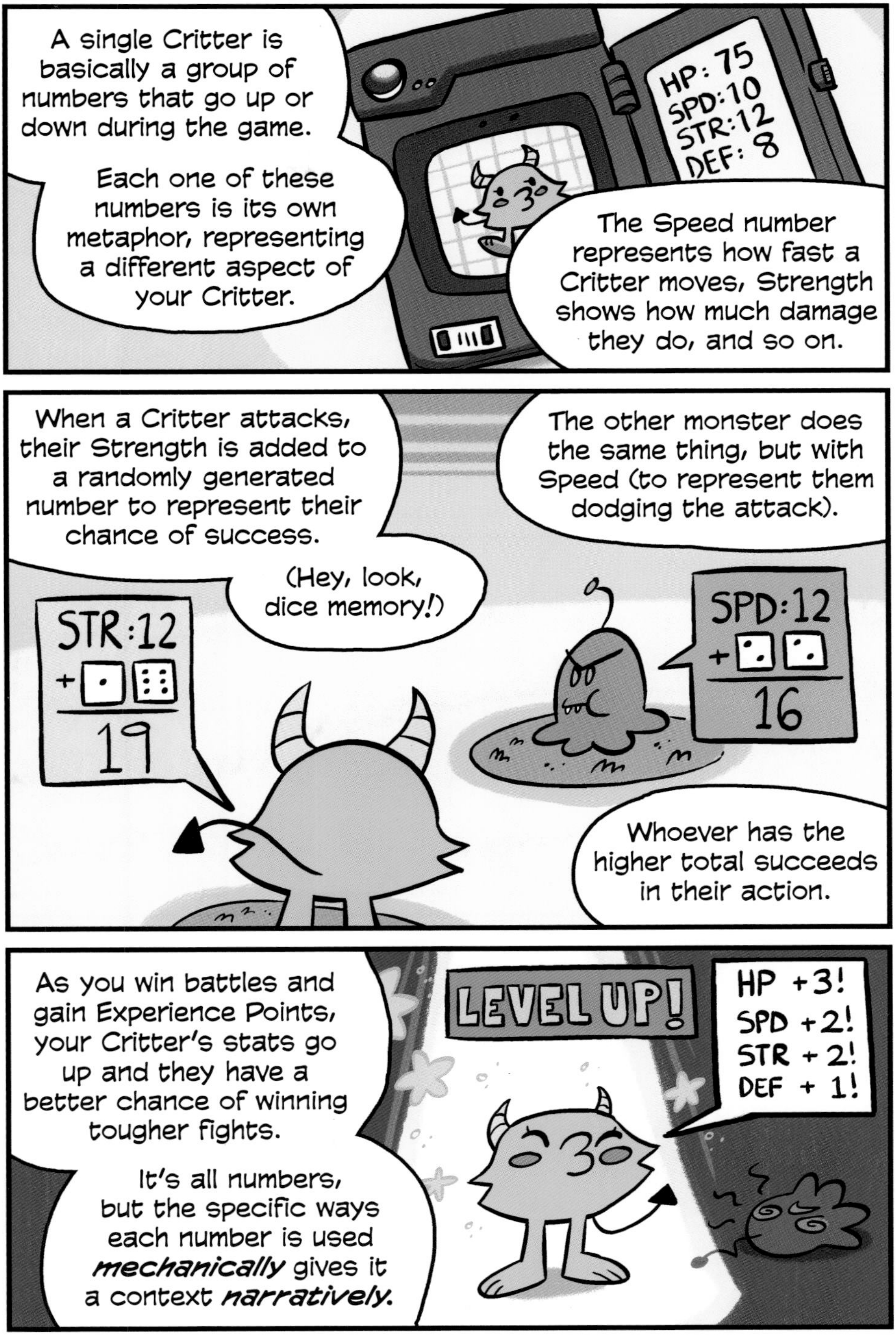

A single Critter is basically a group of numbers that go up or down during the game.
Each one of these numbers is its own metaphor, representing a different aspect of your Critter.
HP: 75
SPD: 10
STR: 12
DEF: 8
The Speed number represents how fast a Critter moves, Strength shows how much damage they do, and so on.
When a Critter attacks, their Strength is added to a randomly generated number to represent their chance of success.
The other monster does the same thing, but with Speed (to represent them dodging the attack).
(Hey, look, dice memory!)
STR: 12
19
SPD: 12
16
Whoever has the higher total succeeds in their action.
As you win battles and gain Experience Points, your Critter's stats go up and they have a better chance of winning tougher fights.
It's all numbers, but the specific ways each number is used *mechanically* gives it a context *narratively*.
LEVEL UP!
HP +3!
SPD +2!
STR +2!
DEF +1!

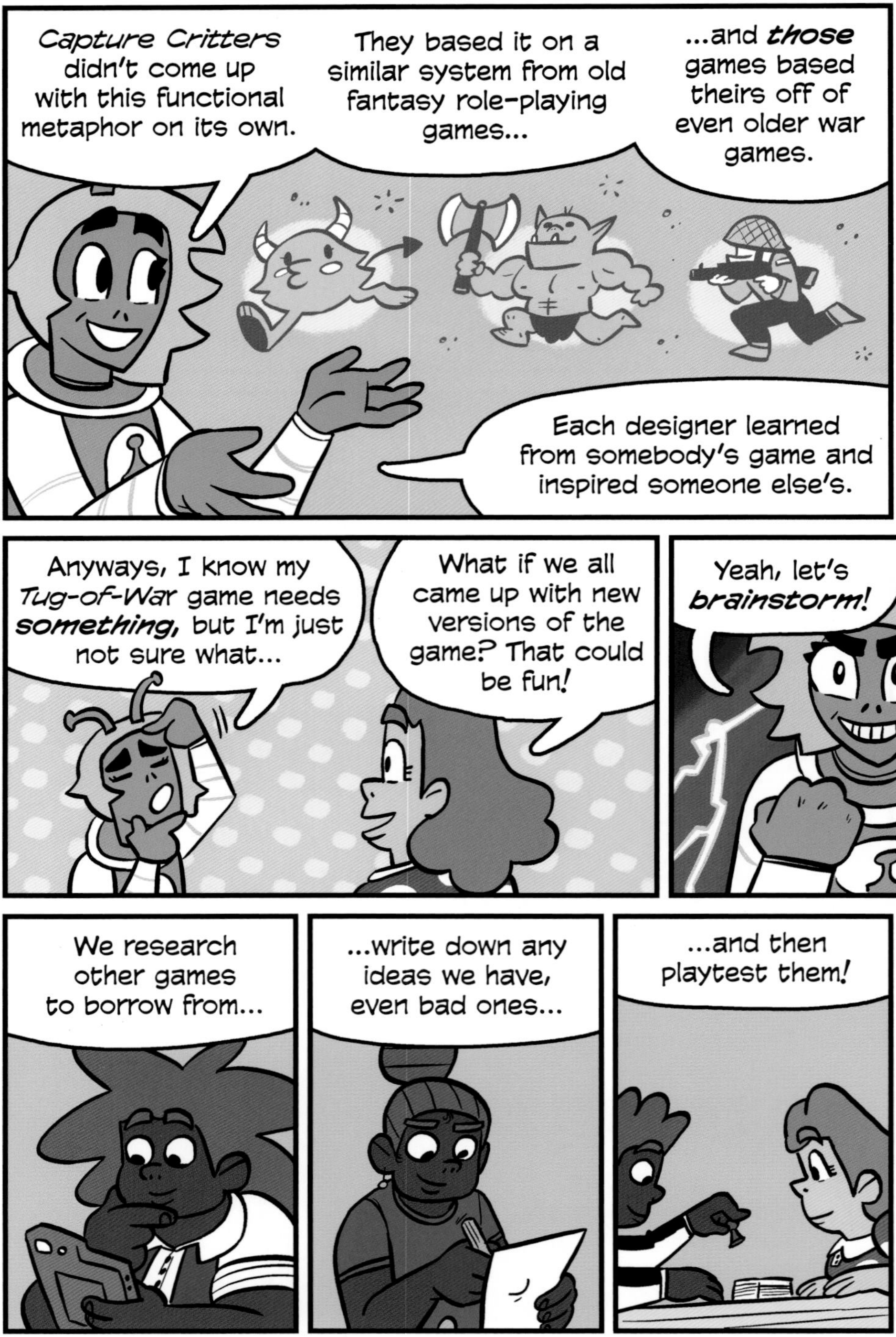
Capture Critters didn't come up with this functional metaphor on its own.
They based it on a similar system from old fantasy role-playing games...
...and ***those*** games based theirs off of even older war games.
Each designer learned from somebody's game and inspired someone else's.
Anyways, I know my *Tug-of-War* game needs ***something,*** but I'm just not sure what...
What if we all came up with new versions of the game? That could be fun!
Yeah, let's ***brainstorm!***
We research other games to borrow from...
...write down any ideas we have, even bad ones...
...and then playtest them!

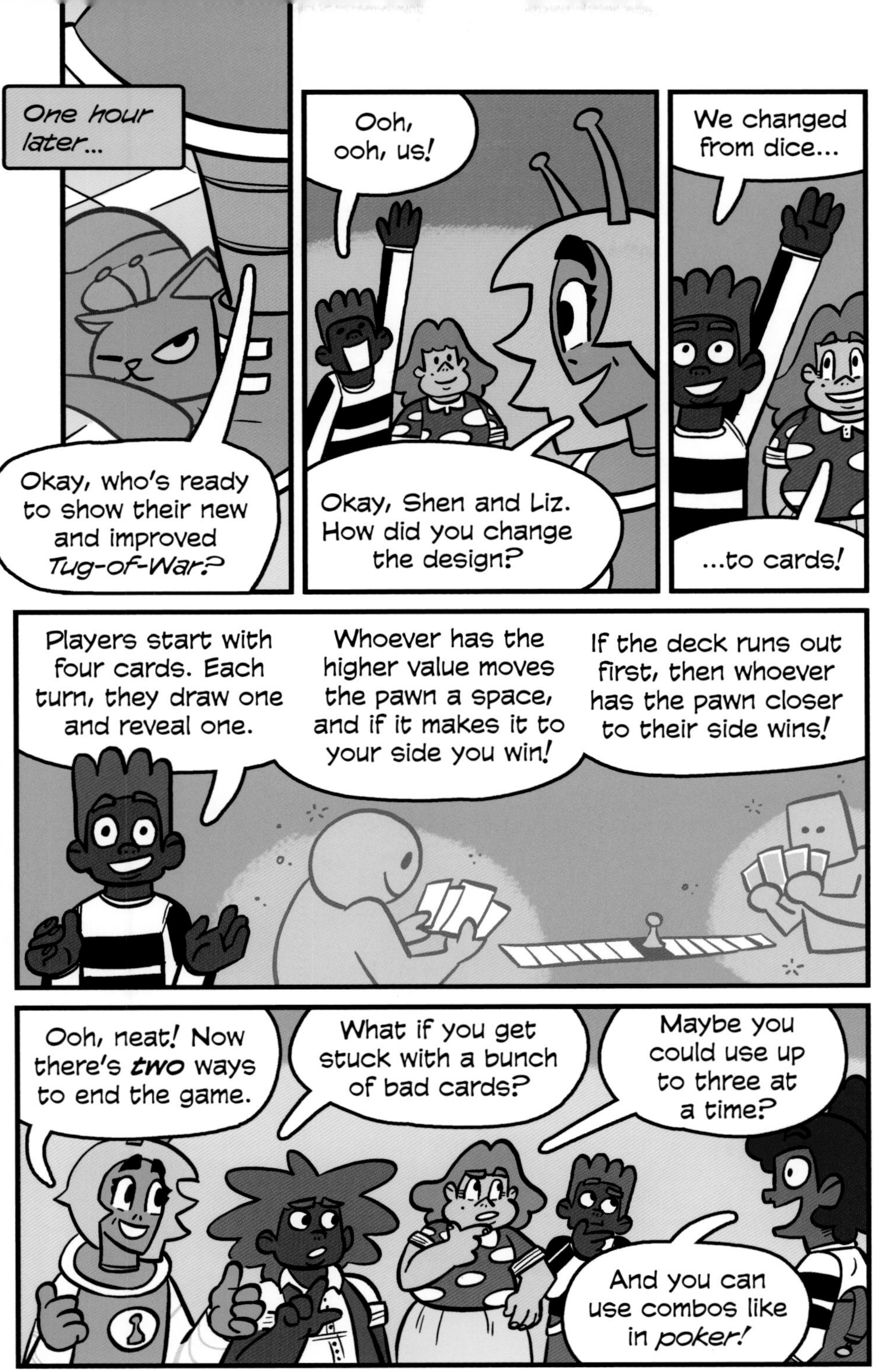
One hour later...
Okay, who's ready to show their new and improved *Tug-of-War?*
Ooh, ooh, us!
Okay, Shen and Liz. How did you change the design?
We changed from dice...
...to cards!
Players start with four cards. Each turn, they draw one and reveal one.
Whoever has the higher value moves the pawn a space, and if it makes it to your side you win!
If the deck runs out first, then whoever has the pawn closer to their side wins!
Ooh, neat! Now there's ***two*** ways to end the game.
What if you get stuck with a bunch of bad cards?
Maybe you could use up to three at a time?
And you can use combos like in *poker!*

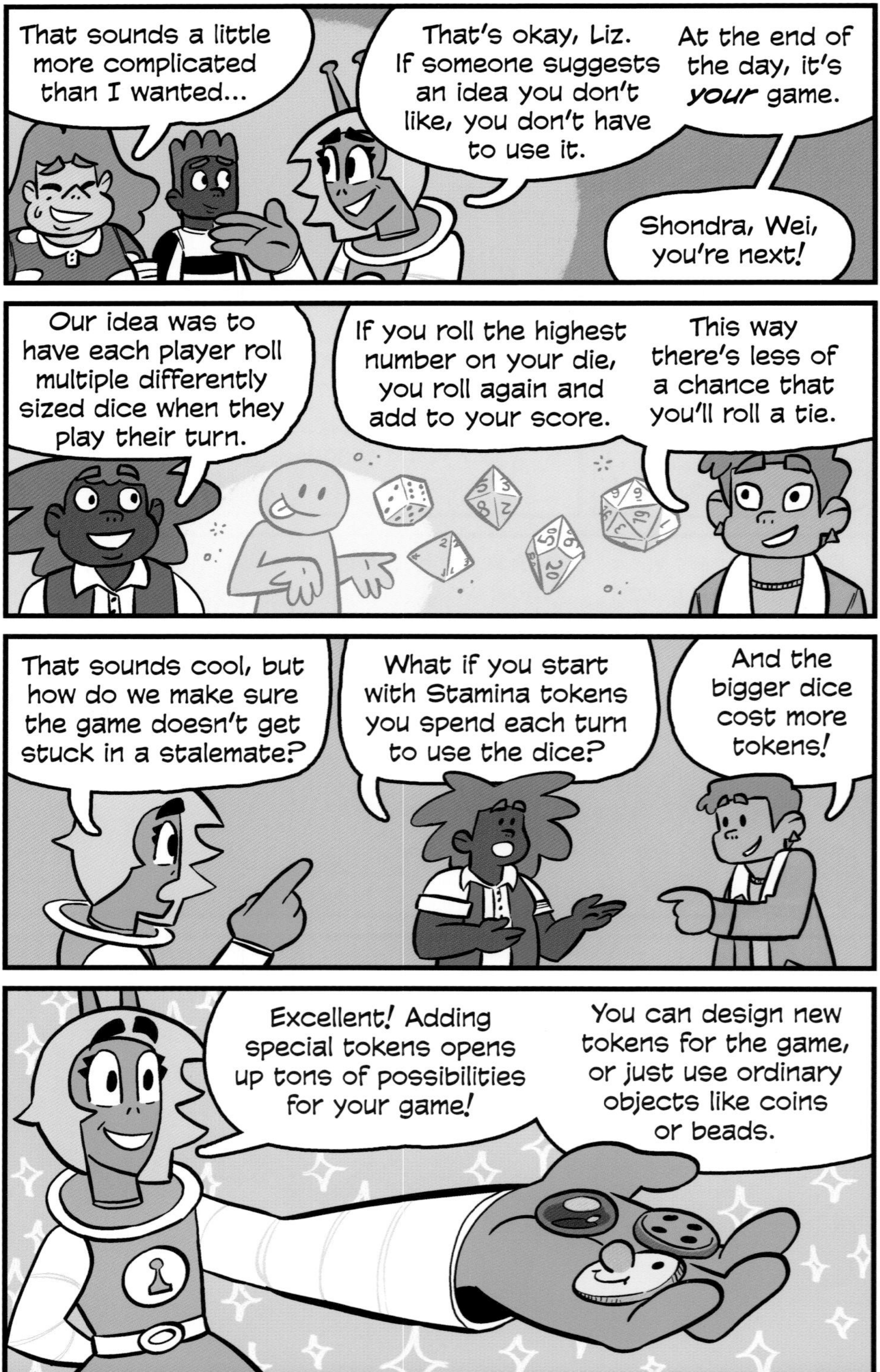

That sounds a little more complicated than I wanted...
That's okay, Liz. If someone suggests an idea you don't like, you don't have to use it.
At the end of the day, it's *your* game.
Shondra, Wei, you're next!
Our idea was to have each player roll multiple differently sized dice when they play their turn.
If you roll the highest number on your die, you roll again and add to your score.
This way there's less of a chance that you'll roll a tie.
That sounds cool, but how do we make sure the game doesn't get stuck in a stalemate?
What if you start with Stamina tokens you spend each turn to use the dice?
And the bigger dice cost more tokens!
Excellent! Adding special tokens opens up tons of possibilities for your game!
You can design new tokens for the game, or just use ordinary objects like coins or beads.

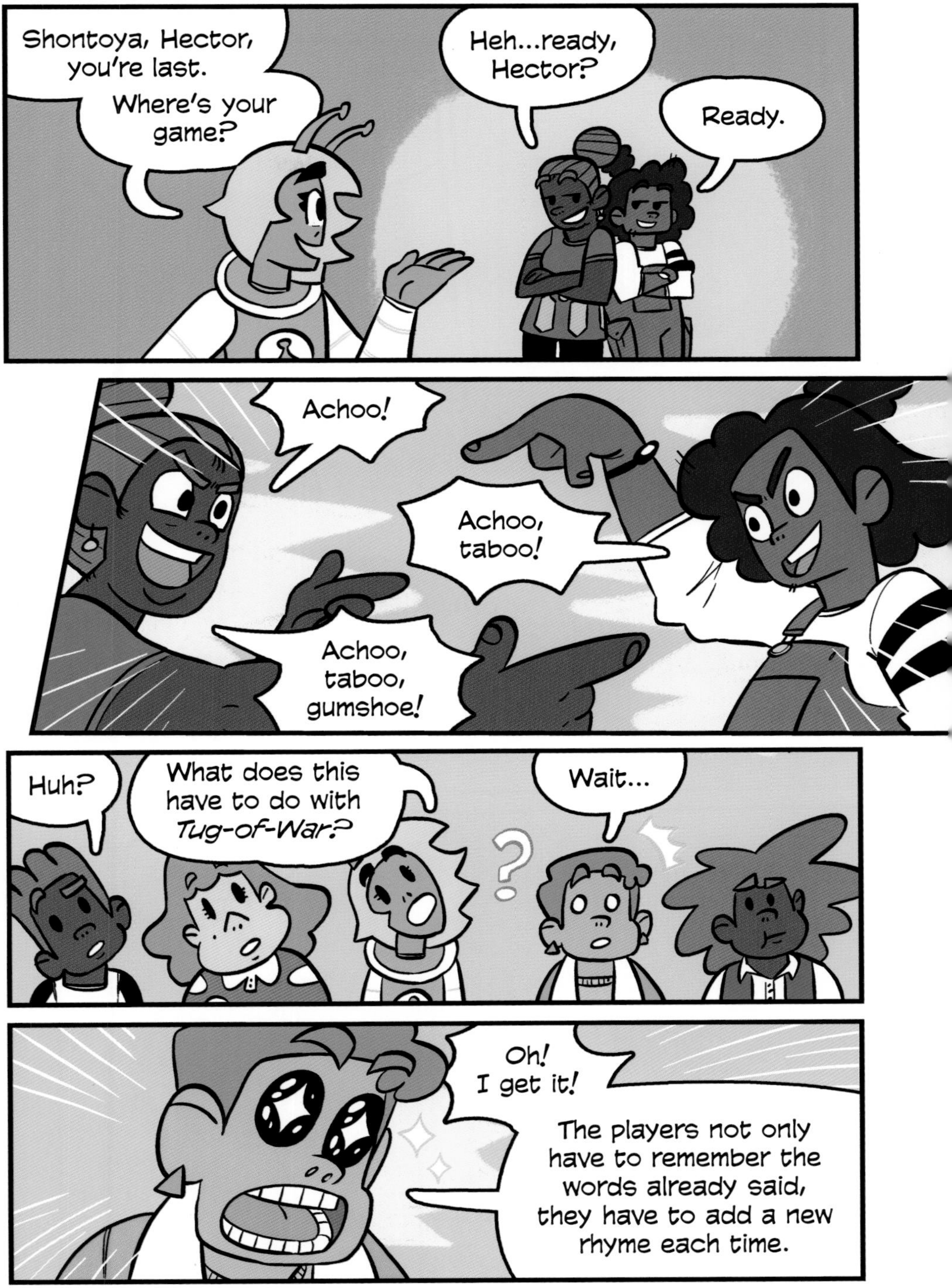
Shontoya, Hector, you're last.
Where's your game?
Heh...ready, Hector?
Ready.
Achoo!
Achoo, taboo!
Achoo, taboo, gumshoe!
Huh?
What does this have to do with *Tug-of-War?*
Wait...
Oh! I get it!
The players not only have to remember the words already said, they have to add a new rhyme each time.

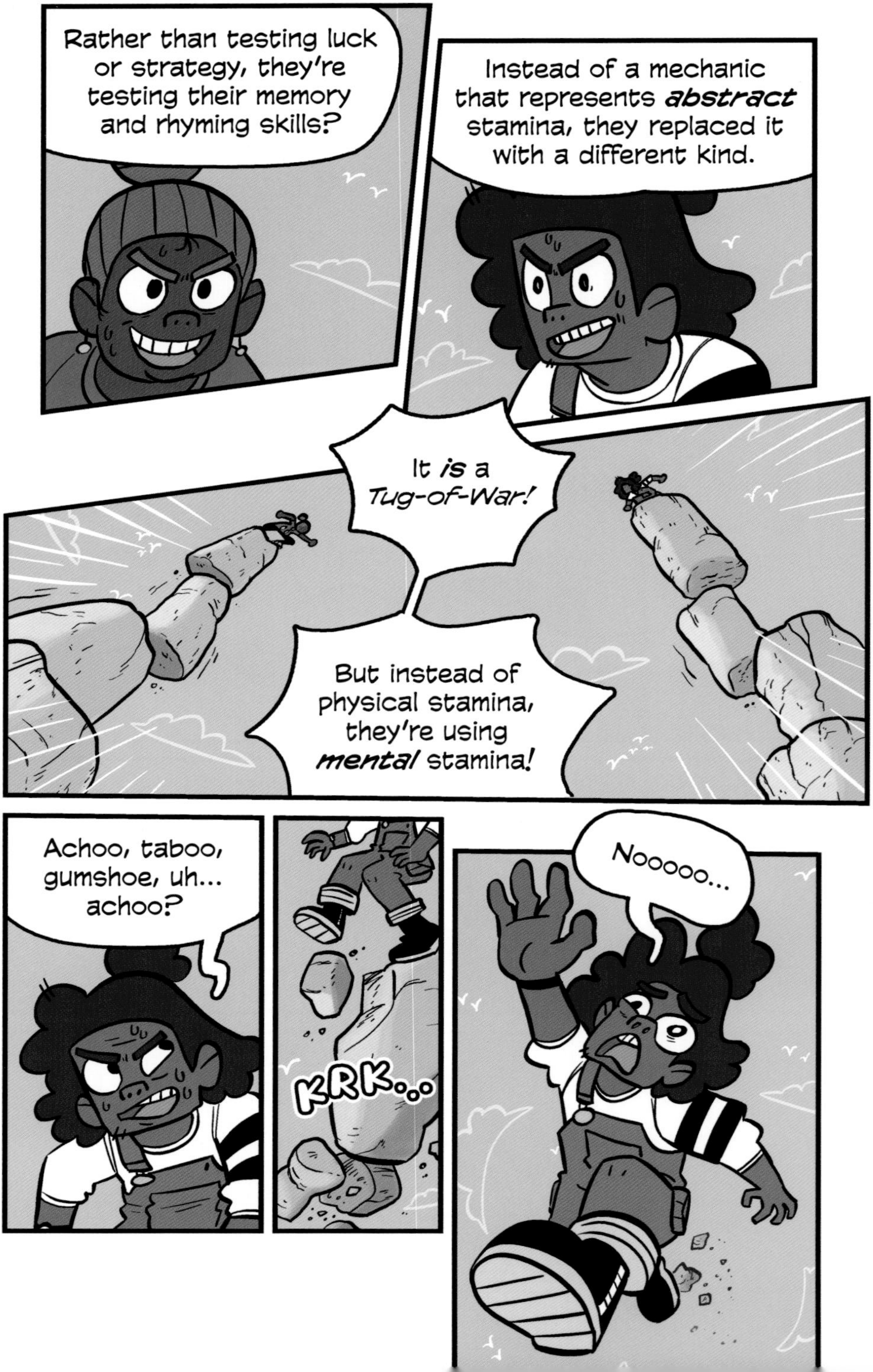

Rather than testing luck or strategy, they're testing their memory and rhyming skills?
Instead of a mechanic that represents *abstract* stamina, they replaced it with a different kind.
It *is* a Tug-of-War!
But instead of physical stamina, they're using *mental* stamina!
Achoo, taboo, gumshoe, uh... achoo?
KRK...
Nooooo...

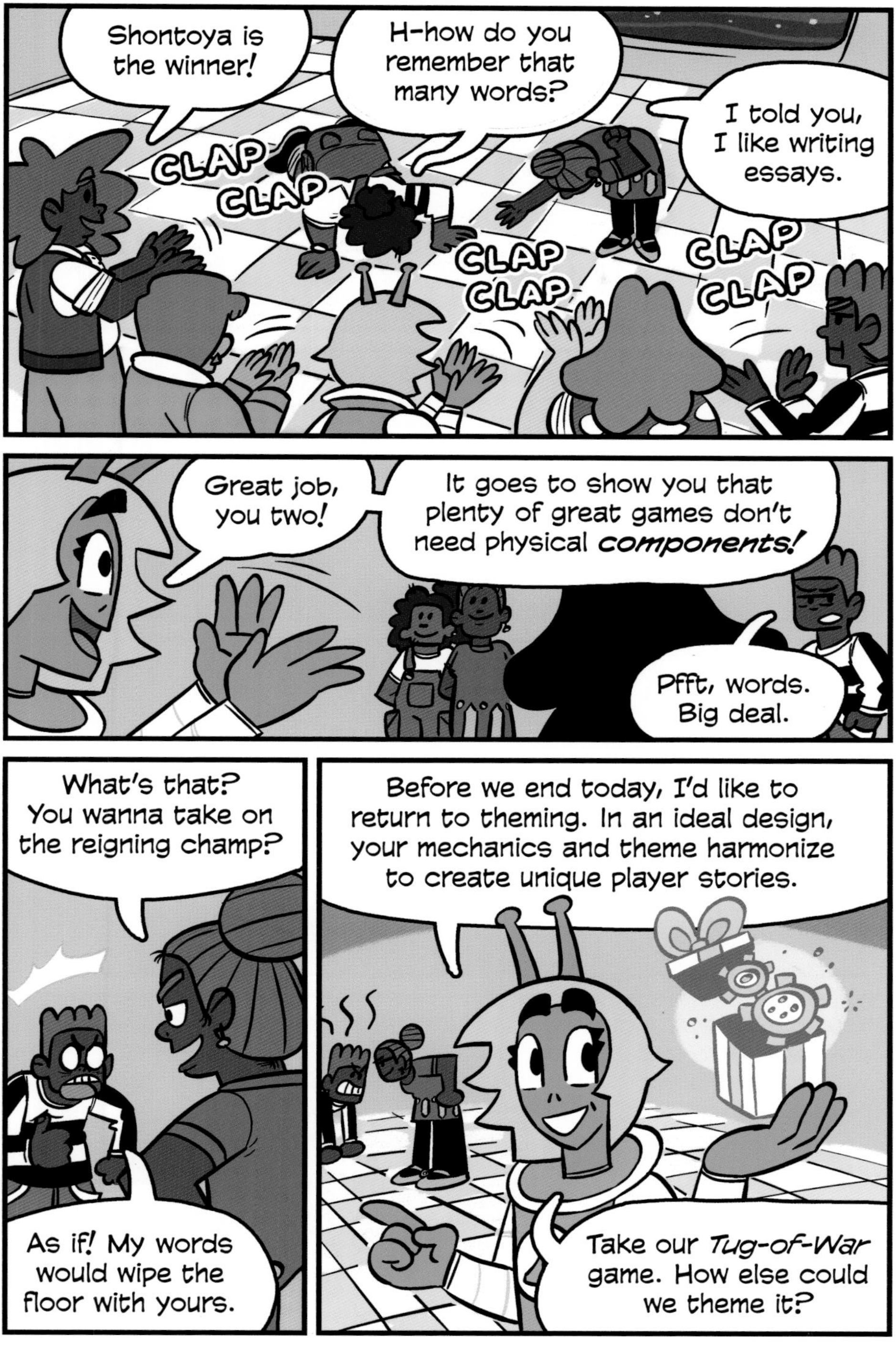
Shontoya is the winner!
H-how do you remember that many words?
I told you, I like writing essays.
CLAP CLAP
CLAP CLAP
CLAP CLAP
Great job, you two!
It goes to show you that plenty of great games don't need physical ***components!***
Pfft, words. Big deal.
What's that? You wanna take on the reigning champ?
As if! My words would wipe the floor with yours.
Before we end today, I'd like to return to theming. In an ideal design, your mechanics and theme harmonize to create unique player stories.
Take our *Tug-of-War* game. How else could we theme it?

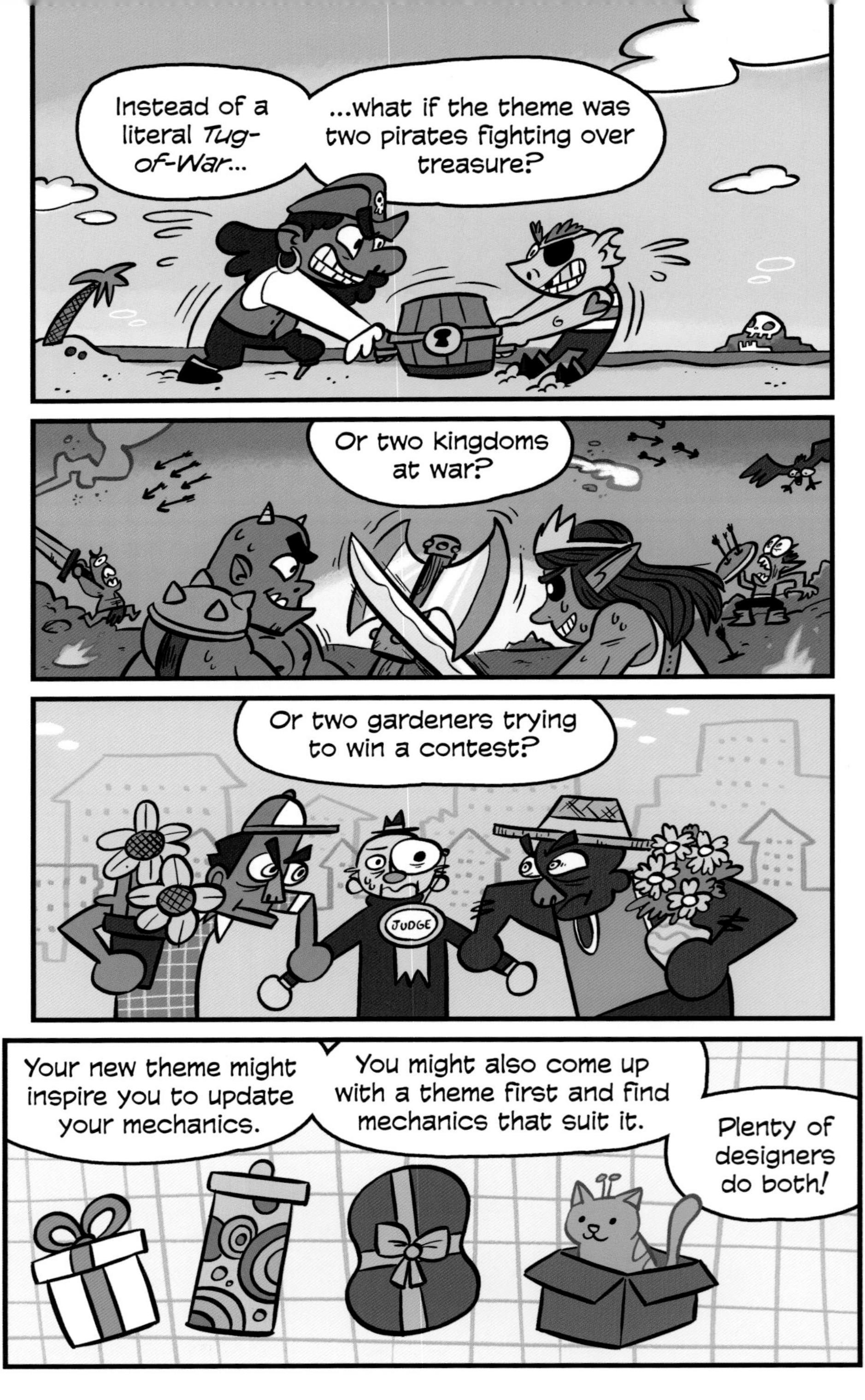
Instead of a literal *Tug-of-War*...
...what if the theme was two pirates fighting over treasure?
Or two kingdoms at war?
Or two gardeners trying to win a contest?
JUDGE
Your new theme might inspire you to update your mechanics.
You might also come up with a theme first and find mechanics that suit it.
Plenty of designers do both!

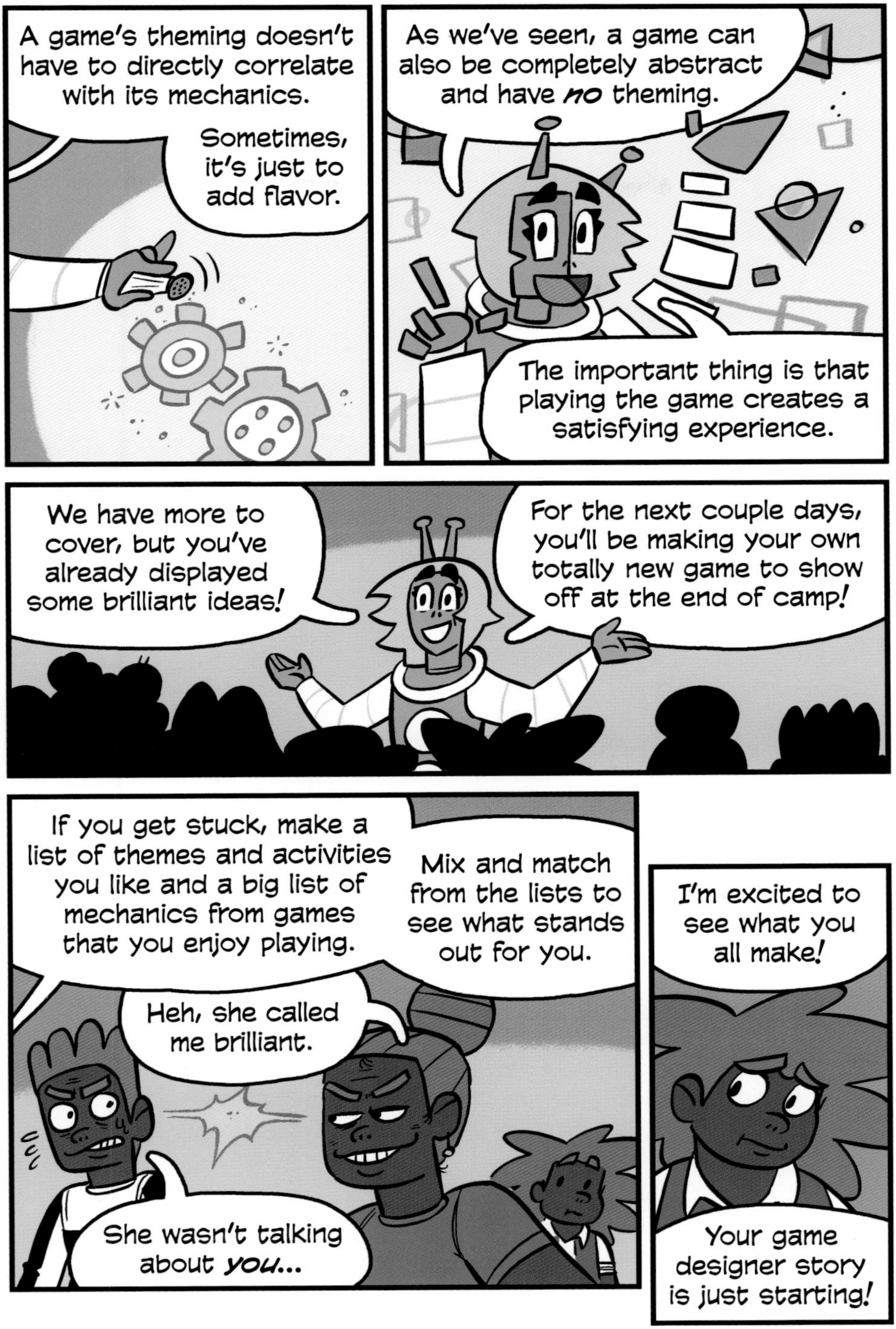
A game's theming doesn't have to directly correlate with its mechanics.
Sometimes, it's just to add flavor.
As we've seen, a game can also be completely abstract and have *no* theming.
The important thing is that playing the game creates a satisfying experience.
We have more to cover, but you've already displayed some brilliant ideas!
For the next couple days, you'll be making your own totally new game to show off at the end of camp!
If you get stuck, make a list of themes and activities you like and a big list of mechanics from games that you enjoy playing.
Mix and match from the lists to see what stands out for you.
Heh, she called me brilliant.
She wasn't talking about *you*...
I'm excited to see what you all make!
Your game designer story is just starting!

Brainstorming and Game Research!

This is a creative exercise to brainstorm ideas for a totally new game project. All you'll need is a couple sheets of paper and a pencil or pen!

Part One: Mind Map

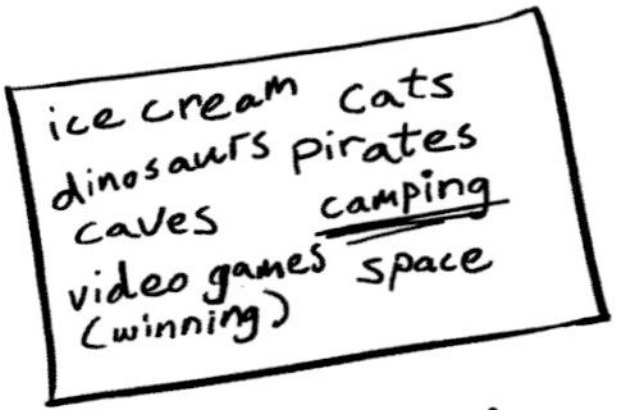
ice cream
cats
dinosaurs
pirates
caves
camping
video games (winning)
space

1. Make a list of topics and activities you enjoy. Try to come up with at least ten items!
2. Choose one of these items to be the subject of your mind map. Write it in the center of a new sheet of paper.
3. Draw lines outward from the center, and add aspects related to your item. Use a highlighter or add a star to aspects you are most interested in.

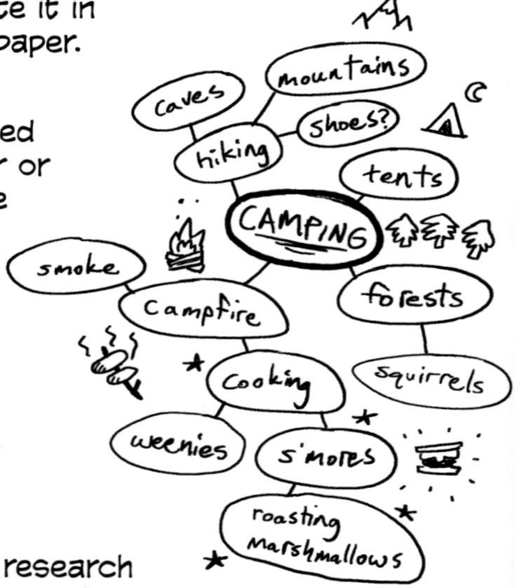
mountains
caves
shoes?
hiking
tents
CAMPING
smoke
forests
Campfire
Cooking
squirrels
weenies
s'mores
roasting marshmallows

Part Two: Research

1. Look up games with your mind map's theme. Hint: add 'bgg' to the end of your search!* If you have trouble finding any, try looking up the associated subjects or concepts.
2. Choose one of the games and research how it plays. Most games will have their manual or video tutorials freely available online. You may also be able to borrow or try the game at a local game store.
3. Describe the game's mechanics. How do they relate to the game's theming? How do the game's aesthetics support this theme? Does playing this game feel like it embodies the theme?

You may repeat these steps with other items from your list. Use these to begin thinking about how you might design a game to embody your favorite things.

* boardgamegeek.com, or BGG, is an online resource for board game and card game enthusiasts.

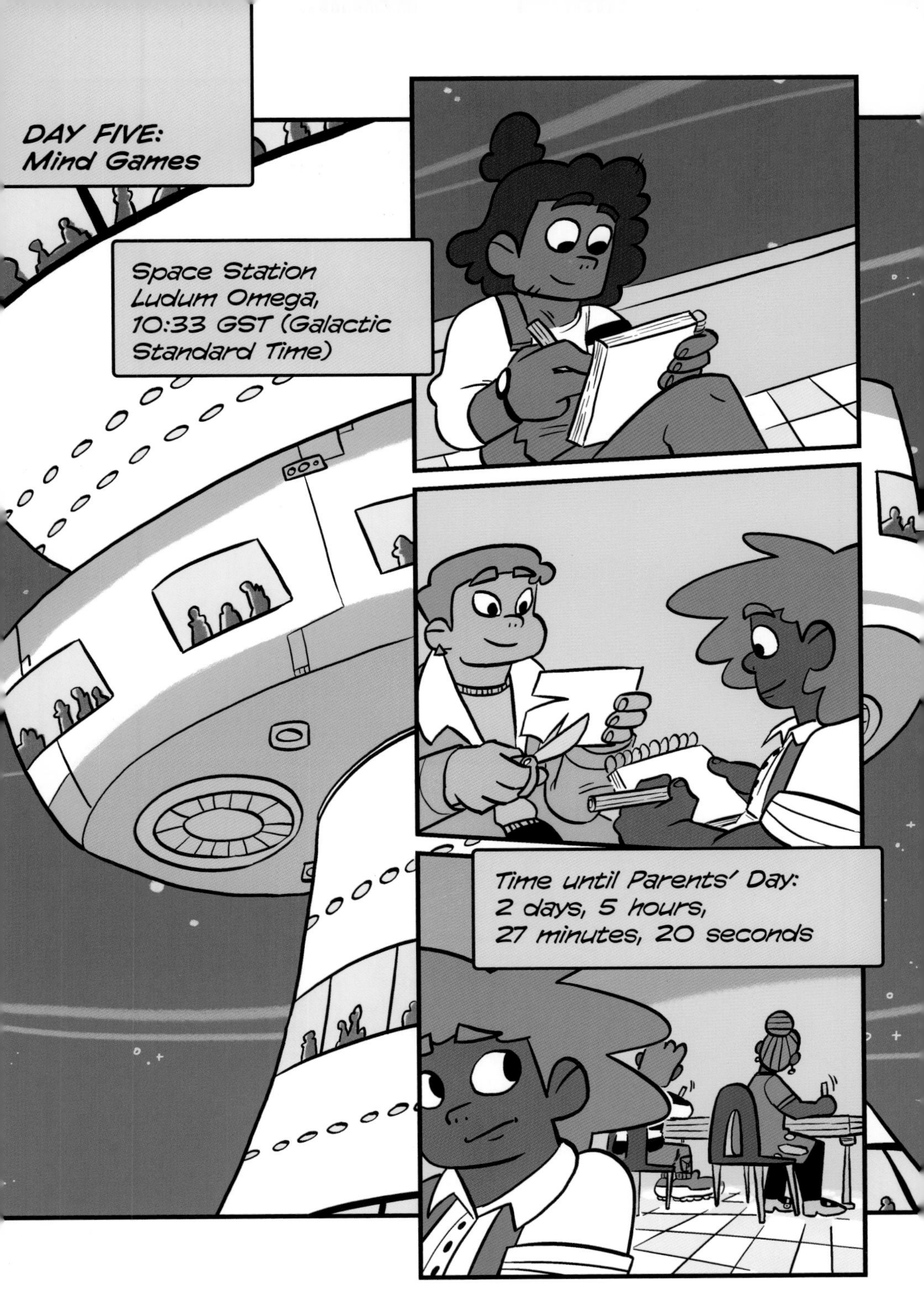
DAY FIVE:
Mind Games
Space Station Ludum Omega, 10:33 GST (Galactic Standard Time)
Time until Parents' Day:
2 days, 5 hours,
27 minutes, 20 seconds

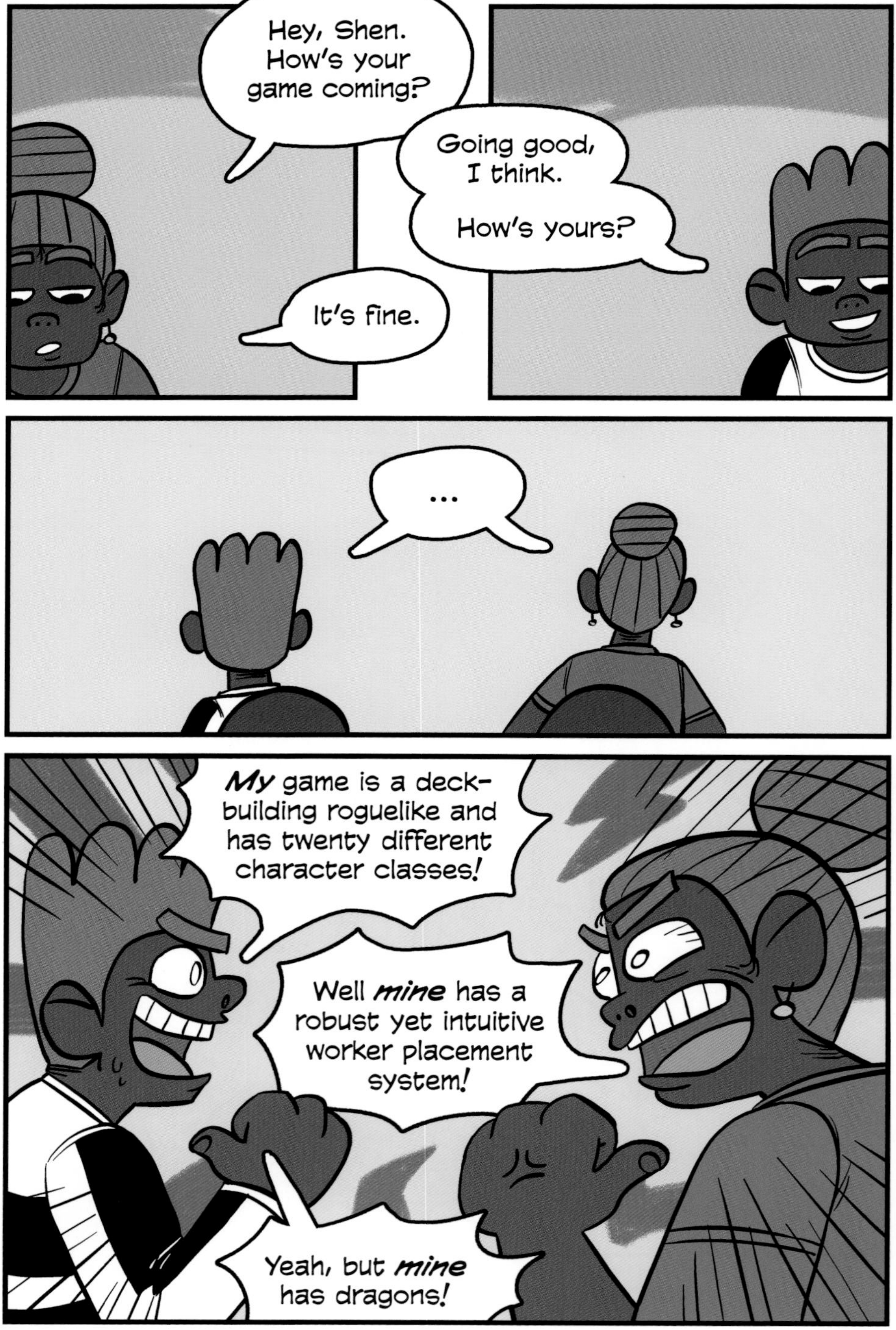
Hey, Shen. How's your game coming?
Going good, I think.
How's yours?
It's fine.
...
My game is a deck-building roguelike and has twenty different character classes!
Well *mine* has a robust yet intuitive worker placement system!
Yeah, but *mine* has dragons!

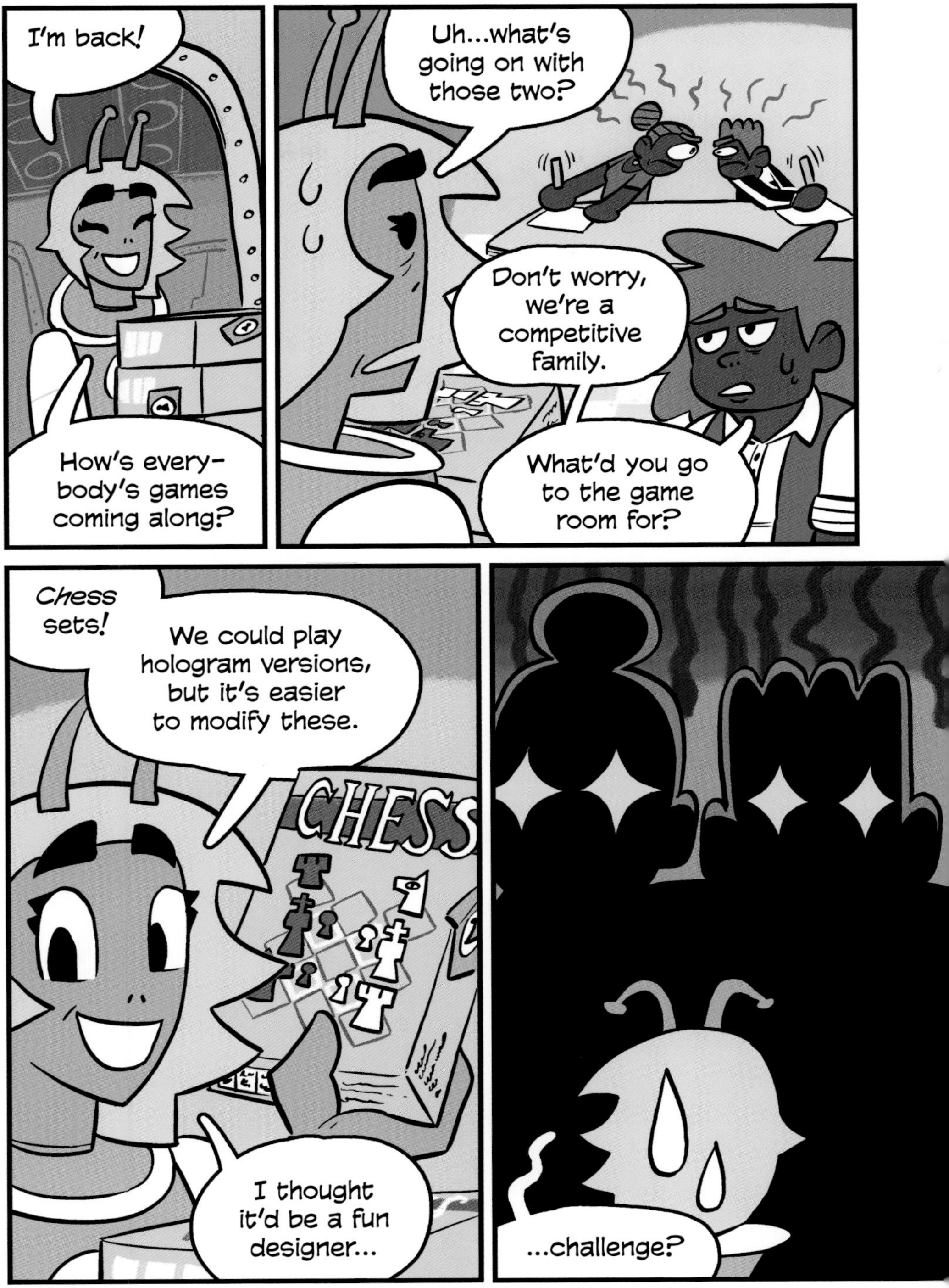
I'm back!
How's every-body's games coming along?
Uh...what's going on with those two?
Don't worry, we're a competitive family.
What'd you go to the game room for?
Chess sets!
We could play hologram versions, but it's easier to modify these.
CHESS
I thought it'd be a fun designer...
...challenge?

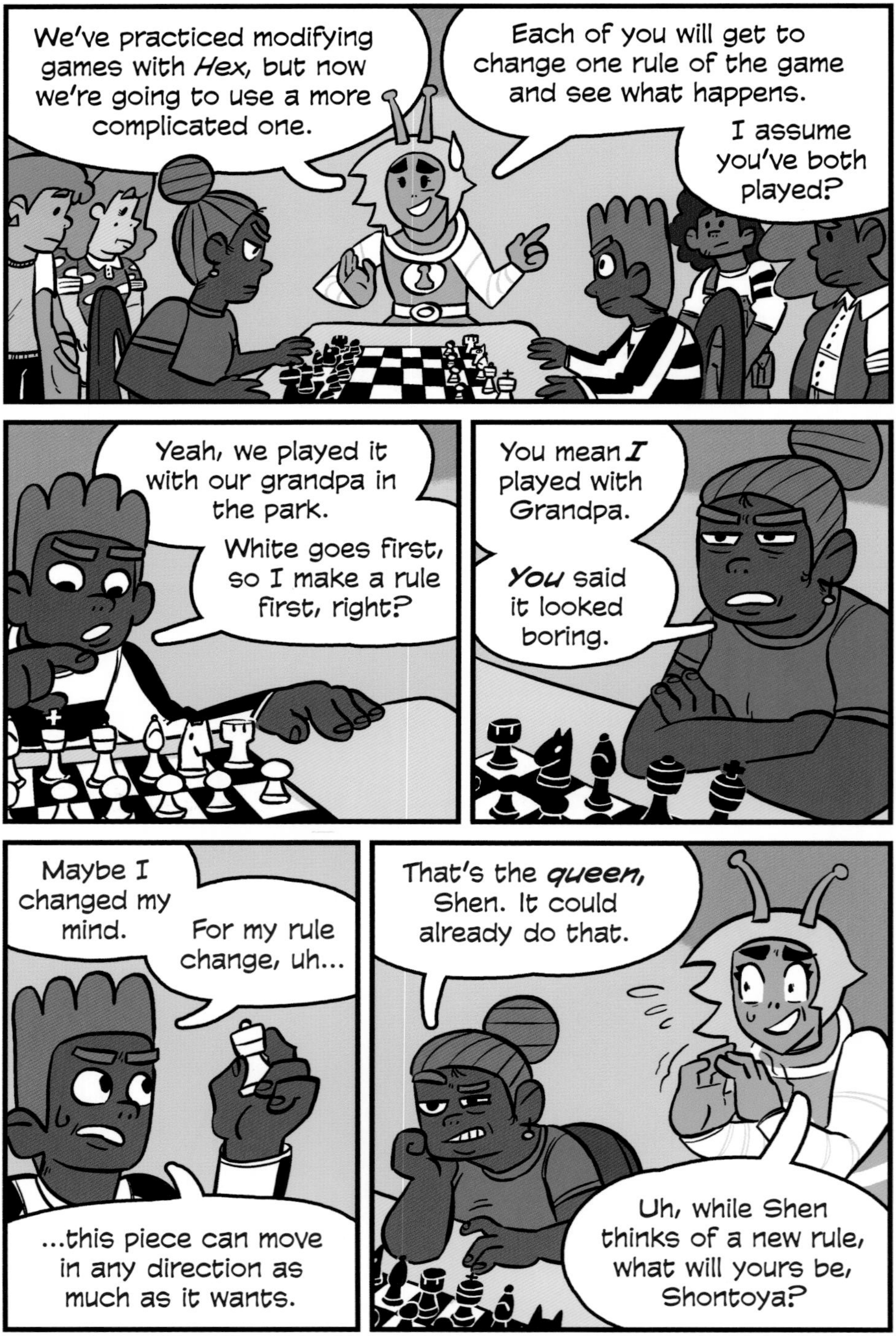
We've practiced modifying games with *Hex*, but now we're going to use a more complicated one.
Each of you will get to change one rule of the game and see what happens.
I assume you've both played?
Yeah, we played it with our grandpa in the park.
White goes first, so I make a rule first, right?
You mean *I* played with Grandpa.
You said it looked boring.
Maybe I changed my mind.
For my rule change, uh...
...this piece can move in any direction as much as it wants.
That's the ***queen,*** Shen. It could already do that.
Uh, while Shen thinks of a new rule, what will yours be, Shontoya?

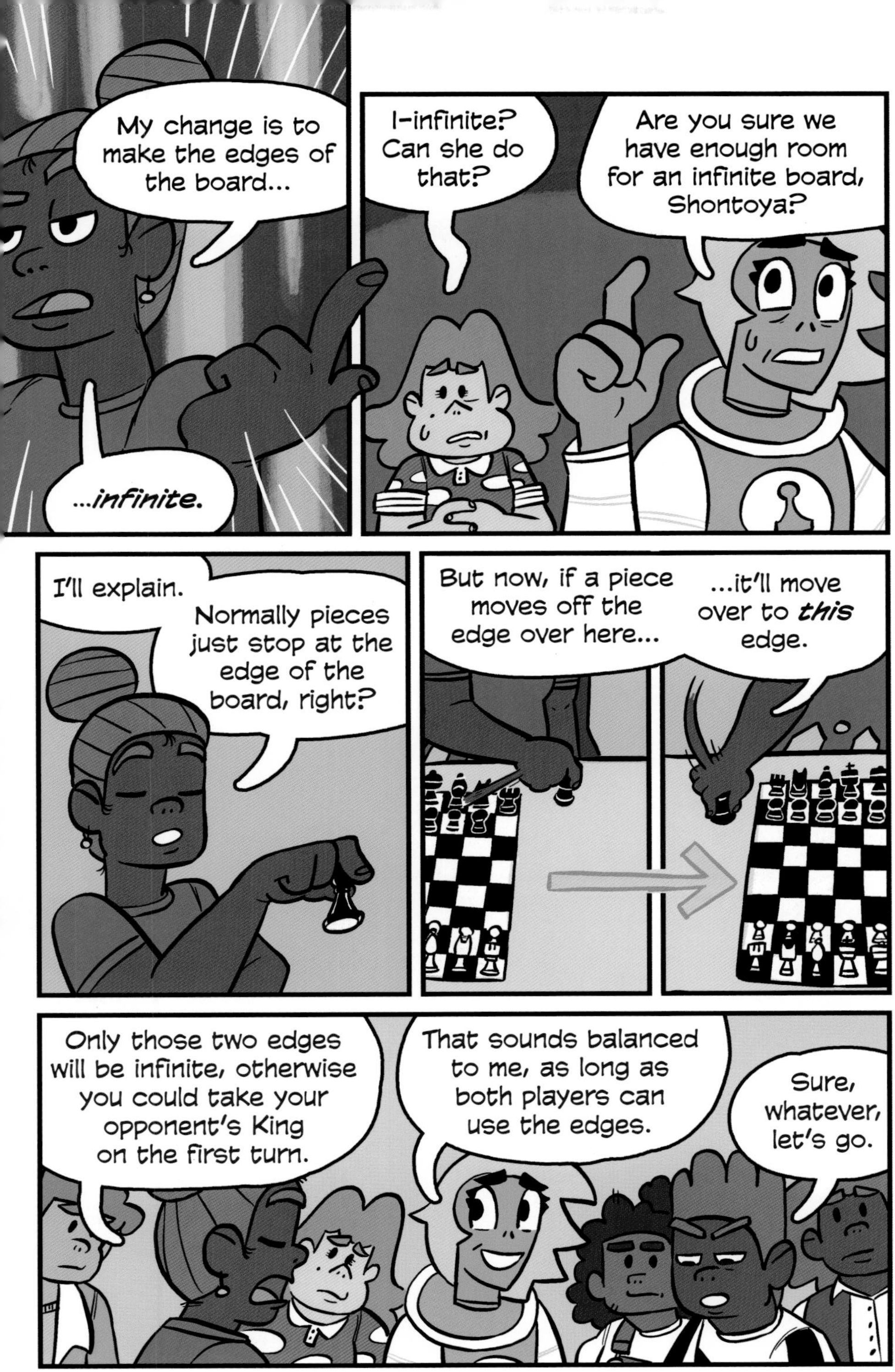
My change is to make the edges of the board...
...*infinite.*
I-infinite? Can she do that?
Are you sure we have enough room for an infinite board, Shontoya?
I'll explain.
Normally pieces just stop at the edge of the board, right?
But now, if a piece moves off the edge over here...
...it'll move over to *this* edge.
Only those two edges will be infinite, otherwise you could take your opponent's King on the first turn.
That sounds balanced to me, as long as both players can use the edges.
Sure, whatever, let's go.

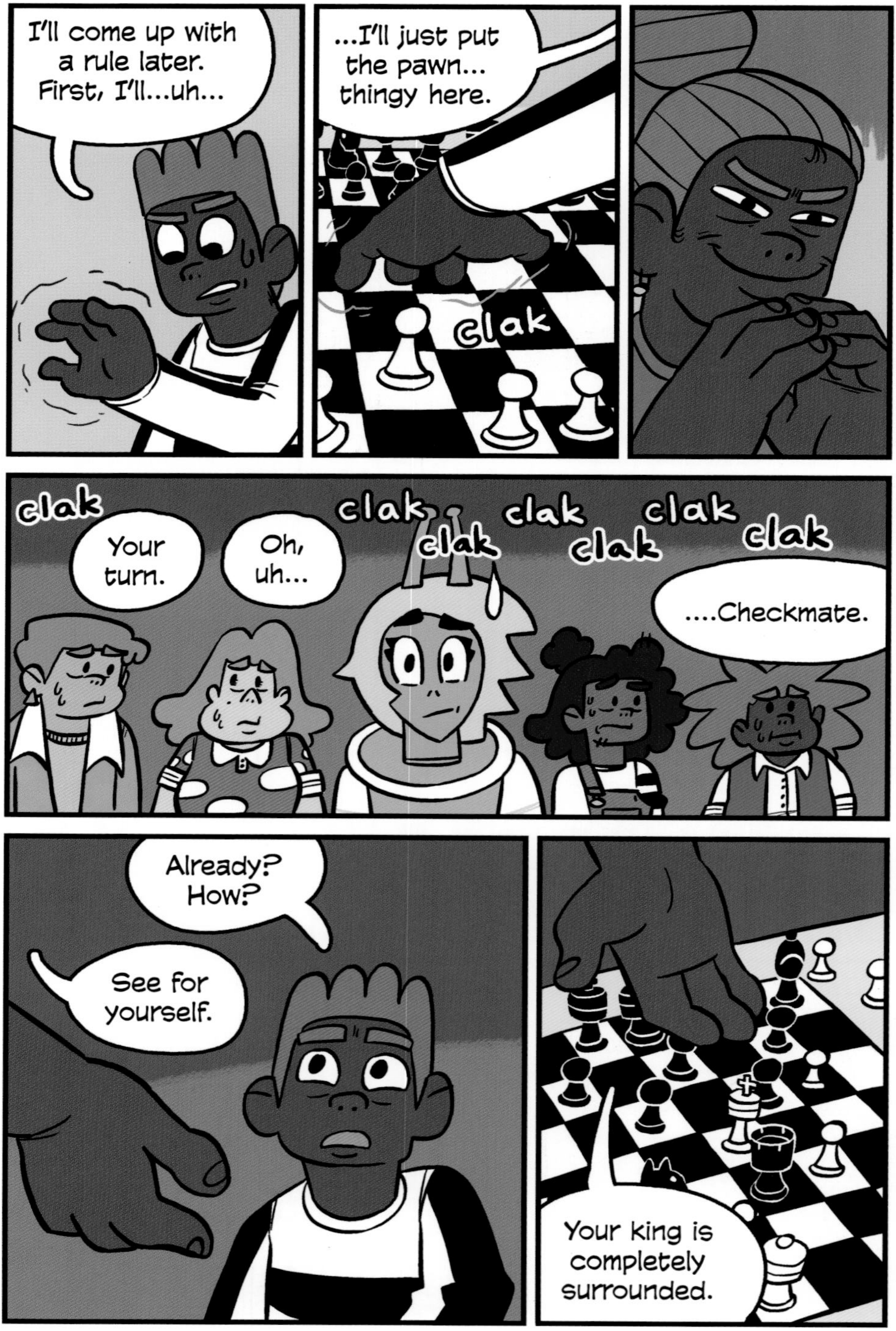
I'll come up with a rule later. First, I'll...uh...
...I'll just put the pawn... thingy here.
clak
clak
Your turn.
Oh, uh...
clak
clak
clak
clak
clak
clak
....Checkmate.
Already? How?
See for yourself.
Your king is completely surrounded.

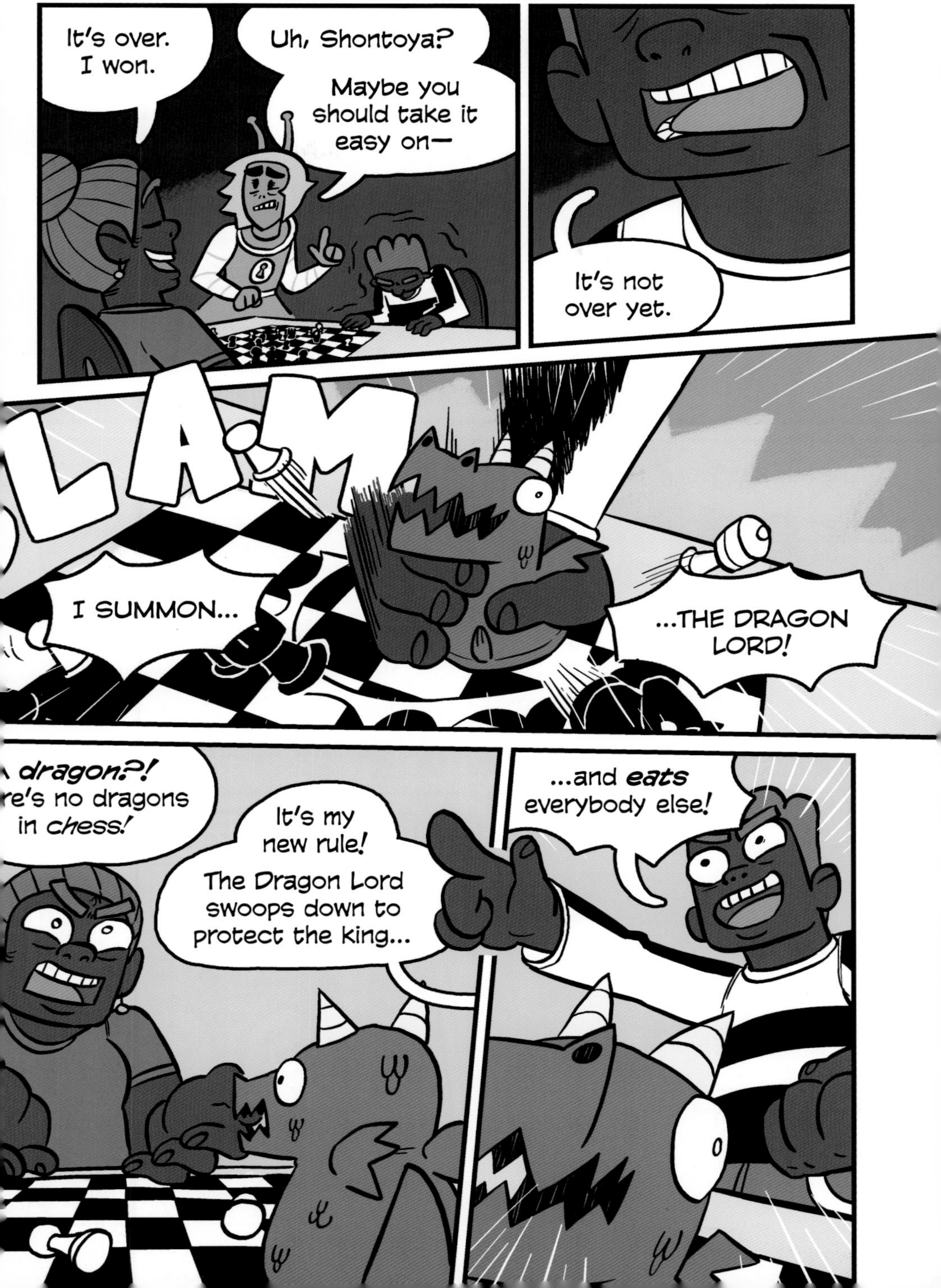
It's over. I won.
Uh, Shontoya?
Maybe you should take it easy on—
It's not over yet.
SLAM
I SUMMON...
...THE DRAGON LORD!
dragon?!
re's no dragons in chess!
It's my new rule!
The Dragon Lord swoops down to protect the king...
...and eats everybody else!

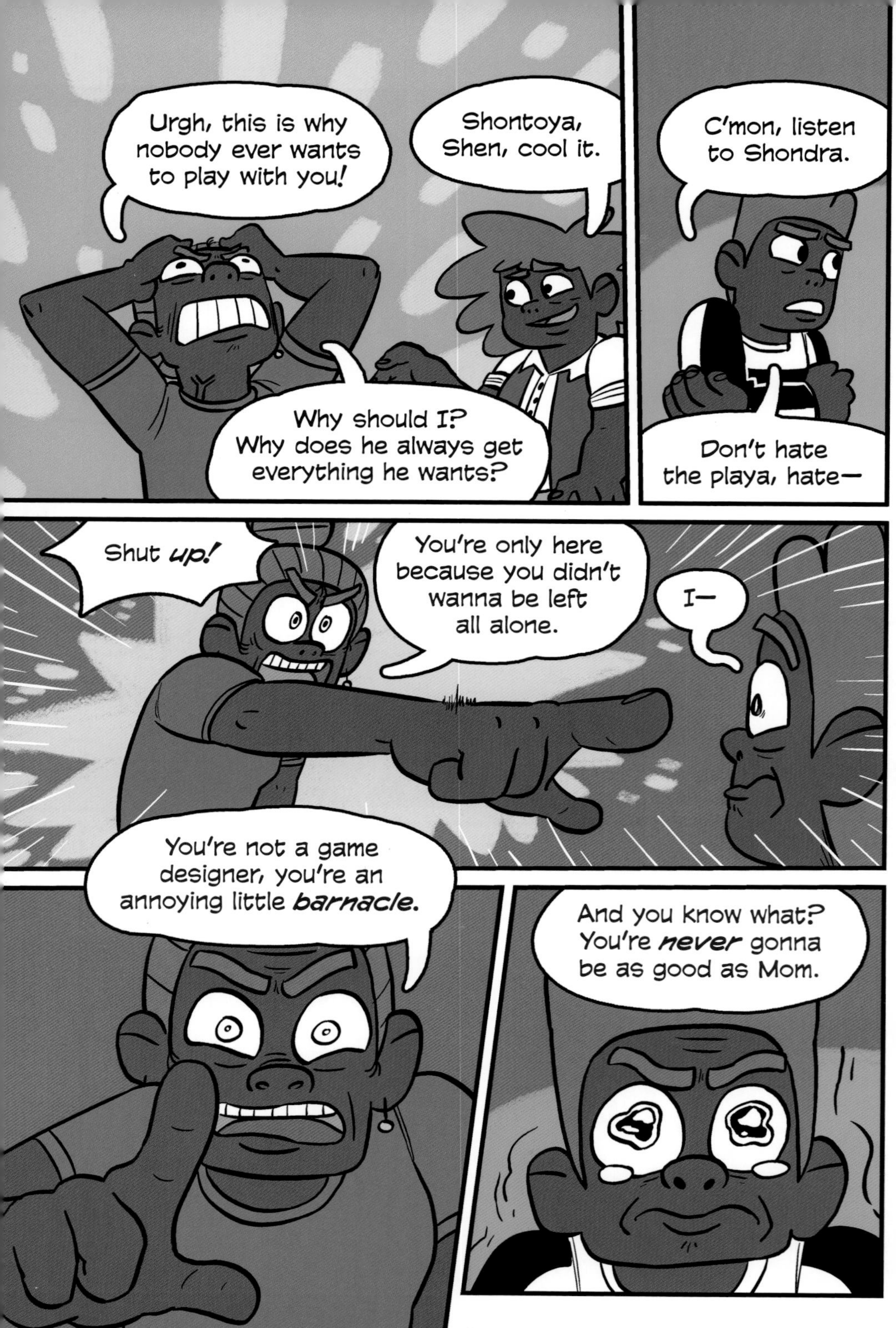

Urgh, this is why nobody ever wants to play with you!
Shontoya, Shen, cool it.
Why should I? Why does he always get everything he wants?
C'mon, listen to Shondra.
Don't hate the playa, hate—
Shut *up!*
You're only here because you didn't wanna be left all alone.
I—
You're not a game designer, you're an annoying little ***barnacle.***
And you know what? You're ***never*** gonna be as good as Mom.

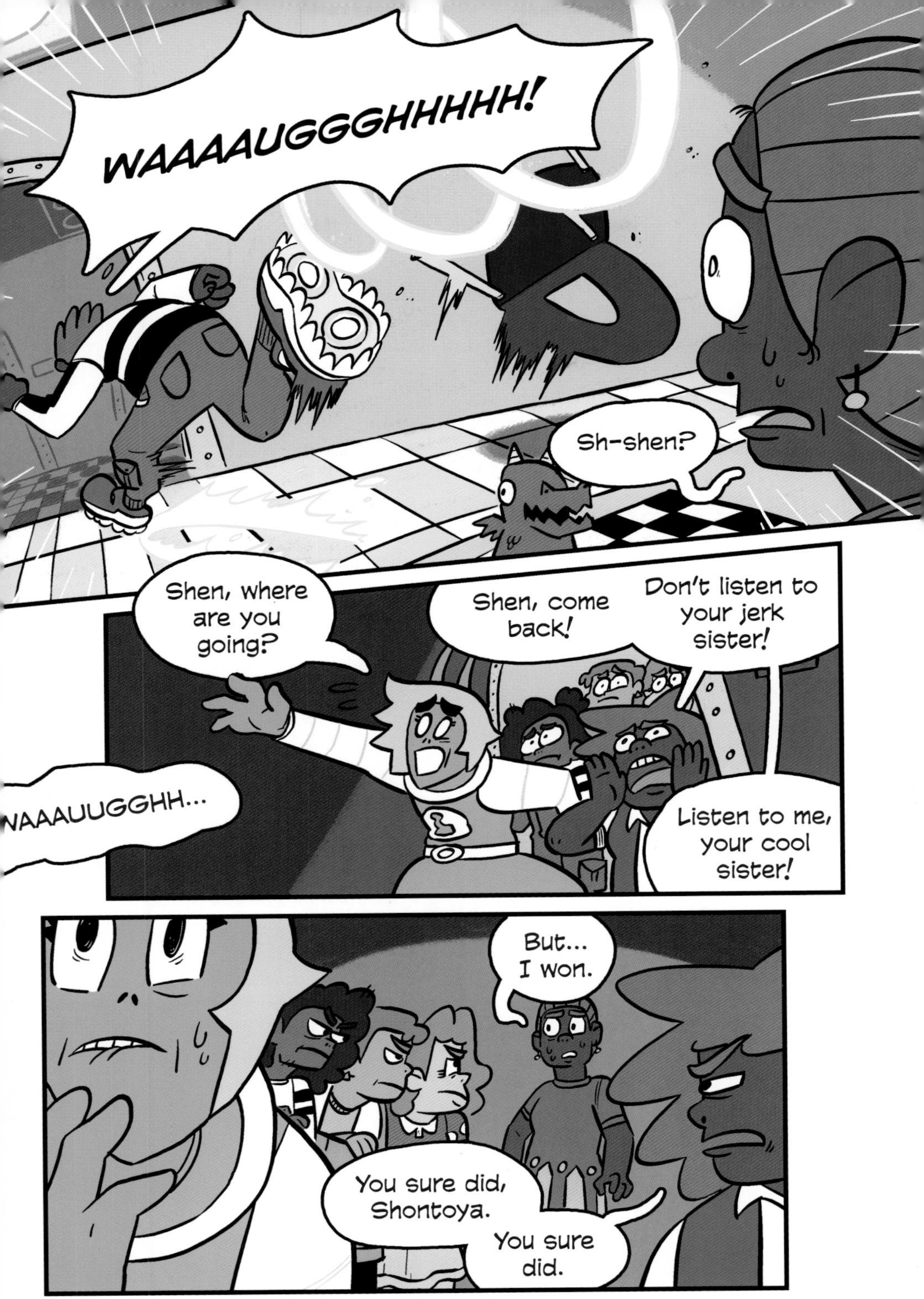

WAAAAUGGGHHHHH!
Sh-shen?
Shen, where are you going?
Shen, come back!
Don't listen to your jerk sister!
WAAAUUGGHH...
Listen to me, your cool sister!
But... I won.
You sure did, Shontoya.
You sure did.

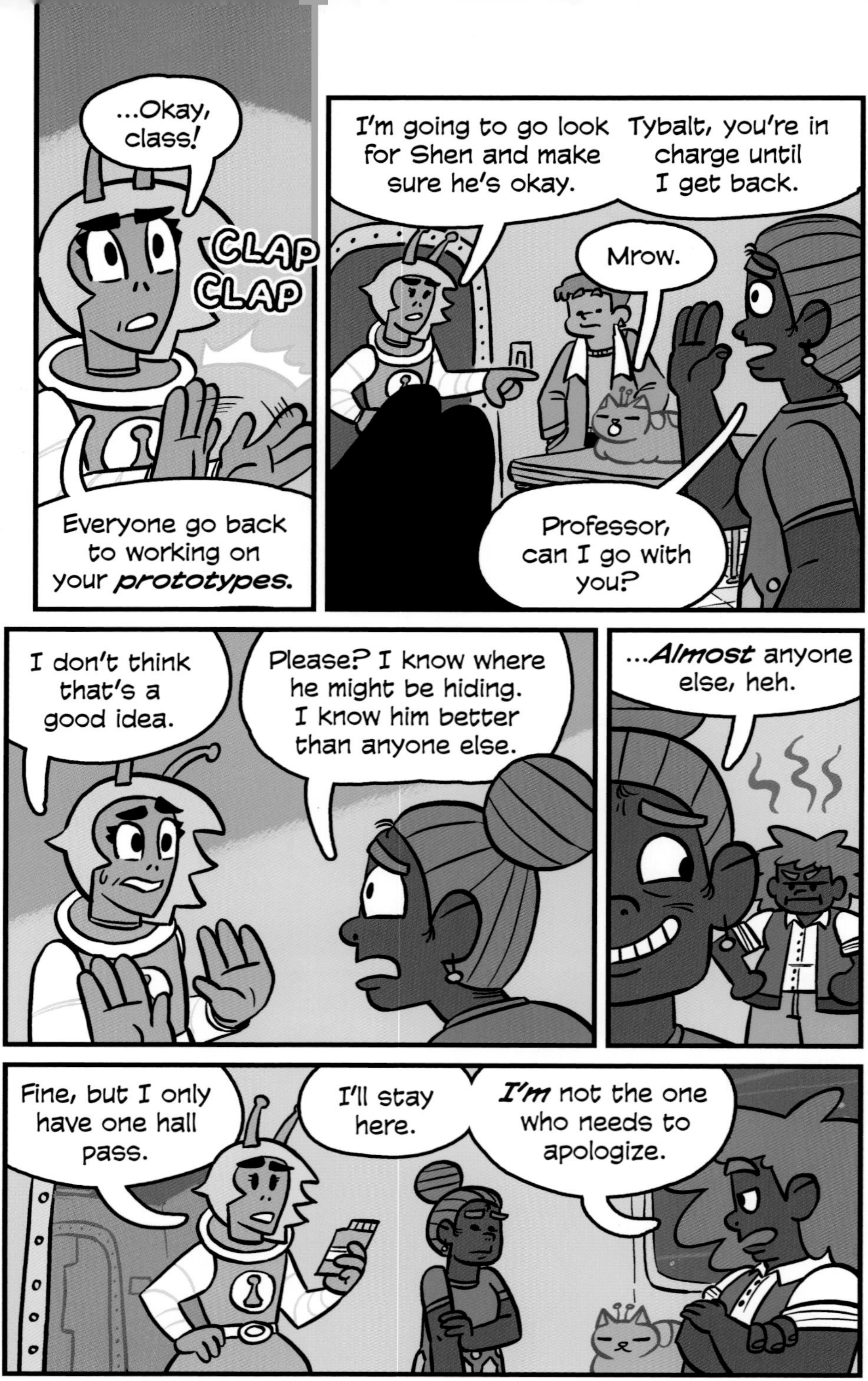
...Okay, class!
CLAP CLAP
Everyone go back to working on your *prototypes.*
I'm going to go look for Shen and make sure he's okay.
Tybalt, you're in charge until I get back.
Mrow.
Professor, can I go with you?
I don't think that's a good idea.
Please? I know where he might be hiding. I know him better than anyone else.
...*Almost* anyone else, heh.
Fine, but I only have one hall pass.
I'll stay here.
I'm not the one who needs to apologize.

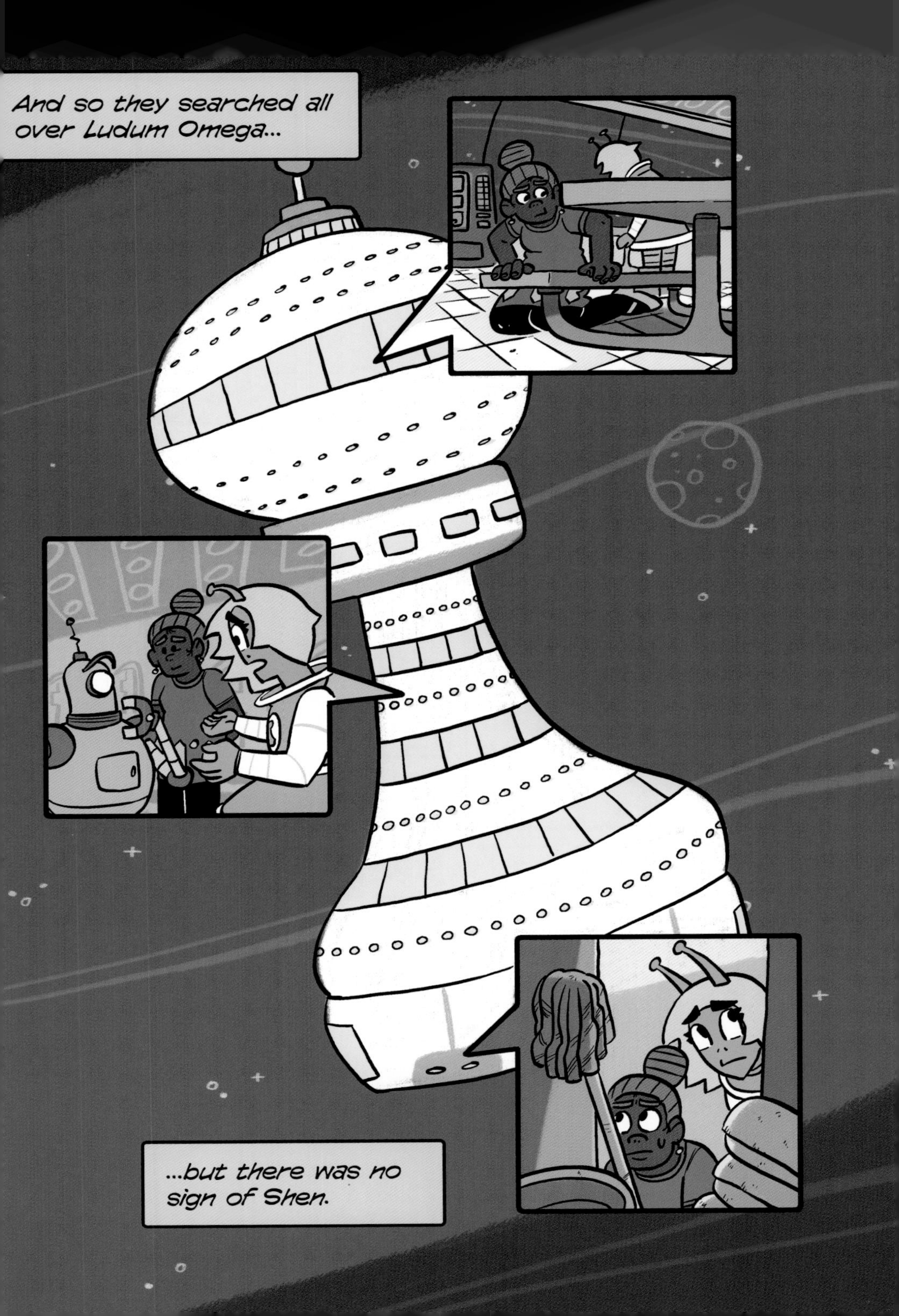
And so they searched all over Ludum Omega...
...but there was no sign of Shen.

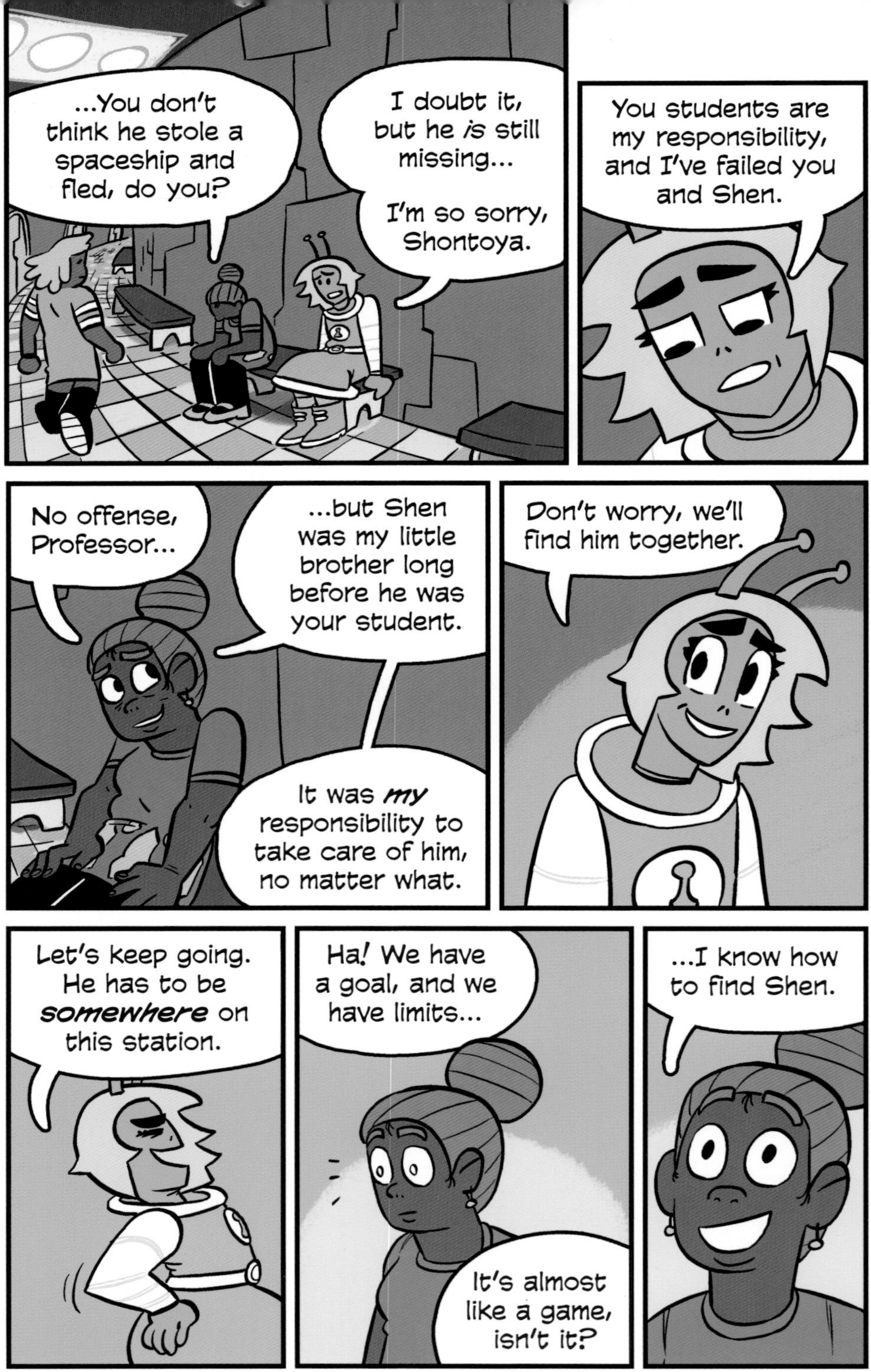
...You don't think he stole a spaceship and fled, do you?
I doubt it, but he *is* still missing...
I'm so sorry, Shontoya.
You students are my responsibility, and I've failed you and Shen.
No offense, Professor...
...but Shen was my little brother long before he was your student.
It was **my** responsibility to take care of him, no matter what.
Don't worry, we'll find him together.
Let's keep going. He has to be **somewhere** on this station.
Ha! We have a goal, and we have limits...
It's almost like a game, isn't it?
...I know how to find Shen.

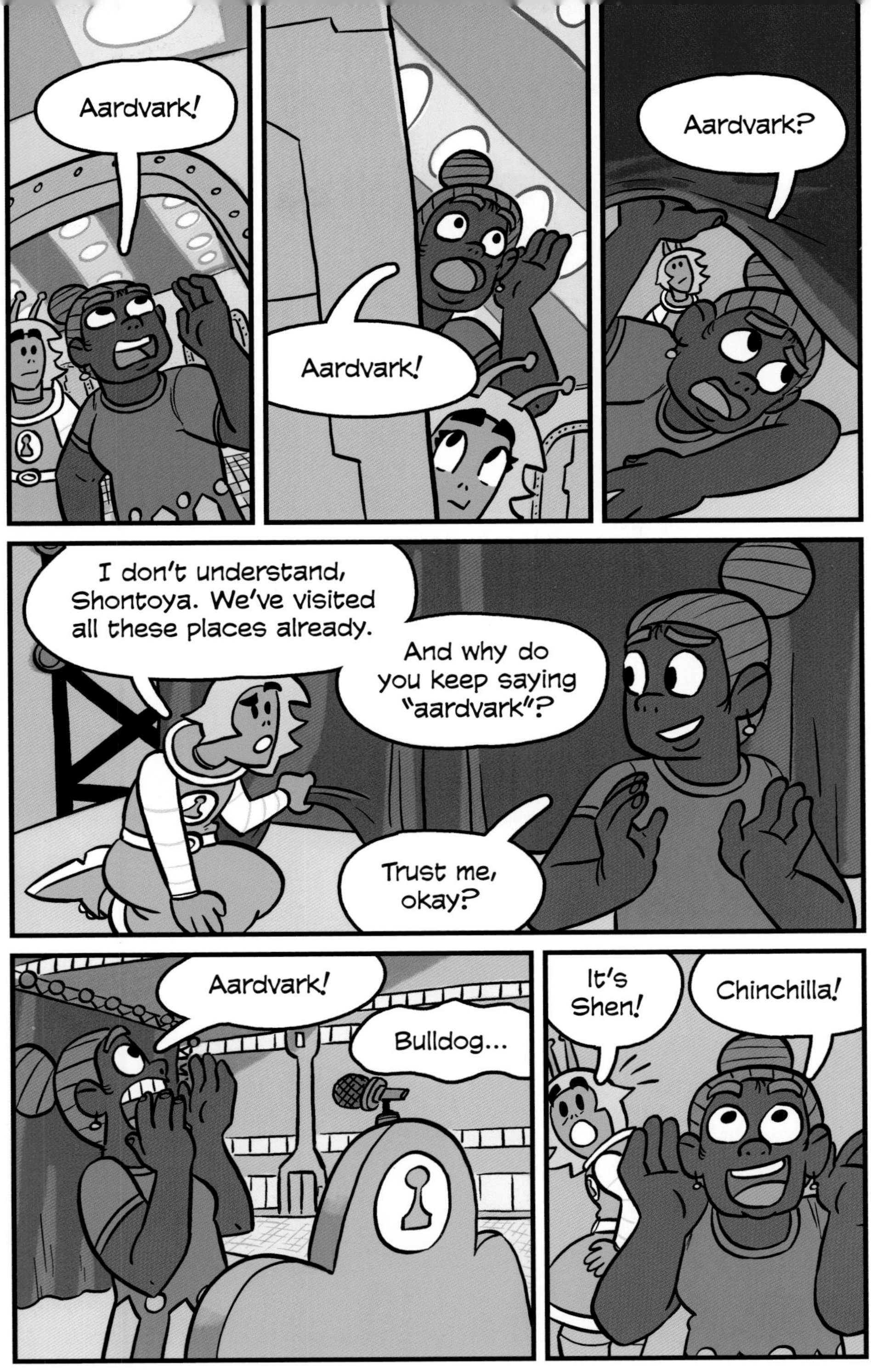
Aardvark!
Aardvark!
Aardvark?
I don't understand, Shontoya. We've visited all these places already.
And why do you keep saying "aardvark"?
Trust me, okay?
Aardvark!
Bulldog...
It's Shen!
Chinchilla!

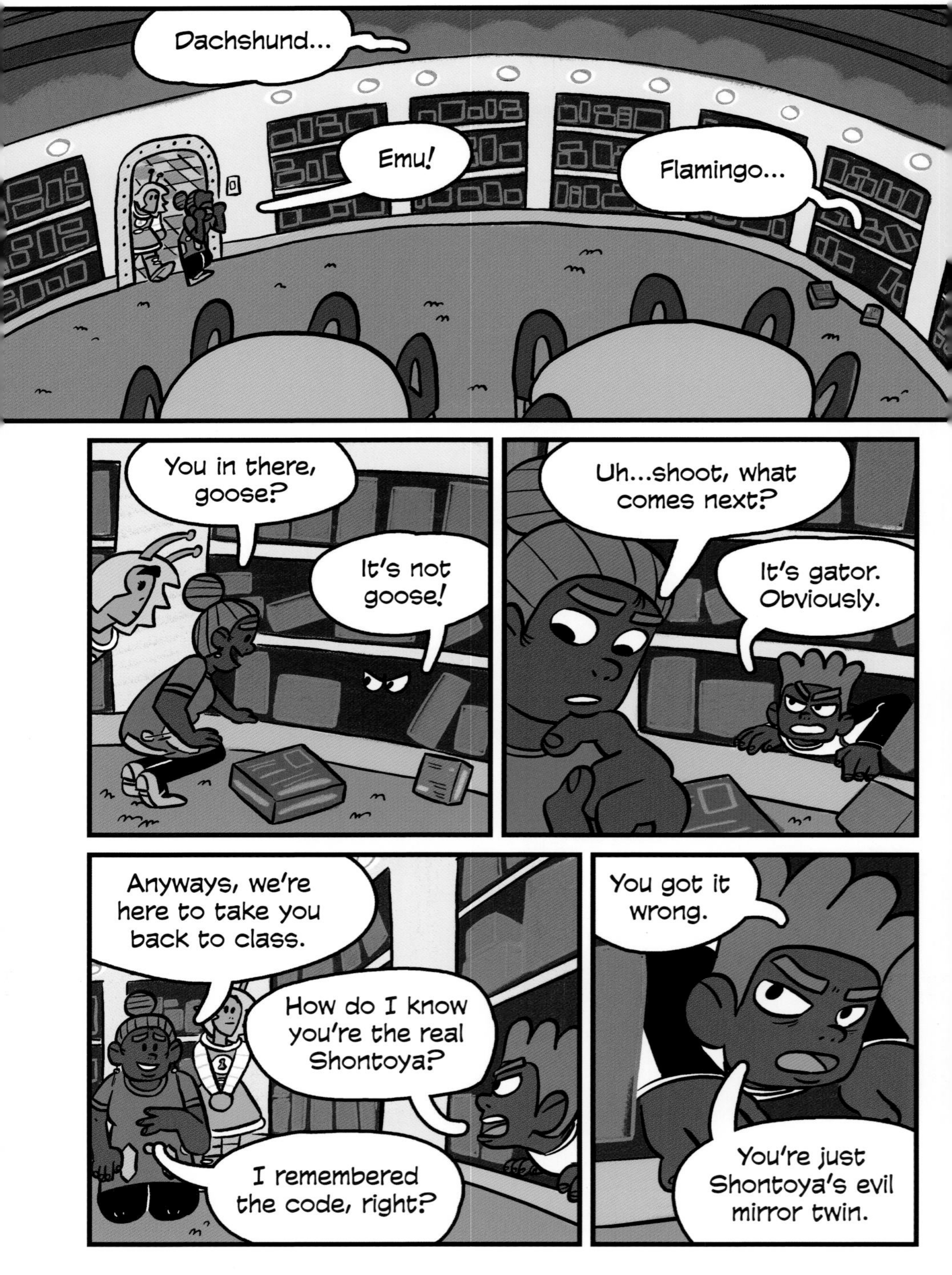
Dachshund...
Emu!
Flamingo...
You in there, goose?
It's not goose!
Uh...shoot, what comes next?
It's gator. Obviously.
Anyways, we're here to take you back to class.
How do I know you're the real Shontoya?
I remembered the code, right?
You got it wrong.
You're just Shontoya's evil mirror twin.

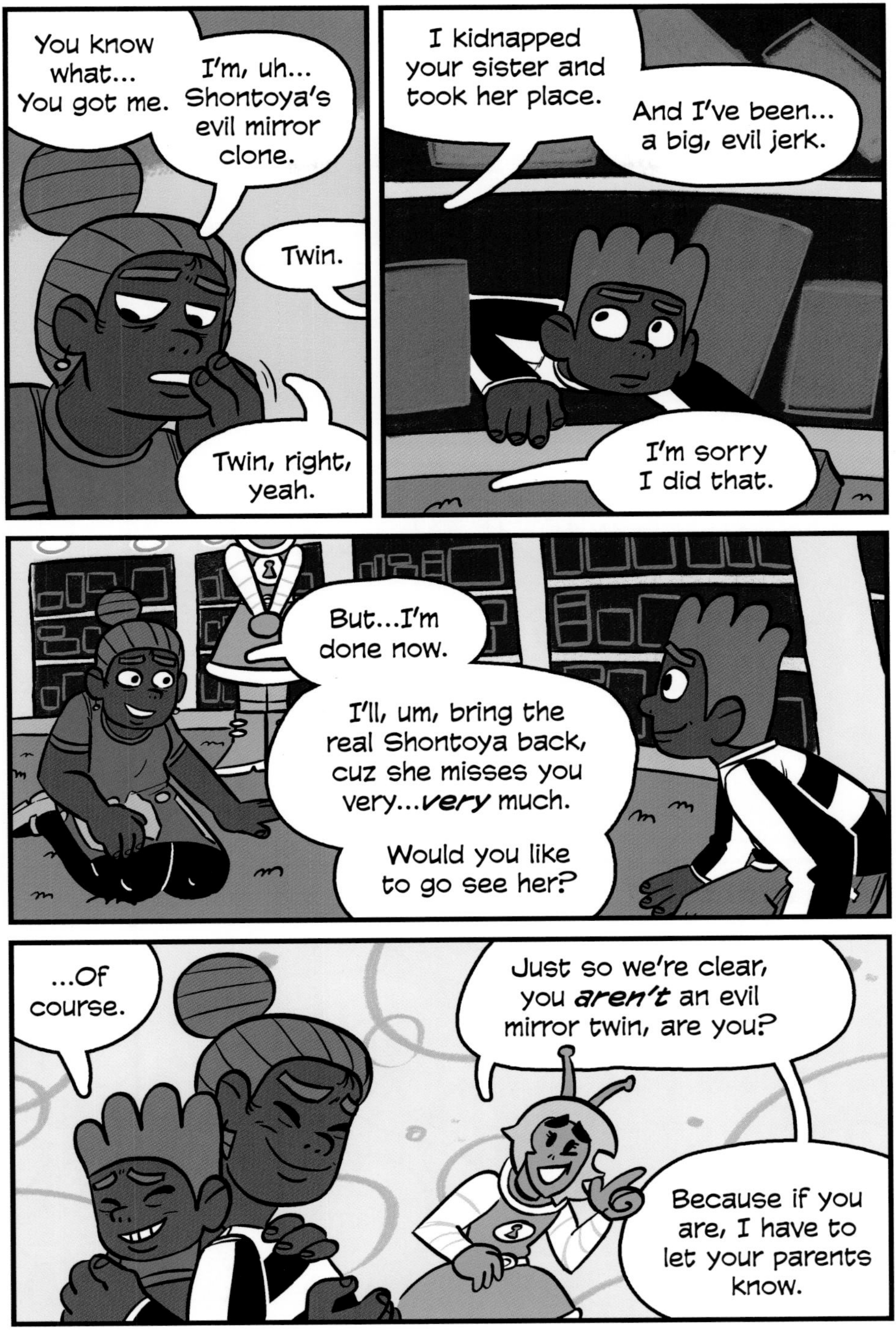
You know what... You got me.
I'm, uh... Shontoya's evil mirror clone.
Twin.
Twin, right, yeah.
I kidnapped your sister and took her place.
And I've been... a big, evil jerk.
I'm sorry I did that.
But...I'm done now.
I'll, um, bring the real Shontoya back, cuz she misses you very...*very* much.
Would you like to go see her?
...Of course.
Just so we're clear, you *aren't* an evil mirror twin, are you?
Because if you are, I have to let your parents know.

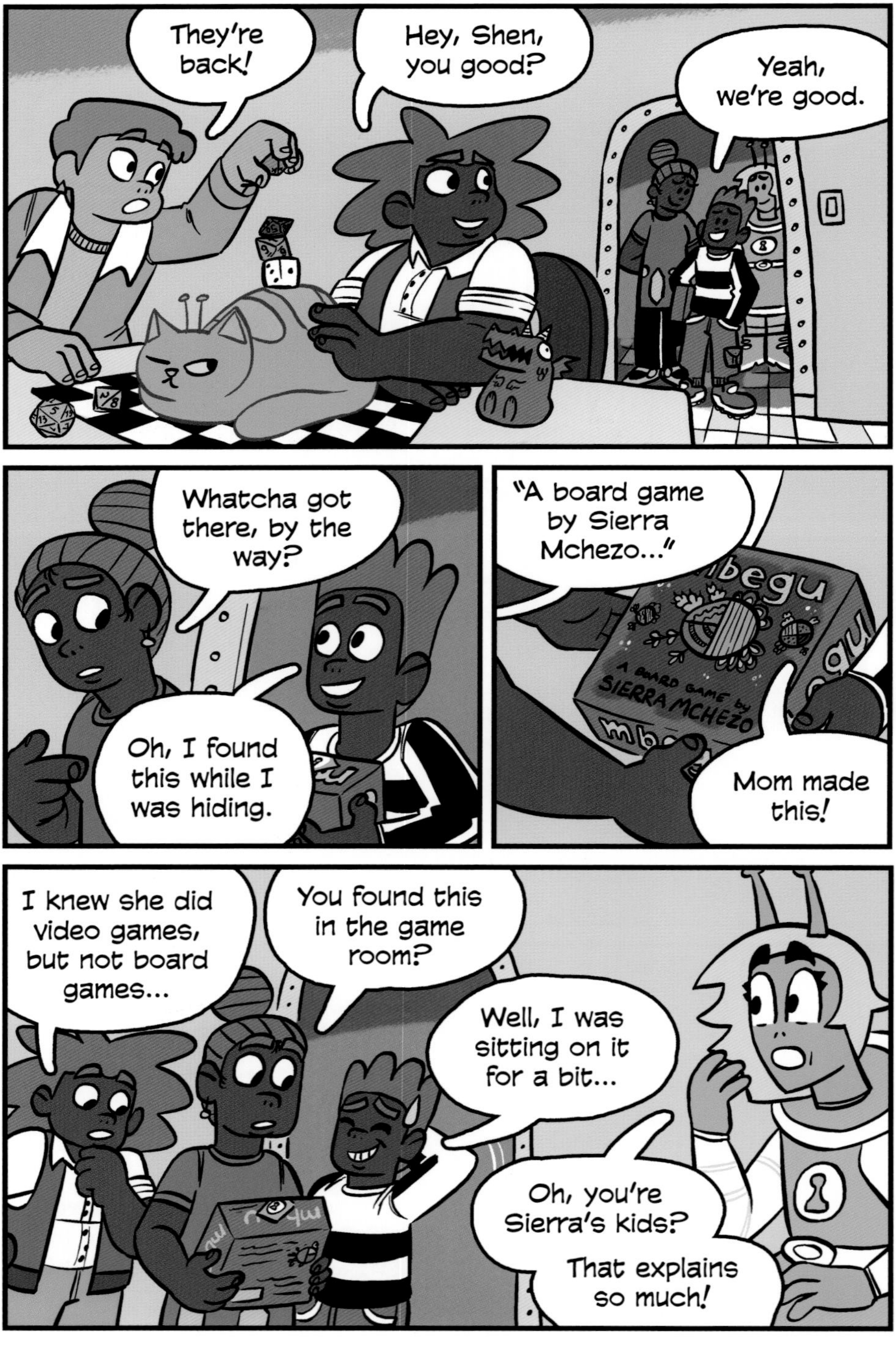
They're back!
Hey, Shen, you good?
Yeah, we're good.
Whatcha got there, by the way?
Oh, I found this while I was hiding.
"A board game by Sierra Mchezo..."
A BOARD GAME by SIERRA MCHEZO
Mom made this!
I knew she did video games, but not board games...
You found this in the game room?
Well, I was sitting on it for a bit...
Oh, you're Sierra's kids?
That explains so much!

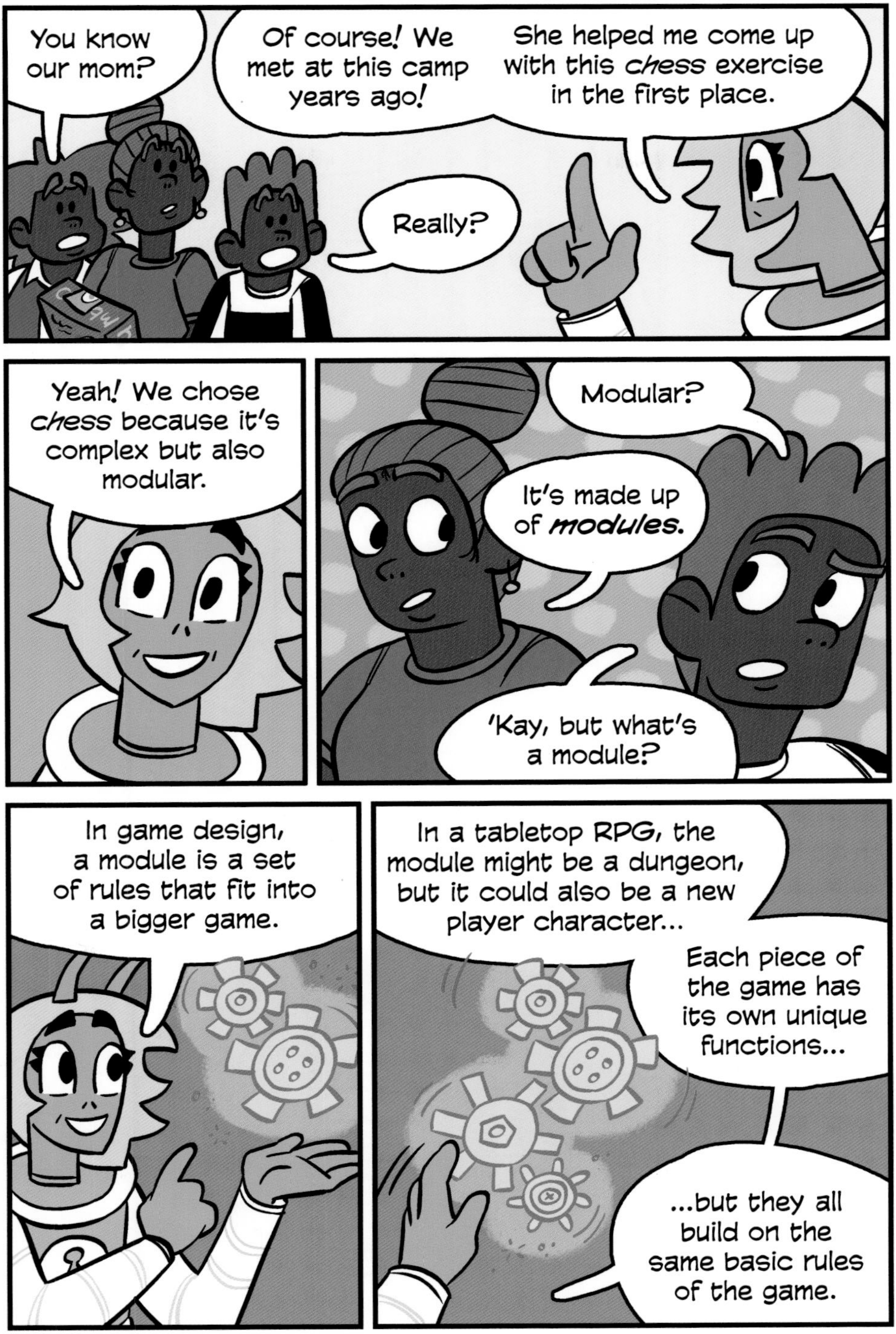
You know our mom?
Of course! We met at this camp years ago!
She helped me come up with this *chess* exercise in the first place.
Really?
Yeah! We chose *chess* because it's complex but also modular.
Modular?
It's made up of ***modules.***
'Kay, but what's a module?
In game design, a module is a set of rules that fit into a bigger game.
In a tabletop RPG, the module might be a dungeon, but it could also be a new player character...
Each piece of the game has its own unique functions...
...but they all build on the same basic rules of the game.

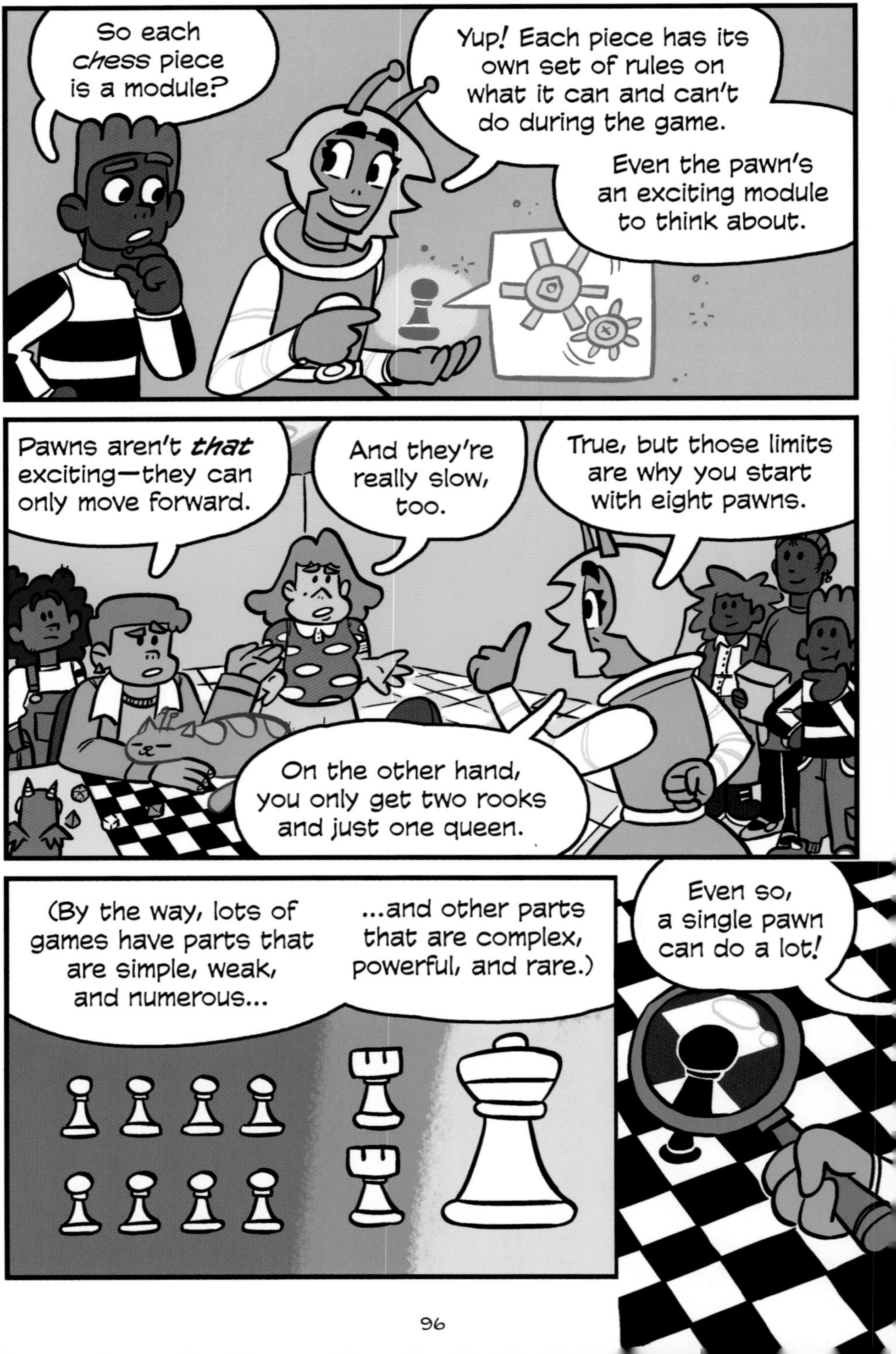
So each *chess* piece is a module?
Yup! Each piece has its own set of rules on what it can and can't do during the game.
Even the pawn's an exciting module to think about.
Pawns aren't ***that*** exciting—they can only move forward.
And they're really slow, too.
True, but those limits are why you start with eight pawns.
On the other hand, you only get two rooks and just one queen.
(By the way, lots of games have parts that are simple, weak, and numerous...
...and other parts that are complex, powerful, and rare.)
Even so, a single pawn can do a lot!

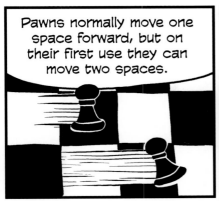

Pawns normally move one space forward, but on their first use they can move two spaces.

They can capture any piece, as long as it's diagonally adjacent.

They can block other pawns and prevent them from moving forward.

If a pawn reaches the other side of the board, they can become a totally new piece!

LEVEL UP!

That's a lot of mechanics crammed into just one piece—

—and *chess* has lots of pieces!

If you replaced the pawn with a different piece that has a different set of abilities, the game would be dramatically altered...

...even though the rest of the rules and pieces are the same.

That's modularity!

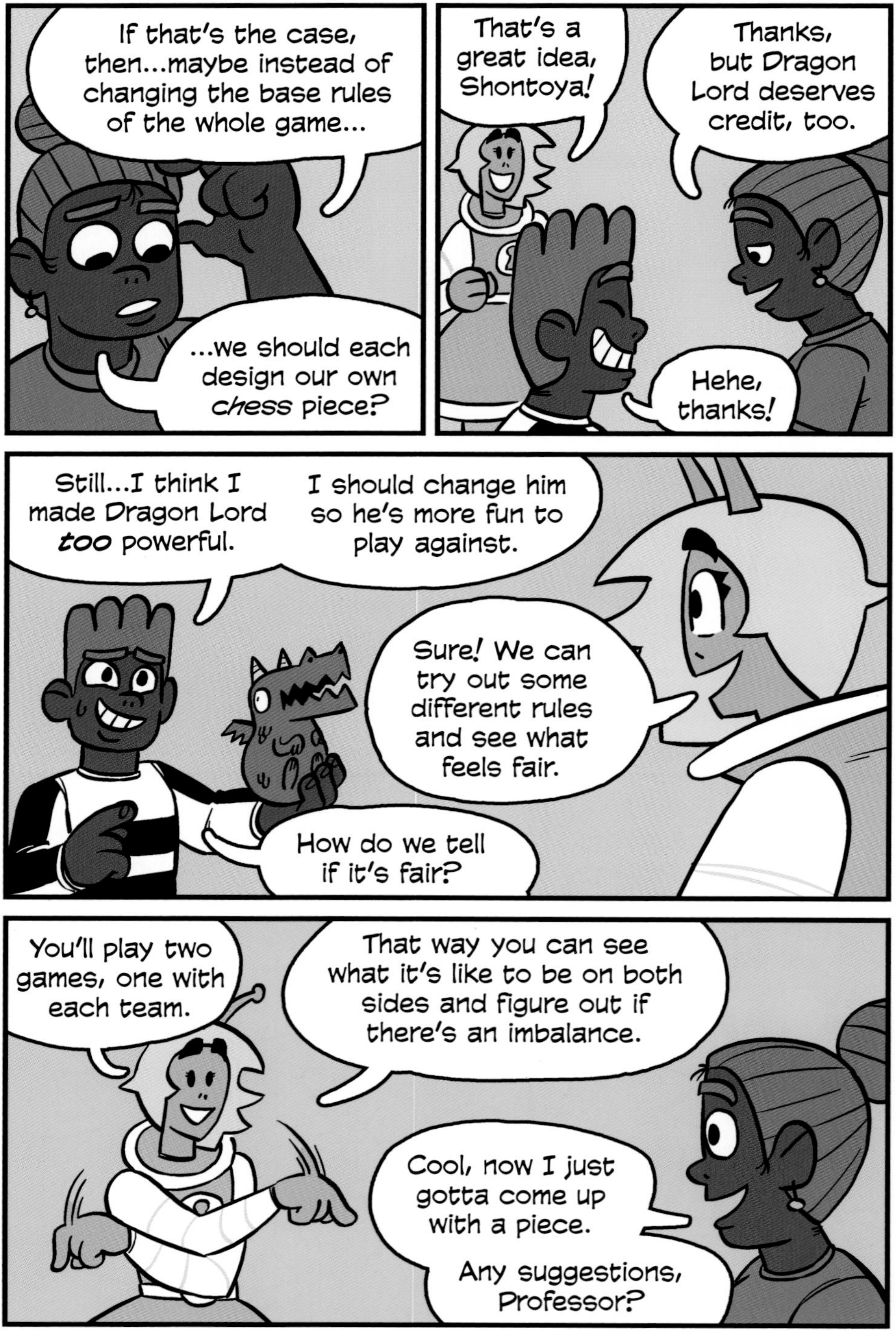

If that's the case, then...maybe instead of changing the base rules of the whole game...
...we should each design our own *chess* piece?
That's a great idea, Shontoya!
Thanks, but Dragon Lord deserves credit, too.
Hehe, thanks!
Still...I think I made Dragon Lord ***too*** powerful.
I should change him so he's more fun to play against.
Sure! We can try out some different rules and see what feels fair.
How do we tell if it's fair?
You'll play two games, one with each team.
That way you can see what it's like to be on both sides and figure out if there's an imbalance.
Cool, now I just gotta come up with a piece.
Any suggestions, Professor?

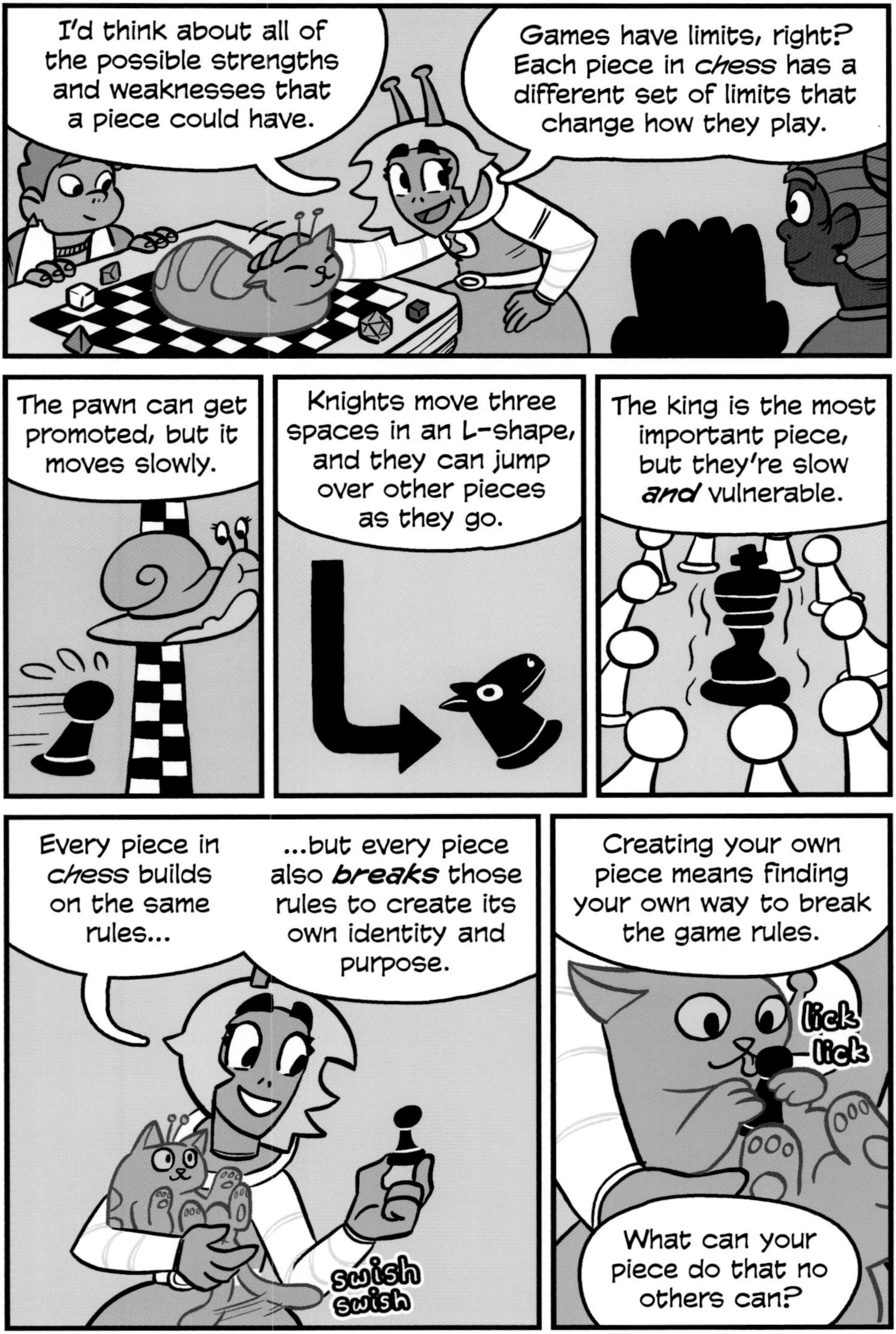
I'd think about all of the possible strengths and weaknesses that a piece could have.
Games have limits, right? Each piece in *chess* has a different set of limits that change how they play.
The pawn can get promoted, but it moves slowly.
Knights move three spaces in an L-shape, and they can jump over other pieces as they go.
The king is the most important piece, but they're slow ***and*** vulnerable.
Every piece in *chess* builds on the same rules...
...but every piece also ***breaks*** those rules to create its own identity and purpose.
swish swish
Creating your own piece means finding your own way to break the game rules.
lick lick
What can your piece do that no others can?

Let's Destroy *Chess!*

Players:	Materials:
2	Standard *chess* set, and whatever else you'd like to add!

This activity will be different from the others. Choose one or more options to flex your game design skills and turn chess *inside out!*

Option One: Change the Rules of *Chess!*

1. Each player chooses a single rule from standard *chess* to modify, or adds a new rule.

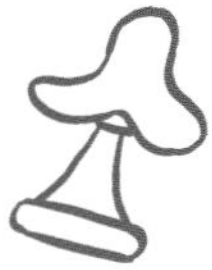

2. Write down your modification and read it out loud to your opponent. Answer any questions they have about your new rule, and make sure you understand theirs, as well.
3. Play a *chess* match with each player using their own modification. Then the players swap seats and try out their opponent's modification. How does this compare to normal *chess?*

Option Two: Alter the *Chess* Teams!

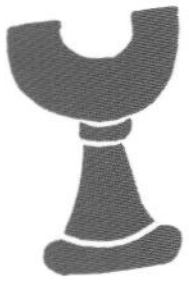

1. Each player builds a unique team of *chess* pieces, swapping pieces from another *chess* set. However, the players can only have one king piece each, and they cannot have more pieces than a normal *chess* team.
2. Play a *chess* match as both teams, swapping seats and noting how the changes affect your game.
3. Take note of how playing each team differed. Did one team feel harder to play against? Which pieces felt the most useful? How might you change the rules to work with these teams?

Option Three: Make a New *Chess* Piece!

1. Each player designs a totally new *chess* piece to replace a standard piece. What are its strengths? What are its weaknesses?

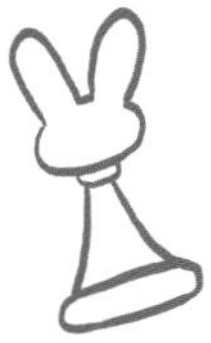

2. Each player makes an object to represent their new piece. They can make it out of any material as long as it fits on a single space of the chessboard.
3. Each player writes down their piece's rules and explains them to their opponent. Play a *chess* match trying out both new pieces. Then swap seats and play again. What is it like playing with or against the piece you created?

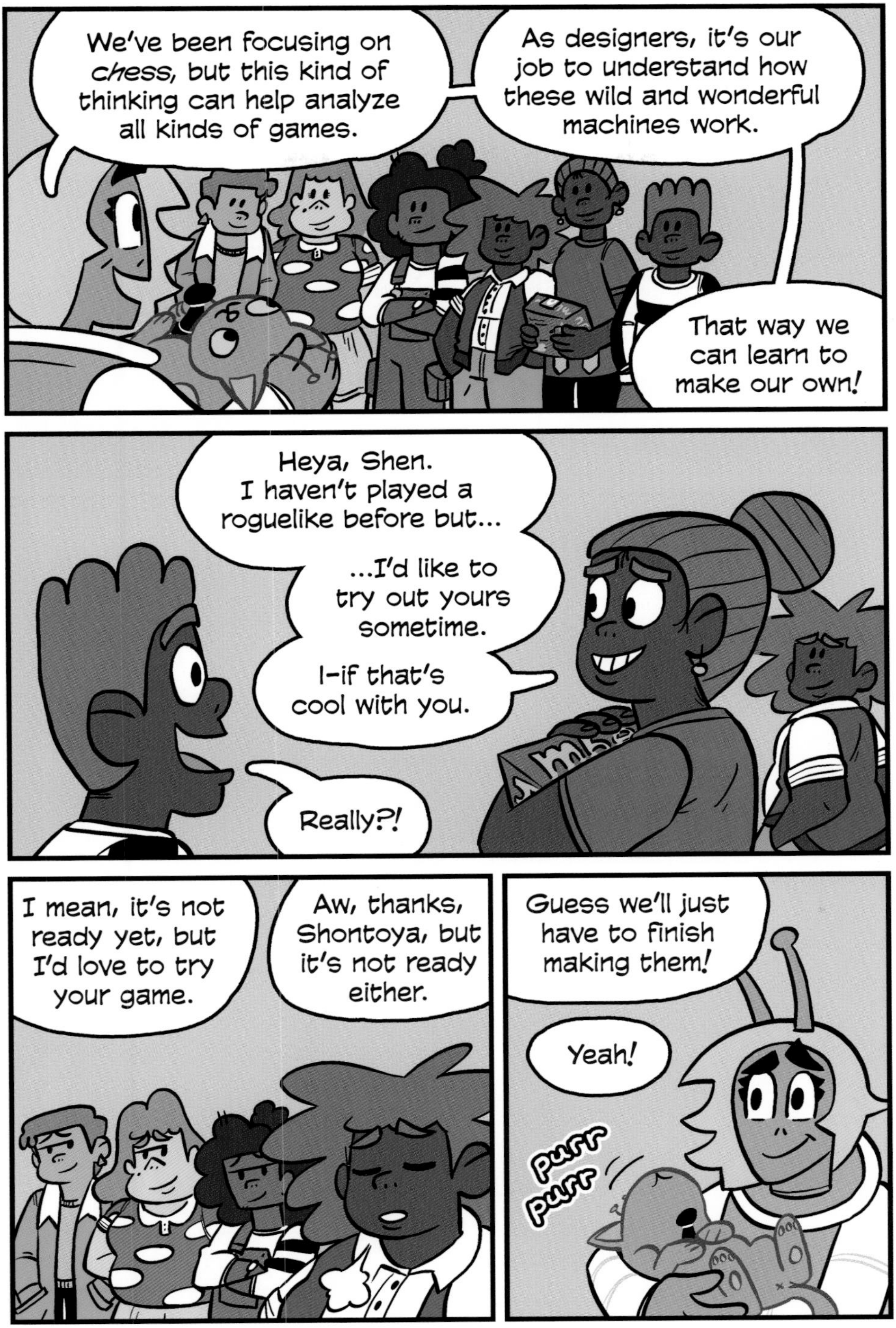
We've been focusing on *chess*, but this kind of thinking can help analyze all kinds of games.
As designers, it's our job to understand how these wild and wonderful machines work.
That way we can learn to make our own!
Heya, Shen. I haven't played a roguelike before but...
...I'd like to try out yours sometime.
I-if that's cool with you.
Really?!
I mean, it's not ready yet, but I'd love to try your game.
Aw, thanks, Shontoya, but it's not ready either.
Guess we'll just have to finish making them!
Yeah!
purr purr

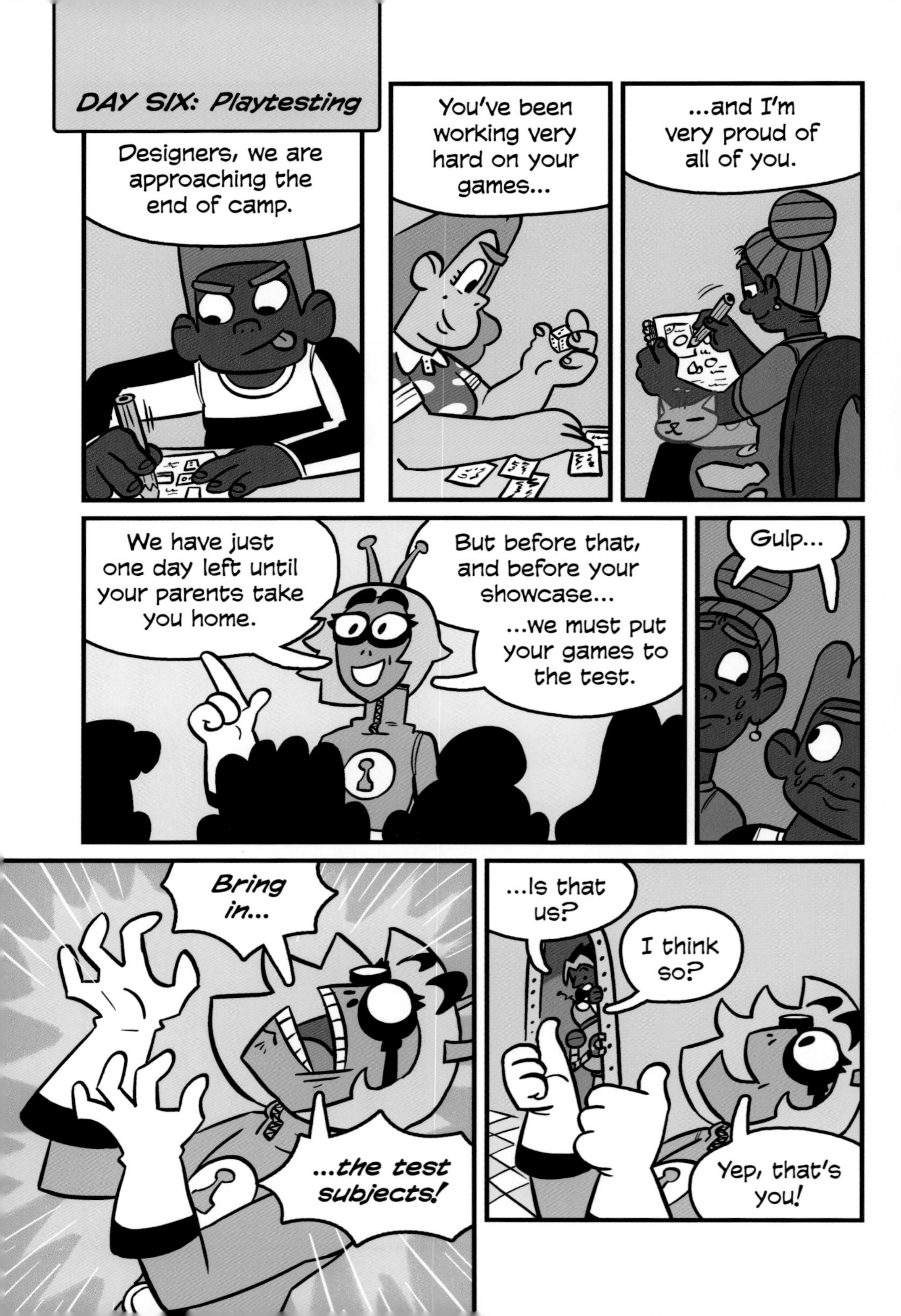
DAY SIX: Playtesting
Designers, we are approaching the end of camp.
You've been working very hard on your games...
...and I'm very proud of all of you.
We have just one day left until your parents take you home.
But before that, and before your showcase...
...we must put your games to the test.
Gulp...
Bring in...
...the test subjects!
...Is that us?
I think so?
Yep, that's you!

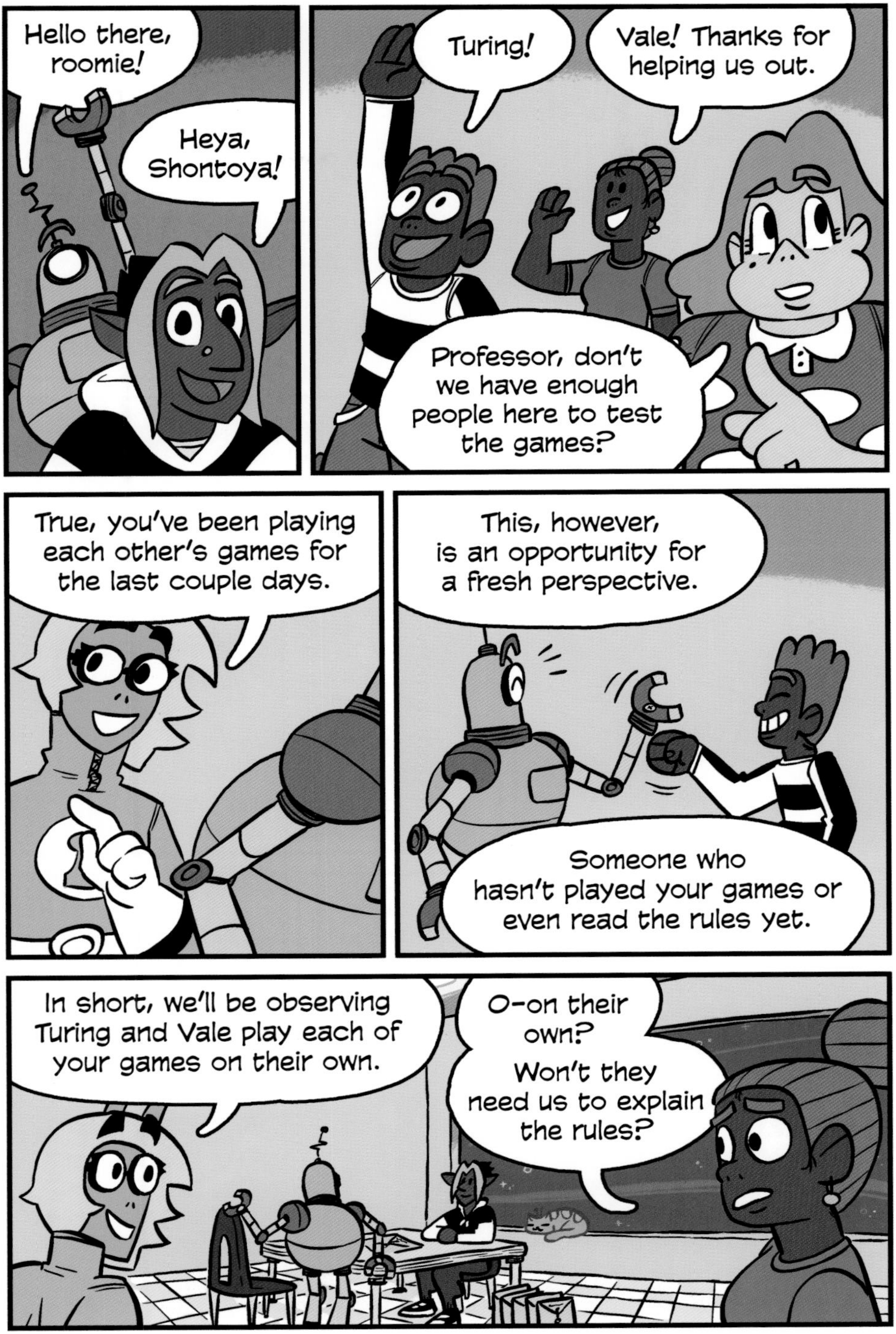
Hello there, roomie!
Heya, Shontoya!
Turing!
Vale! Thanks for helping us out.
Professor, don't we have enough people here to test the games?
True, you've been playing each other's games for the last couple days.
This, however, is an opportunity for a fresh perspective.
Someone who hasn't played your games or even read the rules yet.
In short, we'll be observing Turing and Vale play each of your games on their own.
O-on their own?
Won't they need us to explain the rules?

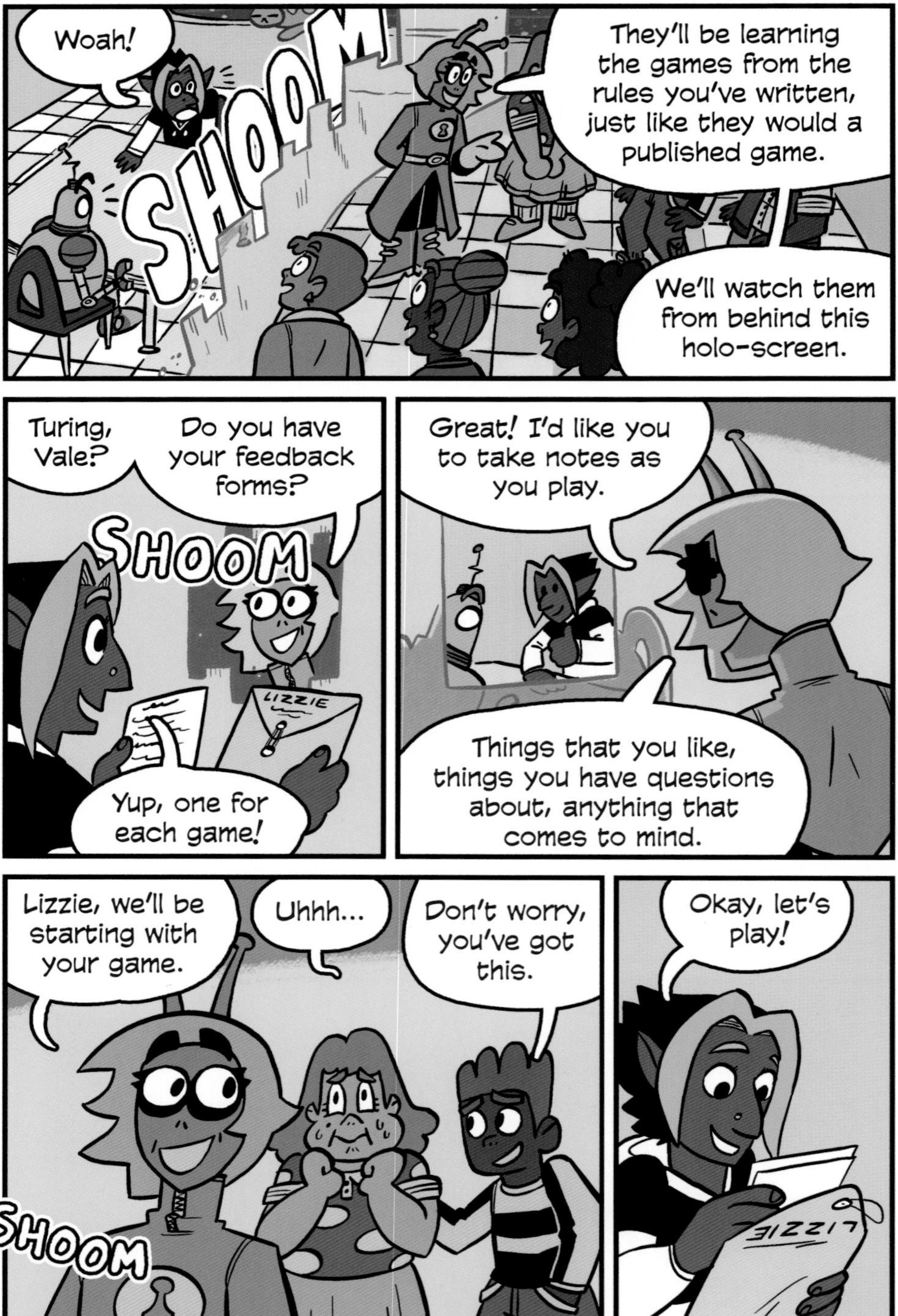

Woah!
SHOOM
They'll be learning the games from the rules you've written, just like they would a published game.
We'll watch them from behind this holo-screen.
Turing, Vale?
Do you have your feedback forms?
SHOOM
LIZZIE
Yup, one for each game!
Great! I'd like you to take notes as you play.
Things that you like, things you have questions about, anything that comes to mind.
Lizzie, we'll be starting with your game.
Uhhh...
Don't worry, you've got this.
SHOOM
Okay, let's play!
LIZZIE

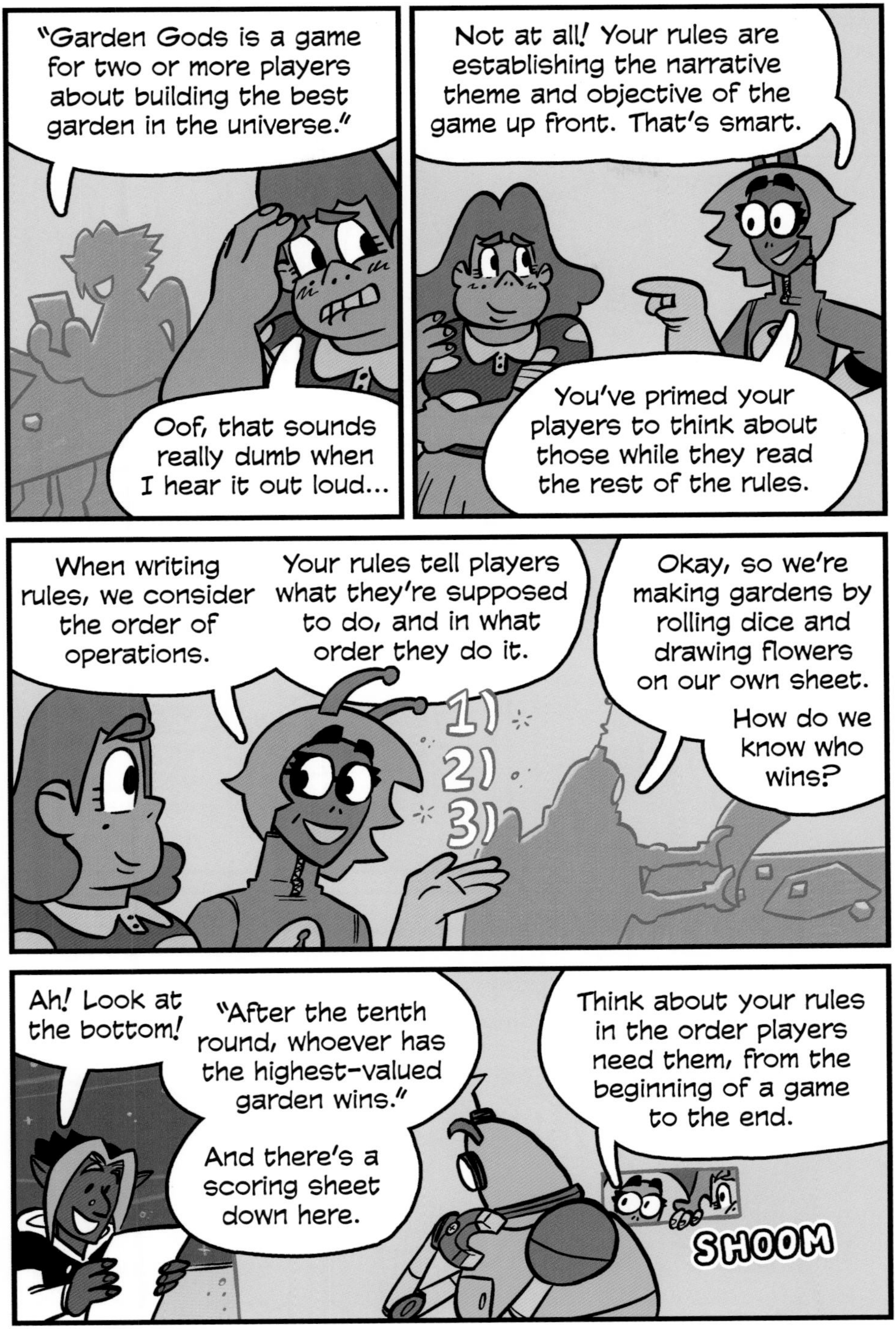

"Garden Gods is a game for two or more players about building the best garden in the universe."
Oof, that sounds really dumb when I hear it out loud...
Not at all! Your rules are establishing the narrative theme and objective of the game up front. That's smart.
You've primed your players to think about those while they read the rest of the rules.
When writing rules, we consider the order of operations.
Your rules tell players what they're supposed to do, and in what order they do it.
1)
2)
3)
Okay, so we're making gardens by rolling dice and drawing flowers on our own sheet.
How do we know who wins?
Ah! Look at the bottom!
"After the tenth round, whoever has the highest-valued garden wins."
And there's a scoring sheet down here.
Think about your rules in the order players need them, from the beginning of a game to the end.
SHOOM

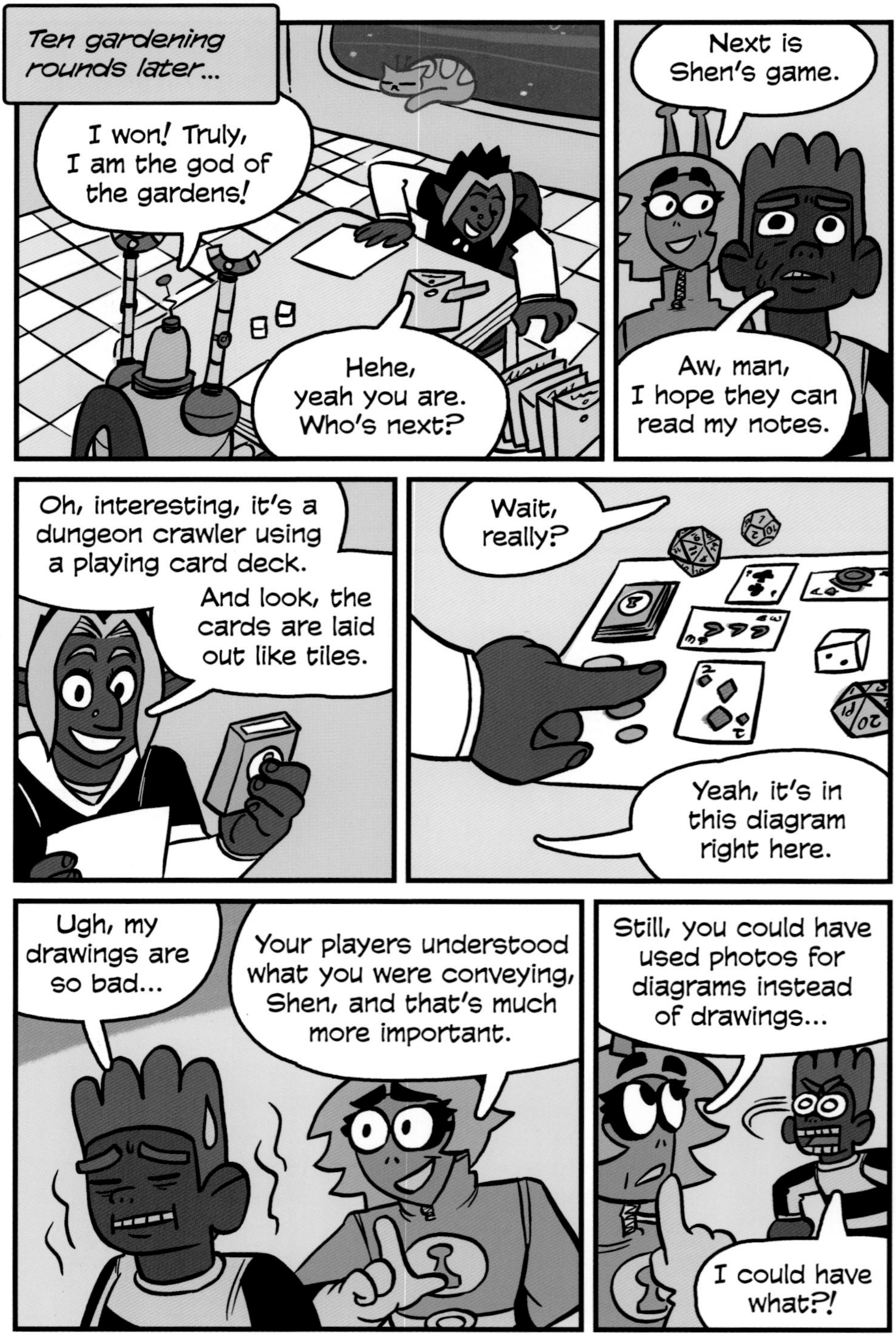
Ten gardening rounds later...
I won! Truly, I am the god of the gardens!
Hehe, yeah you are. Who's next?
Next is Shen's game.
Aw, man, I hope they can read my notes.
Oh, interesting, it's a dungeon crawler using a playing card deck.
And look, the cards are laid out like tiles.
Wait, really?
Yeah, it's in this diagram right here.
Ugh, my drawings are so bad...
Your players understood what you were conveying, Shen, and that's much more important.
Still, you could have used photos for diagrams instead of drawings...
I could have what?!

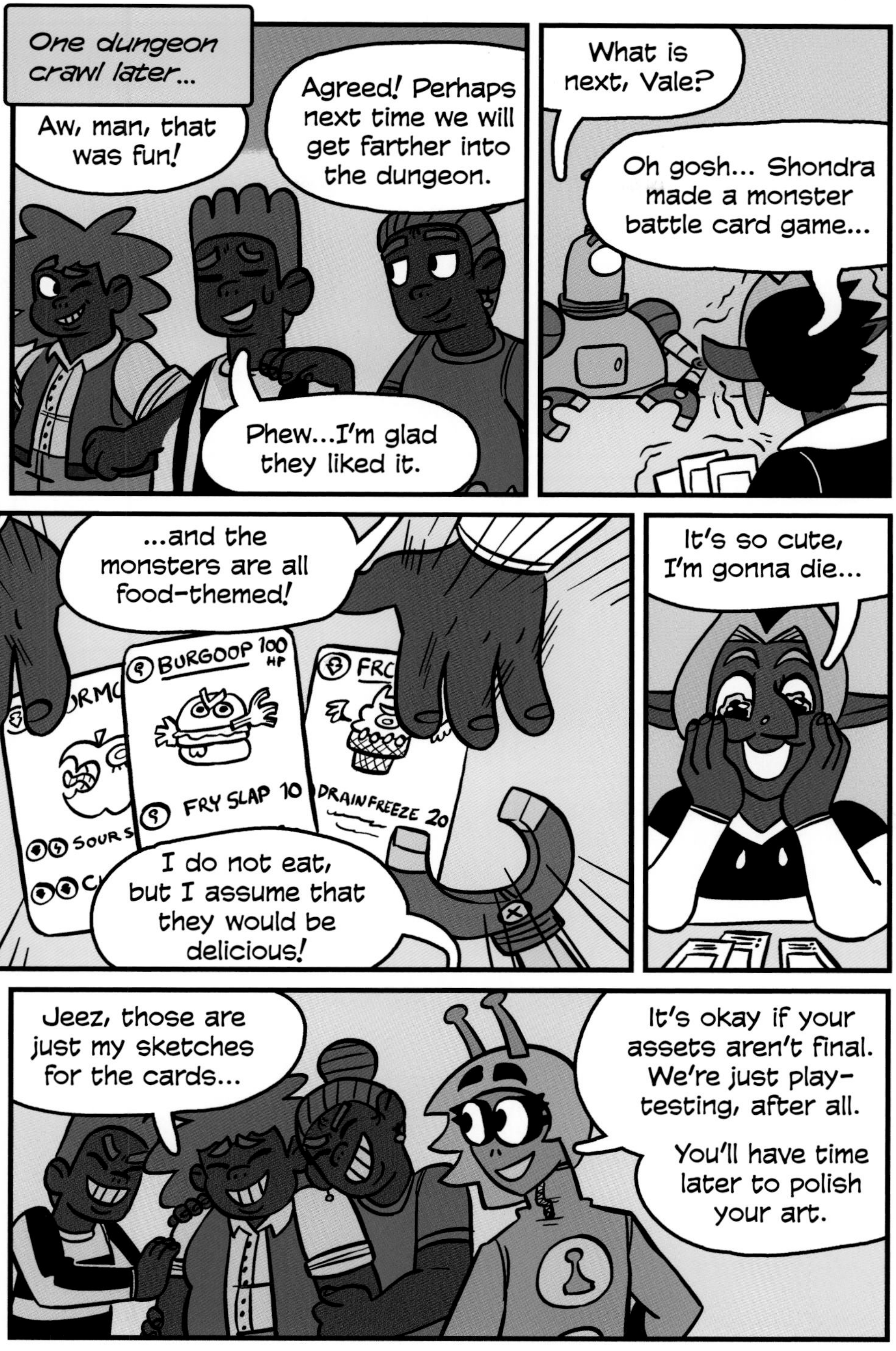
One dungeon crawl later...
Aw, man, that was fun!
Agreed! Perhaps next time we will get farther into the dungeon.
Phew...I'm glad they liked it.
What is next, Vale?
Oh gosh... Shondra made a monster battle card game...
...and the monsters are all food-themed!
BURGOOP 100 HP
FRY SLAP 10
DRAINFREEZE 20
I do not eat, but I assume that they would be delicious!
It's so cute, I'm gonna die...
Jeez, those are just my sketches for the cards...
It's okay if your assets aren't final. We're just play-testing, after all.
You'll have time later to polish your art.

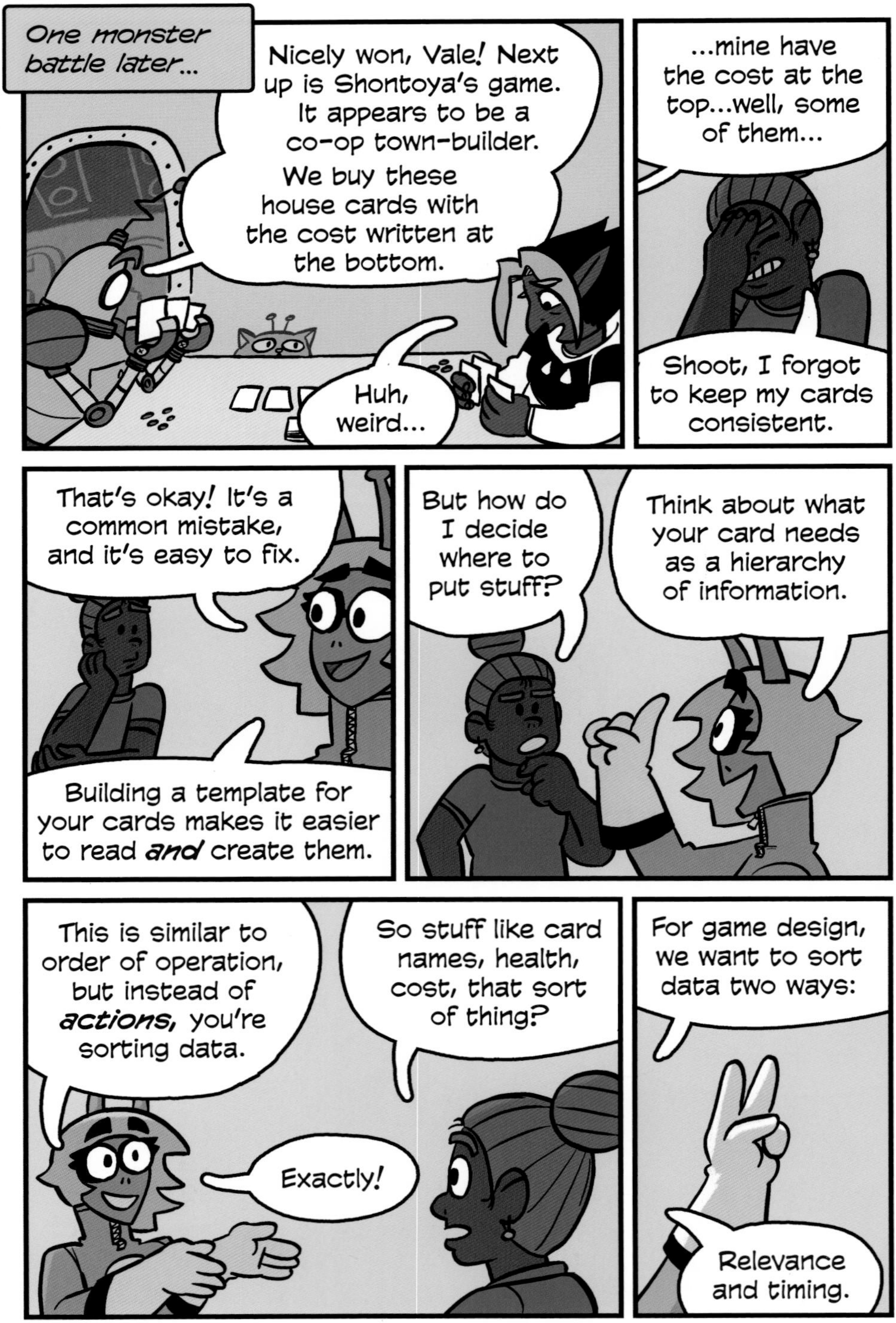
One monster battle later...
Nicely won, Vale! Next up is Shontoya's game. It appears to be a co-op town-builder.
We buy these house cards with the cost written at the bottom.
Huh, weird...
...mine have the cost at the top...well, some of them...
Shoot, I forgot to keep my cards consistent.
That's okay! It's a common mistake, and it's easy to fix.
Building a template for your cards makes it easier to read *and* create them.
But how do I decide where to put stuff?
Think about what your card needs as a hierarchy of information.
This is similar to order of operation, but instead of *actions,* you're sorting data.
So stuff like card names, health, cost, that sort of thing?
Exactly!
For game design, we want to sort data two ways:
Relevance and timing.

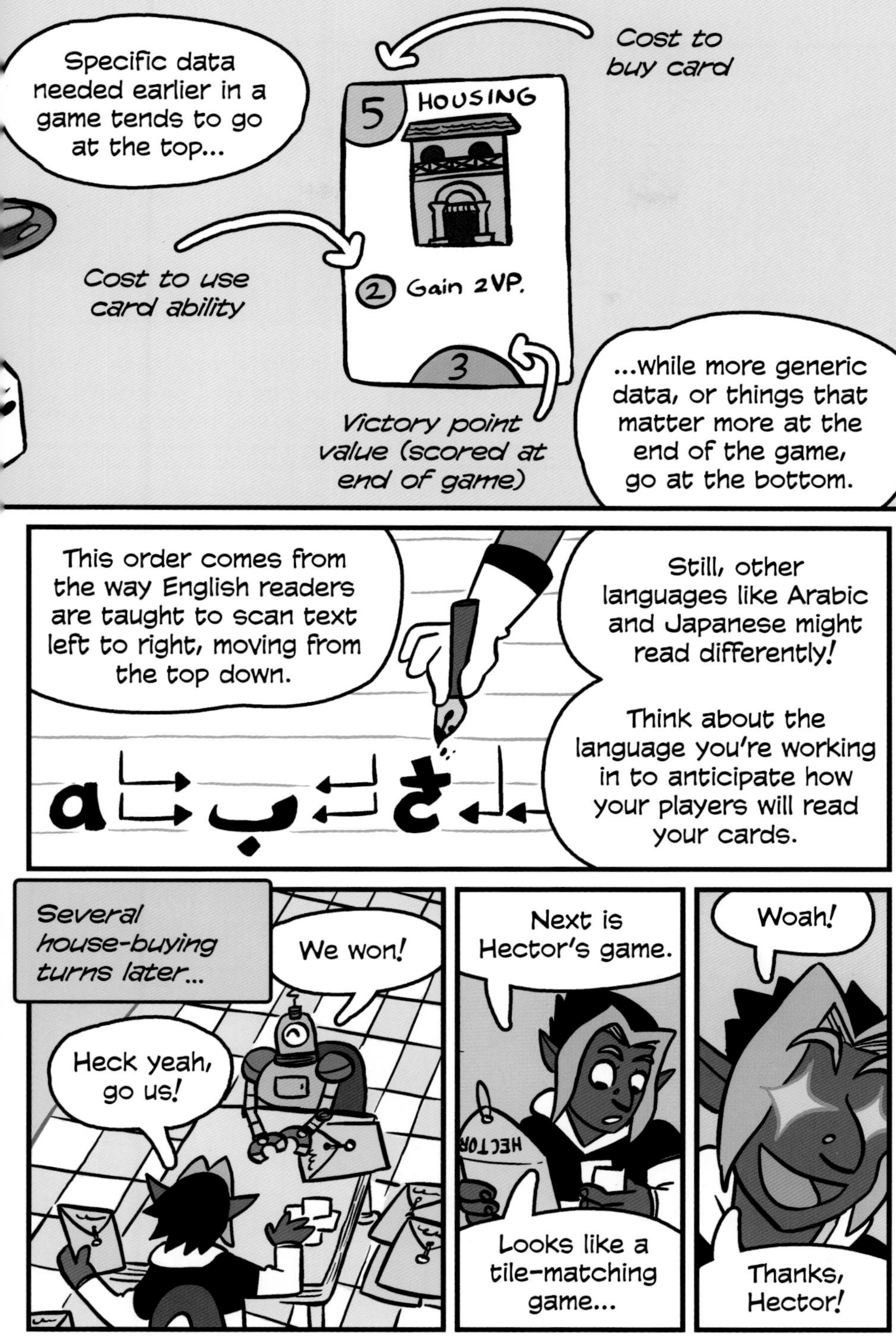
Specific data needed earlier in a game tends to go at the top...
Cost to buy card
5
HOUSING
Cost to use card ability
2 Gain 2VP.
3
Victory point value (scored at end of game)
...while more generic data, or things that matter more at the end of the game, go at the bottom.
This order comes from the way English readers are taught to scan text left to right, moving from the top down.
a
ب
ج
Still, other languages like Arabic and Japanese might read differently!
Think about the language you're working in to anticipate how your players will read your cards.
Several house-buying turns later...
We won!
Heck yeah, go us!
Next is Hector's game.
HECTOR
Looks like a tile-matching game...
Woah!
Thanks, Hector!

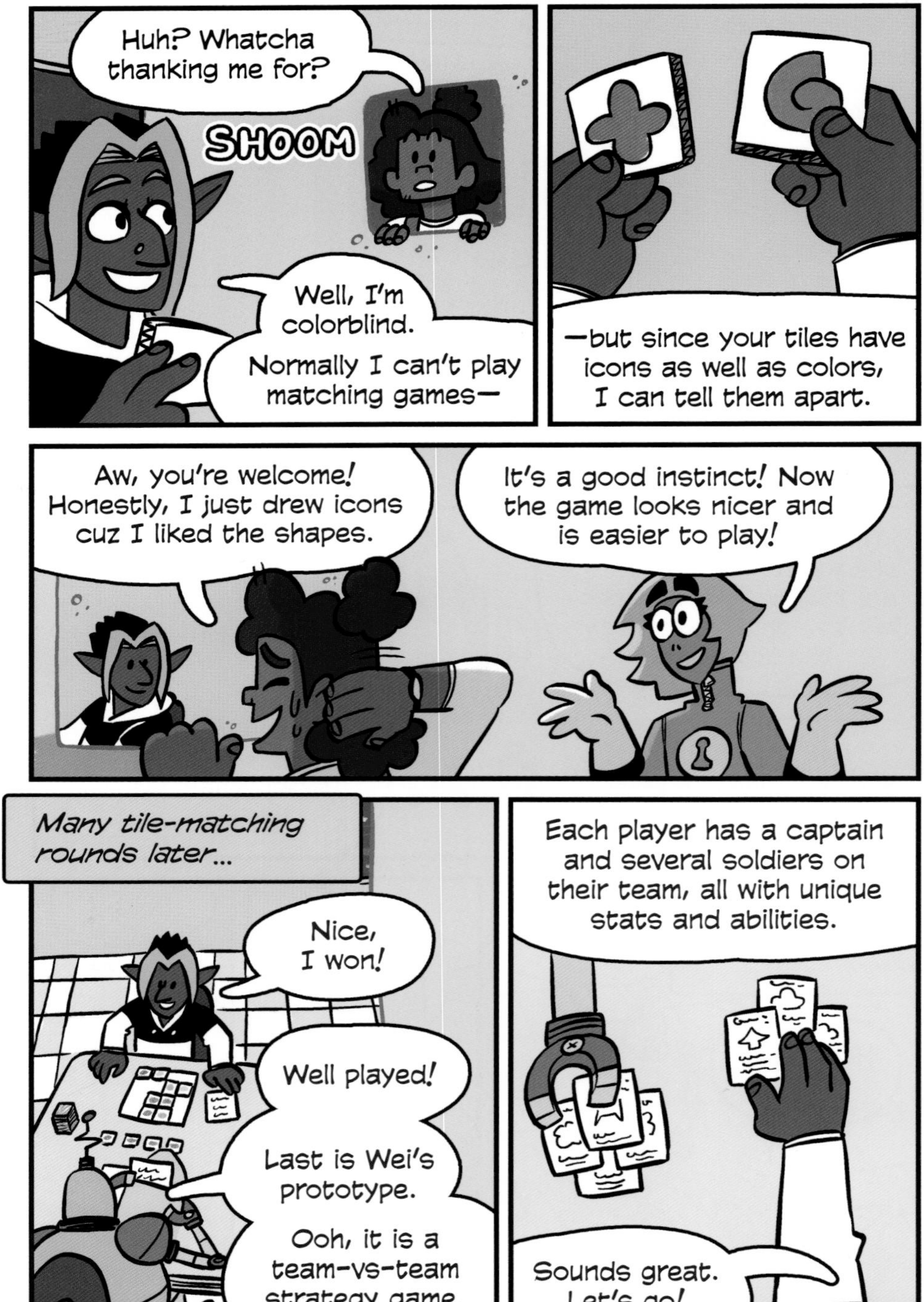
Huh? Whatcha thanking me for?
SHOOM
Well, I'm colorblind.
Normally I can't play matching games—
—but since your tiles have icons as well as colors, I can tell them apart.
Aw, you're welcome! Honestly, I just drew icons cuz I liked the shapes.
It's a good instinct! Now the game looks nicer and is easier to play!
Many tile-matching rounds later...
Nice, I won!
Well played!
Last is Wei's prototype.
Ooh, it is a team-vs-team strategy game.
Each player has a captain and several soldiers on their team, all with unique stats and abilities.
Sounds great. Let's go!

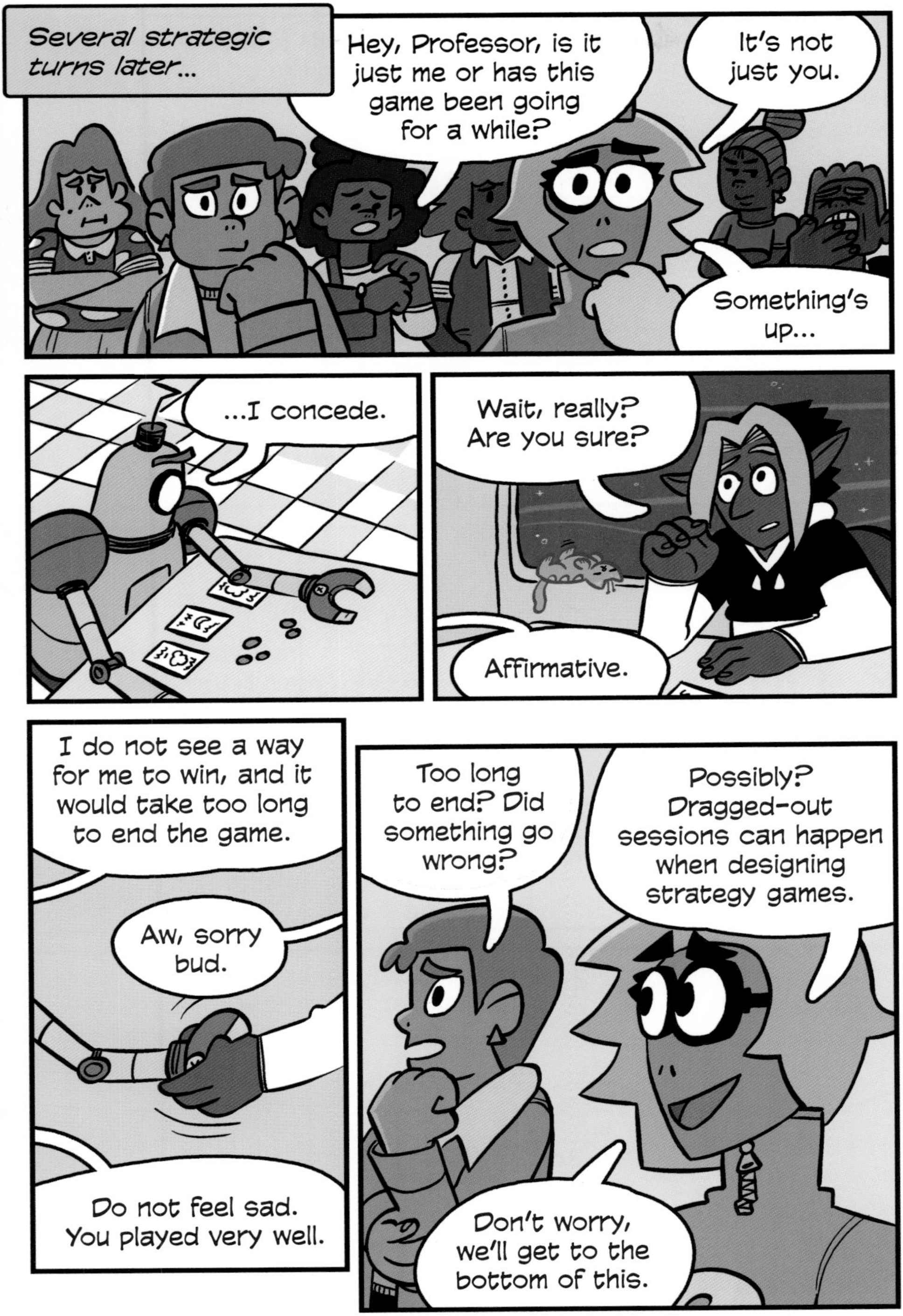
Several strategic turns later...
Hey, Professor, is it just me or has this game been going for a while?
It's not just you.
Something's up...
...I concede.
Wait, really? Are you sure?
Affirmative.
I do not see a way for me to win, and it would take too long to end the game.
Aw, sorry bud.
Do not feel sad. You played very well.
Too long to end? Did something go wrong?
Possibly? Dragged-out sessions can happen when designing strategy games.
Don't worry, we'll get to the bottom of this.

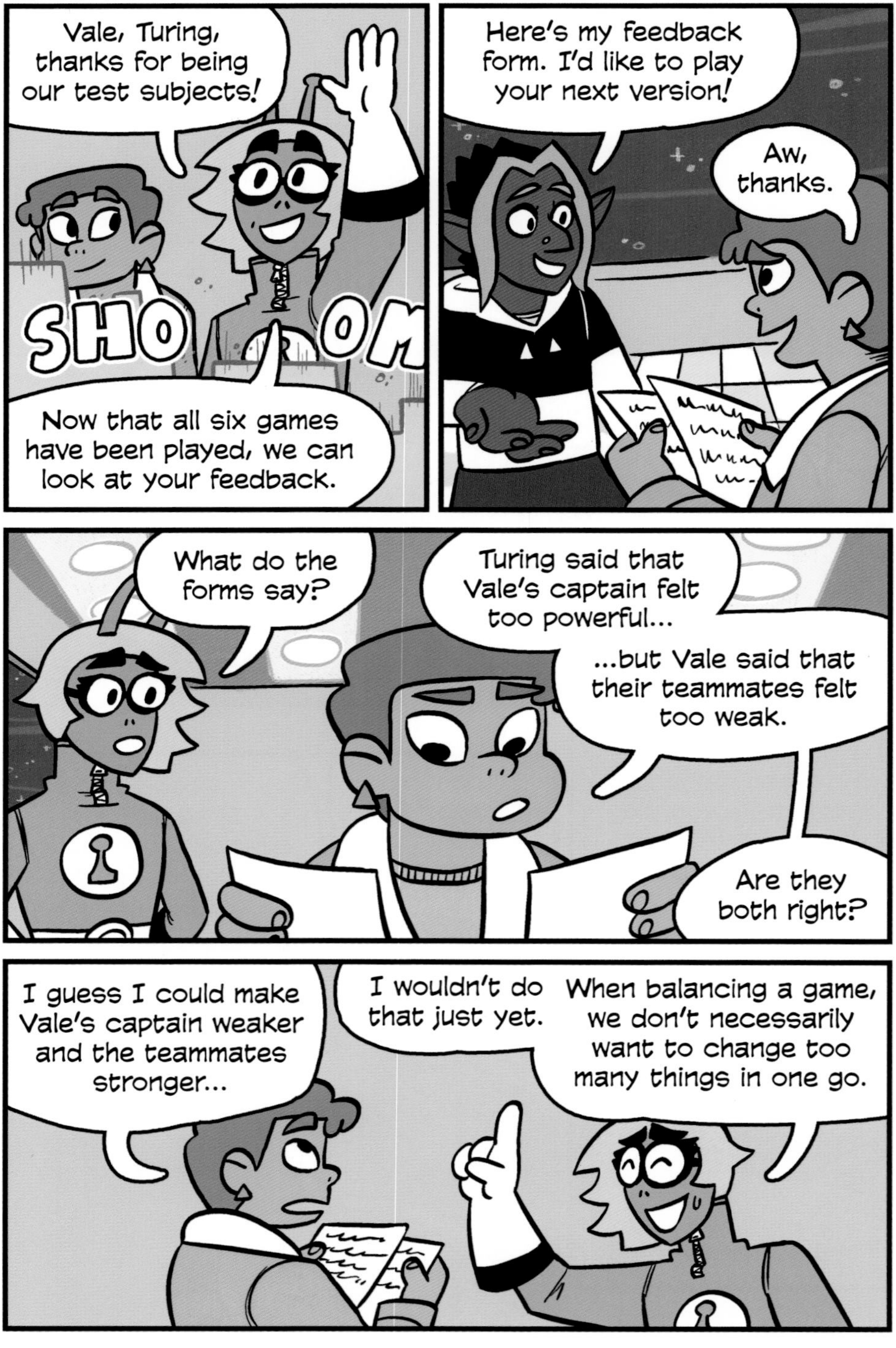
Vale, Turing, thanks for being our test subjects!
SHOOM
Now that all six games have been played, we can look at your feedback.
Here's my feedback form. I'd like to play your next version!
Aw, thanks.
What do the forms say?
Turing said that Vale's captain felt too powerful...
...but Vale said that their teammates felt too weak.
Are they both right?
I guess I could make Vale's captain weaker and the teammates stronger...
I wouldn't do that just yet.
When balancing a game, we don't necessarily want to change too many things in one go.

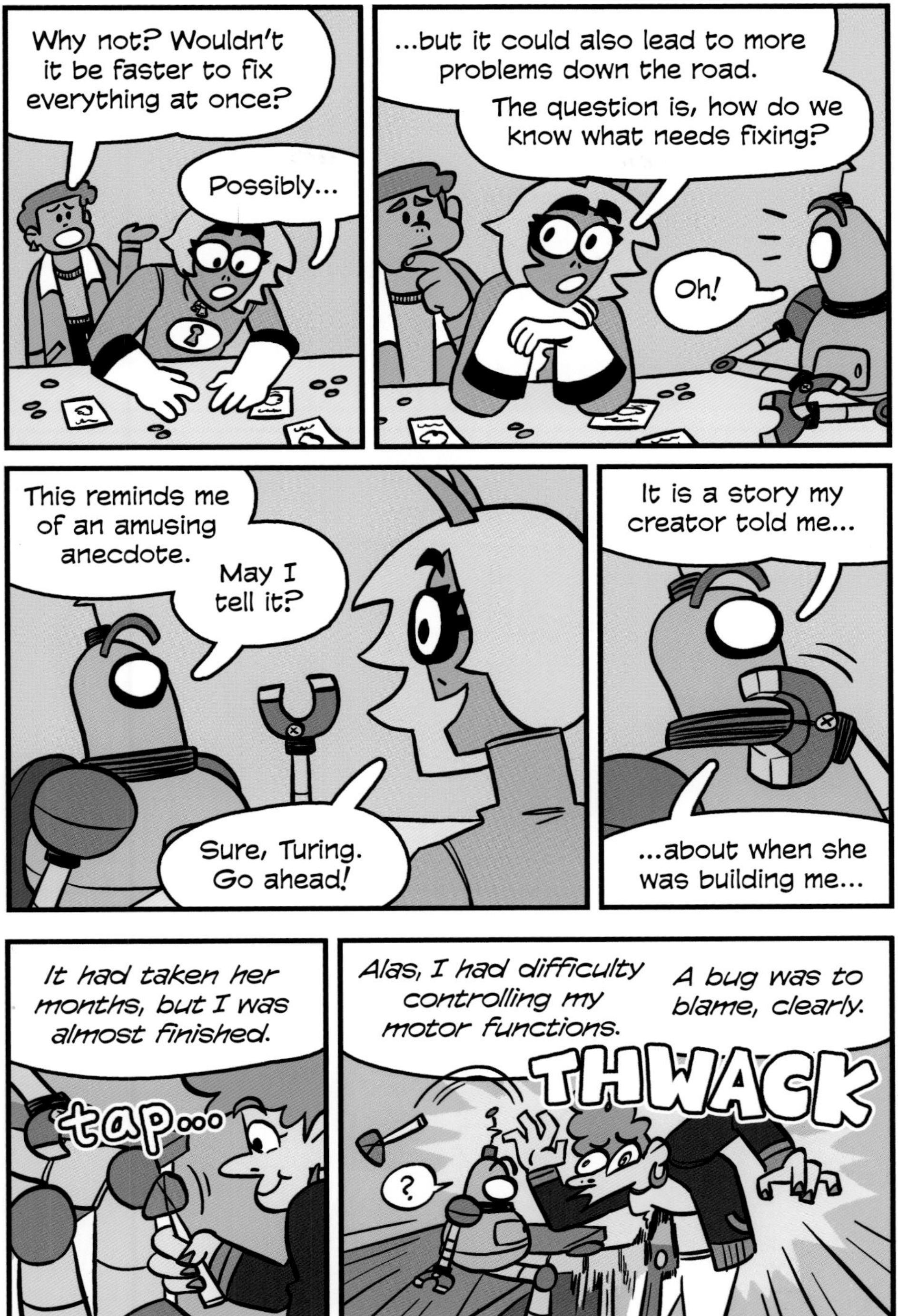

Why not? Wouldn't it be faster to fix everything at once?
Possibly...
...but it could also lead to more problems down the road.
The question is, how do we know what needs fixing?
Oh!
This reminds me of an amusing anecdote.
May I tell it?
Sure, Turing. Go ahead!
It is a story my creator told me...
...about when she was building me...
It had taken her months, but I was almost finished.
tap...
Alas, I had difficulty controlling my motor functions.
A bug was to blame, clearly.
THWACK
?

For weeks, my creator tried to solve the problem.

She fixed every error she could spot—

tap...

—but it always created more.

THWACK

But by adjusting my variables one by one—

—noting how each one affected my programming—

tap...

—she finally discovered the source of all of my bugs!

kick

Astounding how a single parenthesis can make the difference between failure and success!

So...I should test each change in my game on its own, to see how it affects everything?

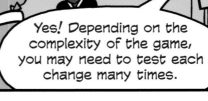

Yes! Depending on the complexity of the game, you may need to test each change many times.

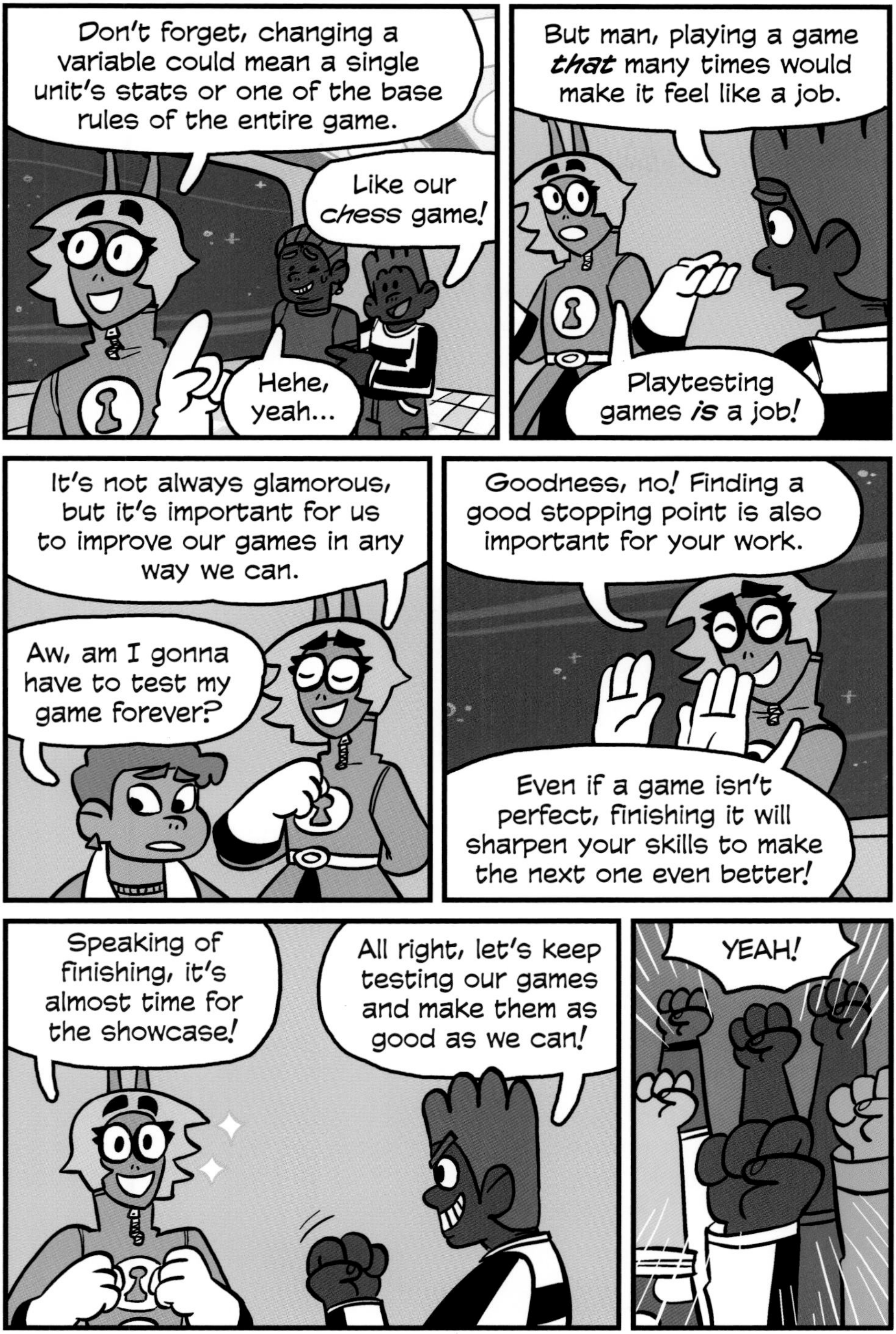
Don't forget, changing a variable could mean a single unit's stats or one of the base rules of the entire game.
Like our *chess* game!
Hehe, yeah...
But man, playing a game ***that*** many times would make it feel like a job.
Playtesting games *is* a job!
It's not always glamorous, but it's important for us to improve our games in any way we can.
Aw, am I gonna have to test my game forever?
Goodness, no! Finding a good stopping point is also important for your work.
Even if a game isn't perfect, finishing it will sharpen your skills to make the next one even better!
Speaking of finishing, it's almost time for the showcase!
All right, let's keep testing our games and make them as good as we can!
YEAH!

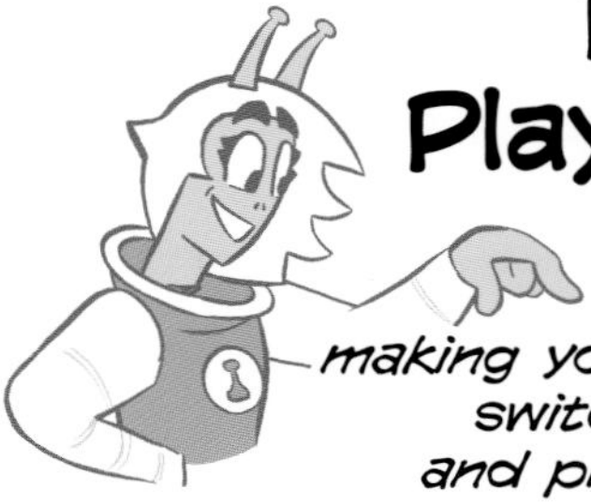

Prototype and Playtest Your Game!

Using your research in Day Four's brainstorming activity, you can begin making your new game a reality. Designers often switch back and forth between prototyping and playtesting, so feel free to do the same!

Part One: Prototype!

1. Write out your game rules. Try to sort your rules in the order that players will need them. Does your game have a theme? What can players do on their turn? How will players know when the game is over?
2. List your components. Your game can use dice and/or playing cards if you wish. If your game needs tokens, list how many your players will need. If you have original art, be as specific as possible with your list so you know what you need to create for your prototype.
3. Create any original assets needed for play. Remember that a prototype doesn't need to have final artwork or materials! You can make prototype components out of note cards, sheets of paper in plastic sleeves, minifigures from other games, etc.

Part Two: Playtest!

1. You can playtest a game by yourself! Try and follow your game's instructions and ask yourself questions while playing it:
   - "How is a single turn organized? What can I do on my turn? What limits are there on what I can do?"
   - "Why would I choose this option on my turn? Do I have too many options on my turn? Too few?"
   - "Does my choice affect what other players can do? How much do I ***want*** players to affect each other?"
2. Invite friends or family members to playtest your game! You can copy the feedback form at the end of this book for them to fill out. Ask them to play using your written instructions to ensure your rules are clear and concise.
3. Observe playtester reactions during the game and listen to their feedback. Discuss what changes you might try in future playtests. Happy designing!

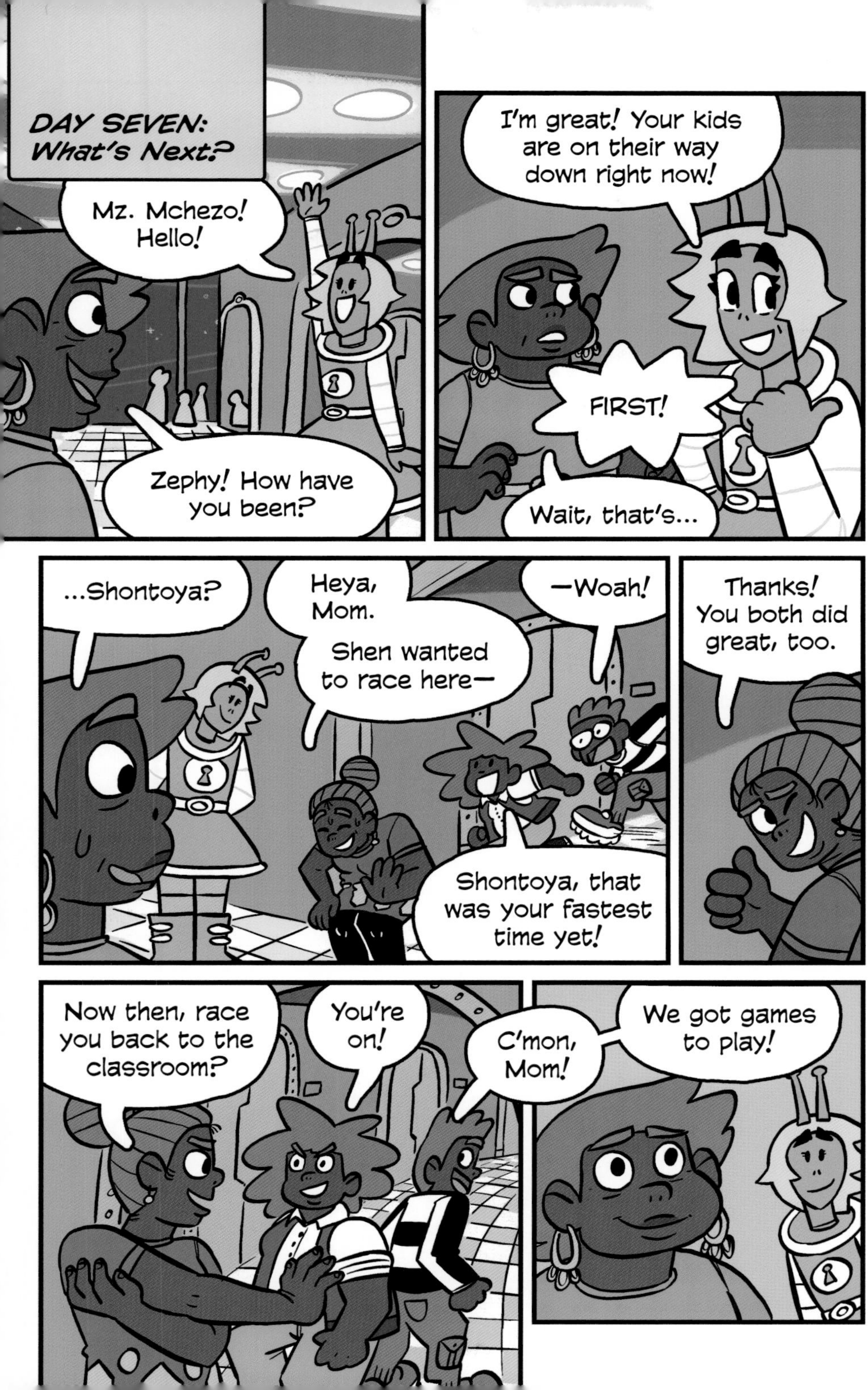
DAY SEVEN:
What's Next?
Mz. Mchezo! Hello!
Zephy! How have you been?
I'm great! Your kids are on their way down right now!
FIRST!
Wait, that's...
...Shontoya?
Heya, Mom.
Shen wanted to race here—
—Woah!
Shontoya, that was your fastest time yet!
Thanks! You both did great, too.
Now then, race you back to the classroom?
You're on!
C'mon, Mom!
We got games to play!

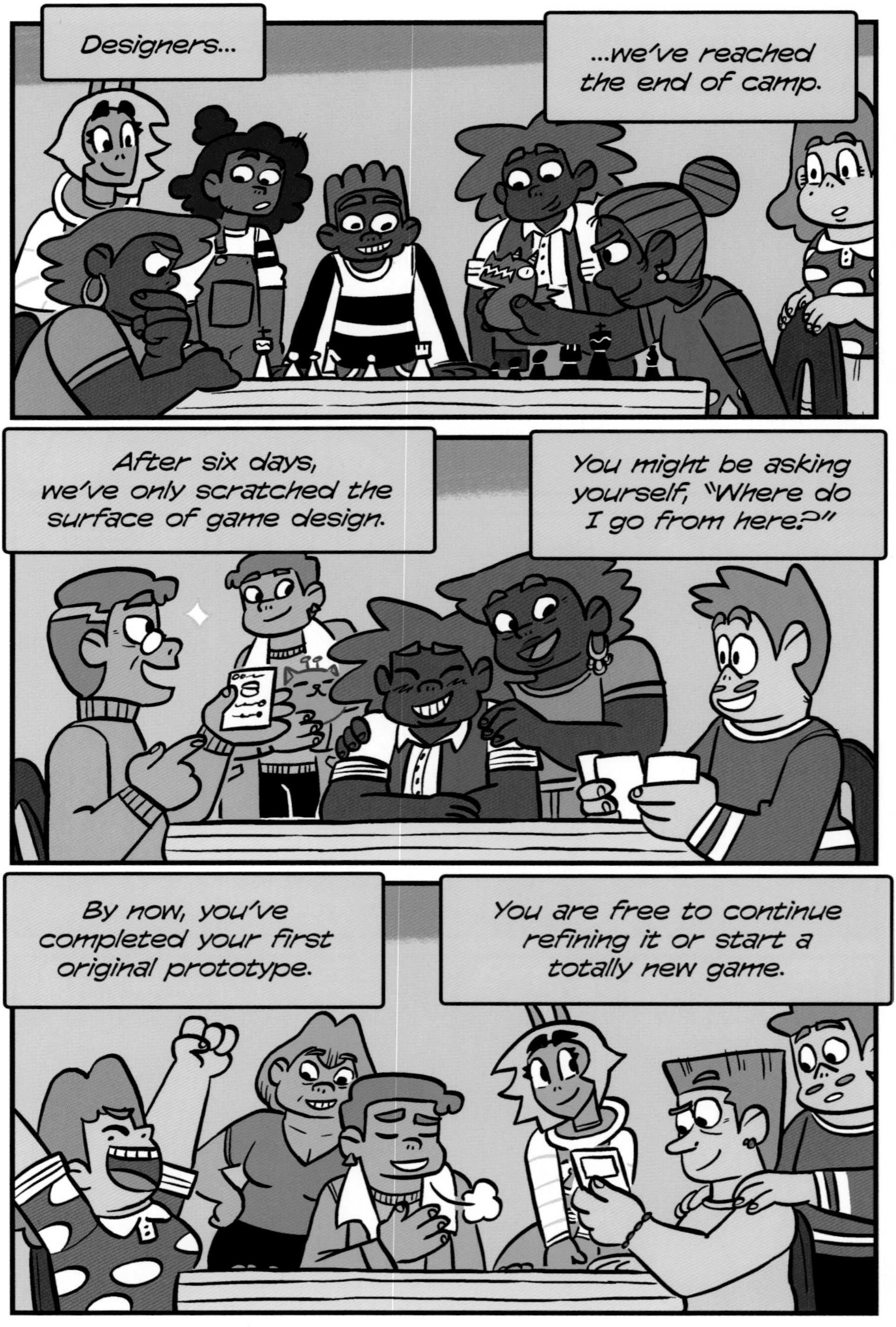

Designers...
...we've reached the end of camp.
After six days, we've only scratched the surface of game design.
You might be asking yourself, "Where do I go from here?"
By now, you've completed your first original prototype.
You are free to continue refining it or start a totally new game.

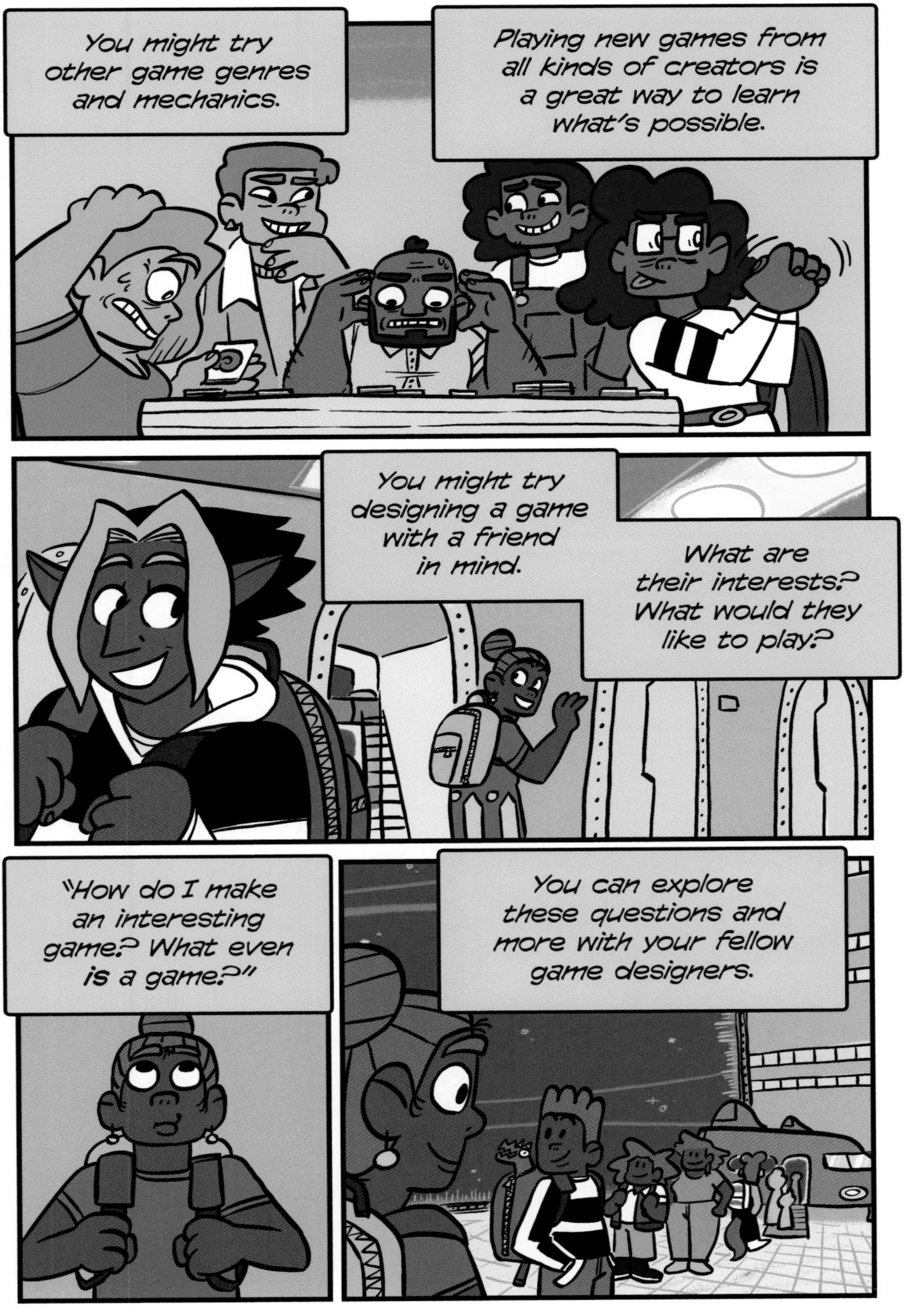
You might try other game genres and mechanics.
Playing new games from all kinds of creators is a great way to learn what's possible.
You might try designing a game with a friend in mind.
What are their interests? What would they like to play?
"How do I make an interesting game? What even is a game?"
You can explore these questions and more with your fellow game designers.

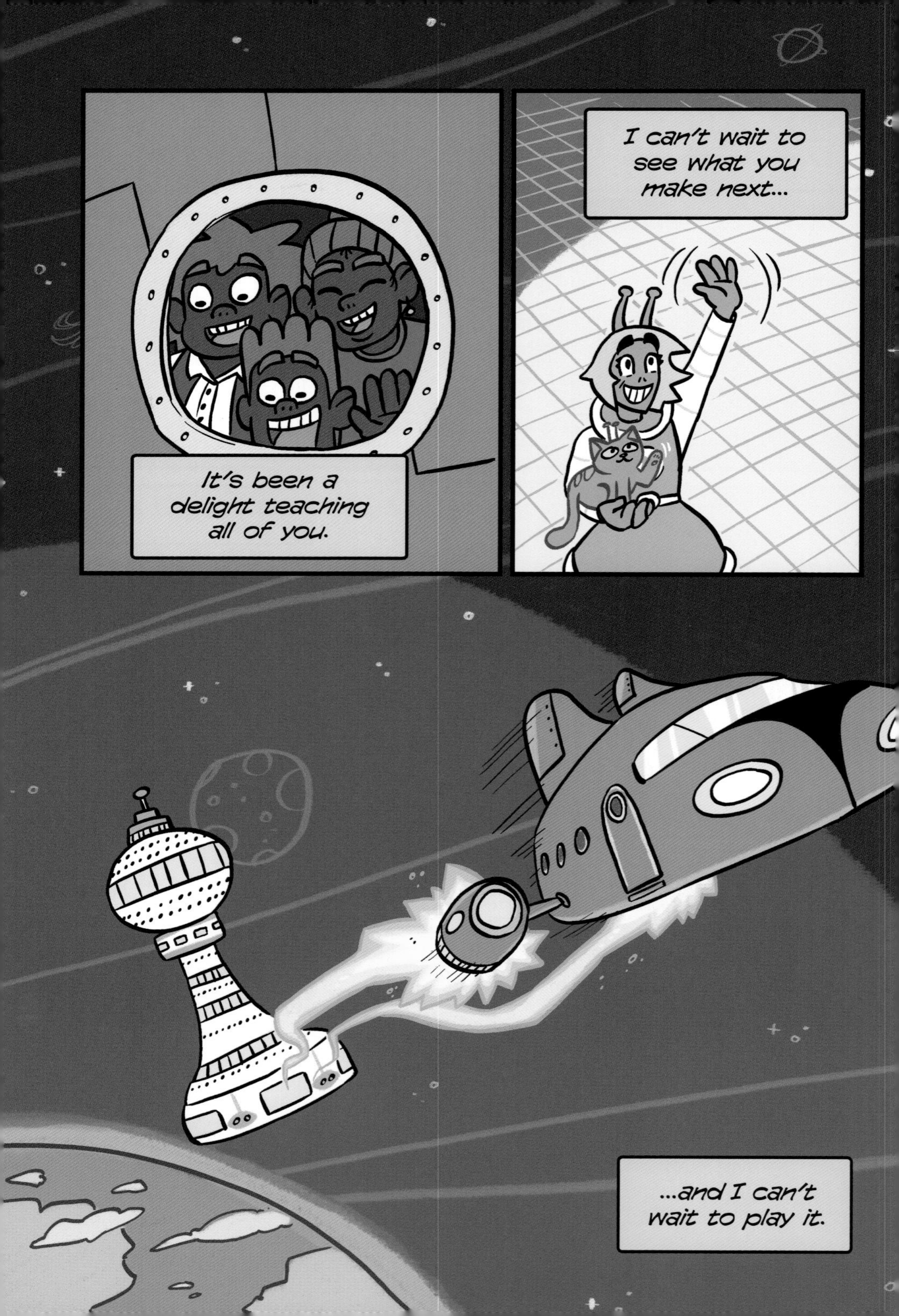
It's been a delight teaching all of you.
I can't wait to see what you make next...
...and I can't wait to play it.

GLOSSARY

Abstract: Distanced from reality. In games, a type of game with no concrete theming. Examples include *go* and *Hex*.

Card Memory: Type of component "memory" where one use affects the chances for the next. Examples include drawing a card from a deck or pulling a tile from a bag.

Component: A physical object necessary for a game such as dice, cards, paper, pencil, board, etc.

Connection: Game mechanic in which players complete paths or otherwise use adjacent pieces to achieve their goal. Examples include *Hex* and *Through the Desert*.

Dice Memory: Type of component "memory" where one use will *not* affect the chances for the next. Examples include rolling a die or spinning a spinner.

Mechanic: Broadly speaking, an action or choice you can make during a game in order to affect it. Games are often made up of multiple mechanics interacting with one another.

Module: A discrete set of rules that fit into a larger game.

Player Interaction: How much players can directly affect each other in a game. A game can be played with varying levels of interaction or even none. Examples of games with no player interaction include *blackjack* and *Ducks in a Row*.

Probability: A process by which one can measure the likelihood of certain outcomes.

Prototype: An early version of a game made for playtesting. Can also describe the process of creating an early version of a game.

Roll and Write: Game mechanic in which dice are rolled and players choose where to write the result on their personal sheet or board.

Roll and Move: Game mechanic in which a die, spinner, or other randomizer determines how many spaces a player can move on their turn. Games using this include *Monopoly, Candy Land,* and *Clue*.

Theming: Elements of a game that give it a narrative context. These can be illustrations, character designs, written lore, etc.

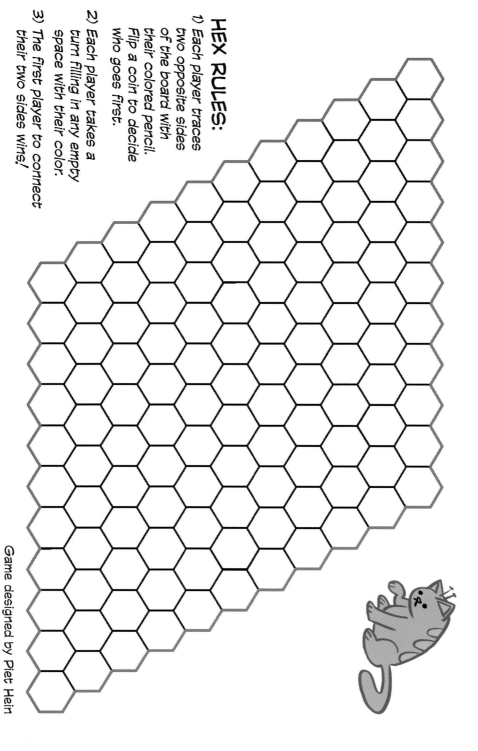

HEX RULES:

1) Each player traces two opposite sides of the board with their colored pencil. Flip a coin to decide who goes first.

2) Each player takes a turn filling in any empty space with their color.

3) The first player to connect their two sides wins!

Game designed by Piet Hein

PLAYTEST FEEDBACK FORM

Name of game: _____   Total game length: _____

First time playing? Yes / No   Did you win? Yes / No / Unsure

Write down any questions or comments you have during the game here:

```
┌─────────────────────────────────────────────────────────┐
│                                                           │
│                                                           │
│                                                           │
│                                                           │
└─────────────────────────────────────────────────────────┘
```

	Least				Most
How clear were the game rules?	1	2	3	4	5
How strategic did the game feel?	1	2	3	4	5
How fair did the game feel?	1	2	3	4	5

What was a memorable decision you made during the game?

What did you do during other players' turns?

How did other players' actions affect your decision-making?

How did the theme affect your enjoyment of the game?

What new features might you be interested in?

What was the most enjoyable part of the game? What was the least enjoyable?

First Second

Published by First Second
First Second is an imprint of Roaring Brook Press,
a division of Holtzbrinck Publishing Holdings Limited Partnership
120 Broadway, New York, NY 10271
firstsecondbooks.com
mackids.com

Library of Congress Control Number: 2022902112

Our books may be purchased in bulk for promotional, educational, or business use.
Please contact your local bookseller or the Macmillan Corporate and Premium Sales Department
at (800) 221-7945 ext. 5442 or by email at MacmillanSpecialMarkets@macmillan.com.

First edition, 2022
Edited by Robyn Chapman and Benjamin A. Wilgus
Cover design by Molly Johanson
Interior book design by Molly Johanson and Madeline Morales
Production editing by Dawn Ryan and Arik Hardin

Penciled and inked in Manga Studio, lettered and colored in Photoshop.

Printed in China by 1010 Printing International Limited, Kwun Tong, Hong Kong

ISBN 978-1-250-75052-5 (paperback)
1 3 5 7 9 10 8 6 4 2

ISBN 978-1-250-75051-8 (hardcover)
1 3 5 7 9 10 8 6 4 2

Don't miss your next favorite book from First Second!
For the latest updates go to firstsecondnewsletter.com and sign up for our enewsletter.

Bree Wolf is an artist, writer, and game designer in Portland, Oregon, who loves every single cat, especially blobby green ones. You can find more of their work online at BreeWolfStuff.com.

Jesse Fuchs is a longtime instructor at the NYU Game Center, where he teaches Introduction To Game Design, Traditional Card Game Literacy and Design, American Computer Games of the 1980s, and other fun things.